The DEFINITIVE MIDDLE SCHOOL GUIDE

• REVISED EDITION •

A Handbook For Success

by Imogene Forte & Sandra Schurr

Incentive Publications, Inc.
Nashville, Tennessee

Edited by Jean K. Signor
Cover: a collaborative effort of the creative KIDS' STUFF™ crew!

ISBN 0-86530-567-6
Library of Congress Control Number: 2002100816

PRINTED IN THE UNITED STATES OF AMERICA
www.incentivepublications.com

Overview

Table Of Contents

INTERDISCIPLINARY TEAMING AND BLOCK SCHEDULING

CURRICULUM AND INSTRUCTION

ADVISORY AND AFFECTIVE EDUCATION

STUDENT ASSESSMENT AND EVALUATION

APPENDIX

PREFACE

Educators agree that *student-centered education* is the most effective approach to meeting young adolescents' needs. Research further indicates that grouping these youngsters together in a supportive environment provides the best climate for learning and growing. After nearly twenty years, the Middle School concept has proven to be the ideal model for educating young adolescents. The Definitive Middle School Guide became an essential tool for educators and administrators at the middle grade level. Now, The Definitive Middle School Guide, Revised Edition has been updated to give middle grade educators the latest and greatest on the state of the middle school concept. While maintaining many of the tips and lists that made the original so invaluable, this revised edition incorporates all of the latest research.

The Definitive Middle School Guide, Revised Edition provides an updated collection of relevant information concerning the middle school philosophy and its essential program components. It is intended to serve as a combination encyclopedia, dictionary, and almanac so that readers can quickly and easily find out "everything they ever wanted to know about middle schools." The book features self-contained modules arranged in a sequence designed to present the evolution of an effective middle school organizational pattern. Each module may also stand on its own to be used independently of the other modules should the need arise. For example, if the reader has a great deal of knowledge of interdisciplinary teaming or cooperative learning, but wants to learn more about advisory programs, he or she can go directly to the advisory module without first working through the previous sections. It should also be noted that the favorite "TOP TEN" format has been utilized once again to allow the user to unearth major concepts without having to sift through extraneous information. The authors have spent considerable time researching and synthesizing the literature on middle schools so that it can be presented in an orderly and timely fashion to meet the needs of the busy teacher, administrator, or others needing "fingertip information" essential to middle school understanding and success.

Educators responsible for setting up or conducting workshops or in-service programs will be delighted to discover that the common format for each of the seven modules provides a complete and workable training package:
- A one-page overview.
- A set of meaningful questions that serve as learning goals as well as pre- and post-tests of the material addressed in the module.
- A glossary of important terms.
- A series of "Top Ten" pages that present the most important and germane material on the module's topic or theme in the form of lists, descriptions, references, tools, and techniques.
- A collection of findings from the published literature to provide motivation and support for the implementation of significant changes in schooling at the middle grade level.
- "Teacher's Wrap-Up À La Bloom": a page of activities, one at each level of Bloom's Taxonomy, that will help the reader wrap up and make use of the information, concepts, and ideas included in the module.

Major topics include:

School Structures and Climate
that Meet the Needs of Middle Grade Students
- Common Denominators of Successful Middle Schools
- Characteristics of Young Adolescents
- School climate
- Facility requirements
- Parent Communication
- Creating a Master Schedule
- Classroom management tips

Interdisciplinary Teaming and Block Scheduling
- Forming teams
- Roles and responsibilities of team members
- Ways to build team identity
- Developing a team handbook
- Evaluating a team's effectiveness
- Promoting the Block Schedule
- Ways to Flex a Block Schedule

Curriculum and Instruction
- Characteristics of Learning Styles
- In-Class Grouping
- Understanding Standards-Based Education
- Elements of Lesson Planning
- Methods for Differentiating Instruction
- Tips for Effective Discussions

Advisory and Affective Education
- Goals for effective advisory programs
- Krathwohl's Affective Taxonomy
- Responsibilities of advisors
- Ways to schedule advisory time
- Instruments for evaluating an advisory program's success

Student Assessment and Evaluation
- Peer editing
- Helping Students Become Test-wise
- Assessing Student Understanding
- Assessment Tips, Tools, and Test Formats

SCHOOL STRUCTURES AND CLIMATE THAT MEET THE NEEDS OF MIDDLE GRADES STUDENTS

Overview of School Structures and Classroom Climate that Meet the Needs of Middle Grade Students

A school that meets the needs of Middle School Students:
- is based on the unique needs and characteristics of the young adolescent, including physical, psychological, intellectual, social, and moral and ethical needs.
- has a well developed mission statement that is understood and accepted by administrators, teachers, students, and parents.
- is structured around the widely varying needs and characteristics of young adolescents.
- is student-centered rather than subject-centered.
- includes provision for pre-service and in-service teacher training to meet the exceptionalities in interests, abilities, and experiences of students in transition.
- accepts and respects each student and teacher as an individual of worth and dignity in his or her own right; celebrates differences and encourages creativity and freedom of expression in keeping with ethnic genealogy and background experiences.
- requires the same teachers to share the same students over the same block of time in the same part of the building.

The effective middle school organizational structure affords:
- articulation between the elementary school and the middle school that is enhanced by increased communication and a student-centered focus. Articulation between the middle school and the high school is also an important aspect of the program.
- flexible block scheduling to allow for varied learning activities, grouping and regrouping students for instruction, and common planning time for teachers.
- interdisciplinary approaches in disciplines and integration of all curricular areas.
- a varied range of exploratory opportunities for students.
- opportunities for focusing on affective education as a regular part of the daily schedule.
- emphasis placed on intramural rather than interscholastic athletics with cooperation and participation encouraged.
- educators who have been especially trained and are committed to the education of the young adolescent.
- classroom teachers who have mastered strategies that promote positive classroom management and active student participation.
- forward thinking, outcome-based, and devotion to excellence in classroom instruction, student motivation, the quest for life skills, broad-based learning, and creative thinking.

10 PLUS 3

Guiding Questions for School Structures and Climate

1. What are the unique needs and characteristics of the middle grade student?

2. What are some characteristics of under-achieving middle grade students?

3. What are some indicators of gifted students at the middle grade level?

4. What are some characteristics of schools that meet the needs of at-risk middle level students?

5. Why have young adolescents in our society today been labeled as "Kids Caught In The Middle?"

6. What are some guidelines for establishing a student-centered rather than subject-centered middle school mission statement?

7. What are the important common denominators?

8. How should the physical plant best be arranged to facilitate the middle school philosophy and program?

9. How can successful practices and strategies in effective middle school classrooms be identified and how can teachers, students, and administrators work together to nurture and maximize these characteristics for the good of all students?

10. Why are interdisciplinary approaches to curriculum and instruction desirable?

11. How would you define an authentic exploratory offering? Give examples of five to ten content areas in which exploratory offerings could be developed.

12. What are some steps middle grades teachers can take to be more effective as positive rather than negative disciplinarians?

13. What are some ways that parents and caregivers can be involved in the decision-making and day-to-day operations of the middle school program?

10 PLUS 10

School Structure and Climate Terms That Meet the Needs of Middle Grade Students

1. **Student-Centered School Structures:** The organizational patterns unique to middle school philosophy which includes flexible block schedule, interdisciplinary team, advisory, exploratory program, intrascholastic sports, and team space allocations.

2. **Transescence:** The stage of development which begins prior to the onset of puberty and extends through the early stages of adolescence.

3. **Early Adolescence:** The stage of development between ages 10 and 14 when the student begins to reach puberty.

4. **At-Risk Student:** A student who demonstrates academic learning and achievement problems is under motivated and lacks structure and organization.

5. **Gifted/Talented Student:** A student who demonstrates a wide range of abilities and interests, is an avid reader, solves problems creatively, and is self-motivated, and needs little outside control.

6. **English as a Second Language Student (ESL):** A student whose first language is one other than English.

7. **Heterogeneous Grouping:** A grouping of students that does not divide learners on the basis of ability or academic achievement.

8. **Homogeneous Grouping:** Grouping of students that divides learners on the basis of specific levels of ability, achievement, or interest. Sometimes referred to as tracking.

9. **Interdisciplinary Program:** Instruction that integrates and combines subject matter ordinarily taught separately into a single organizational structure.

10. **Common Planning (Team Duty) Time:** Regularly-scheduled time during the school day during which a given team of teachers who are responsible for the same group of students is available for joint planning, parent conferencing, and/or lesson preparation.

11. **School Mission Statement:** A brief but concise statement that clearly conveys the overall intent and focus for the schooling process in a given educational setting.

12. **Classroom Management:** A term that includes everything teachers must manipulate in order to produce successful student involvement and cooperation. This means such variables as room arrangement, curriculum, instructional techniques, and classroom rules and expectations.

13. **Classroom Climate:** Refers to the human exchanges and interactions that regularly occur between and among students and teachers during the learning process.

14. **Behavior:** The manner of conducting oneself or what one "does."

15. **Discipline:** A process developed to guide the actions and behaviors of students within their learning environment.

16. **Assertive Discipline:** A disciplinary system of externally imposed rewards and punishments.

17. **Conflict Resolution:** A process which is designed to teach students the constructive tools and techniques for solving conflicts through both mediation and negotiation of disputes so as to foster collaborative problem solving within the classroom setting.

18. **Behavior Management:** A system of rules, sanctions, and rewards that encourage students to exhibit specific behavior and/or accomplish required tasks.

19. **Extrinsic Motivation:** Emphasizes the value an individual places on the ends of an action. In extrinsic motivation, the goal rather than the doing is the reason for performing behavior.

20. **Intrinsic Motivation:** Refers to the pleasure or value associated with an activity itself. In intrinsic motivation, the "doing" is considered the primary reason for the performance of the behavior.

10 PLUS 3

School Structures that Meet the Needs of Middle Grade Students

1. Eliminates the middle grades as a mini- or junior high school organization by providing its own identity as a middle level school.

2. Provides a comfortable and supportive physical classroom setting conducive to learning.

3. Removes the constraints and limitations of a rigid schedule and bell system to a flexible block schedule with no predetermined time periods.

4. Places students together who are more alike in their needs and characteristics through a 6–8 grade configuration rather than a 7–9 grade configuration.

5. Promotes the integration of subject matter through the interdisciplinary team and common planning period concepts.

6. Creates "smallness within bigness" by forming teams of teachers and students into surrogate families.

7. Takes into account and plans curriculum and instruction based on individual differences.

8. Empowers both teachers and students to make decisions.

9. Discourages the "winner/loser" or "star" system through emphasis on cooperation and collaboration.

10. Provides variety through alternative delivery systems, multi-media resources, and exploratory offerings.

11. Shows a balance between a student-centered program and a subject-centered program.

12. Values potential student involvement in all areas of the schooling and places high priority on self-direction, self-description, and self-assessment.

13. Provides a logical transition from the self-contained classroom of the elementary school setting to the departmentalization of the high school setting.

SO, You Think You Have A Good Middle School!

Directions:

Listed below are fifteen essential elements most often associated with successful middle school programs. Read each statement and its qualifying sub points carefully. Then react to each statement in terms of its stage of implementation for your school setting. Be honest in your assessment and be ready to cite several examples that document or validate your implementation rating.

Common Denominators of Successful Middle Schools
[rating scale]

1. Middle level educators are knowledgeable about the unique needs and characteristics of the early adolescent.

Sub points:

○ *Not Yet*

a. Every educator in my building knows the needs and characteristics associated with the intellectual, moral, physical, emotional/psychological, and social development of the students they serve.

○ *Trying*

○ *OK*

○ *Almost There*

b. Every educator in my building understands how the growth and development of their students affect student outcomes in these affective and cognitive areas.

○ *WOW!*

c. Every educator in my building plans and teaches around these developmental needs of the students they serve.

---

2. Middle level educators maintain a balance between cognitive and academic goals and non-cognitive or affective goals.

Sub points:

○ *Not Yet*

a. Every educator in my building is knowledgeable about the philosophy of the middle school, which places equal value on a student-centered and a subject-centered environment.

○ *Trying*

○ *OK*

○ *Almost There*

b. Every educator in my building works hard to meet both the cognitive and the affective goals of our program.

○ *WOW!*

c. Every educator in my building places a high priority on building a school, team, and classroom climate that is conducive to learning and a culture that accepts mistakes as an integral part of that learning process.

Common Denominators of Successful Middle Schools
[rating scale]

3. Middle level educators support a wide range of organizational patterns or structures including block scheduling, multi-age grouping, interdisciplinary teaming, developmental or academic grouping, thematic houses, exploratory programs, and school-within-a-school options.

   ○ *Not Yet*

   ○ *Trying*

   ○ *OK*

   ○ *Almost There*

   ○ *WOW!*

Sub points:

a. Every educator in my building is supportive of the flexible block schedule and uses it appropriately.

b. Every educator in my building is associated with an interdisciplinary team that has a strong team identity, regular team meetings/student conferences, team rules, team celebrations, and team roles.

c. Every educator in my building is comfortable with grouping and regrouping of students for instruction.

---

4. Middle level educators insist on both team planning and personal planning time for teachers, recognizing that cooperative planning is essential to the middle school philosophy.

   ○ *Not Yet*

   ○ *Trying*

   ○ *OK*

   ○ *Almost There*

   ○ *WOW!*

Sub points:

a. Every educator in my building is a willing and effective team leader or team member.

b. Educators in my building make optimal use of their team planning time.

c. Every educator in my building is committed to team planning sessions which focus equal time on both discipline and classroom management techniques, as well as integrated instruction and team teaching opportunities.

---

5. Middle level educators are committed to a physical plant where teams are housed together to support interdisciplinary teaming, collaborative team planning, team teaching, and team gatherings/celebrations.

   ○ *Not Yet*

   ○ *Trying*

   ○ *OK*

   ○ *Almost There*

   ○ *WOW!*

Sub points:

a. Educators in my building strive to create an attractive and safe "house" for their team of students.

b. Every educator in my building values the teaming concept that specifies "an effective team is responsible for the same students, for the same extended period of time each day, in the same part of the facility, and with the same team of teachers."

6. **Middle level educators push for high academic goals and expectations through a challenging curriculum and through high performance standards for students.**

○ *Not Yet*

○ *Trying*

Sub points:

○ *OK*

a. Every educator in my building accepts the rigors of their assigned discipline and strives to help each student reach his/her potential.

○ *Almost There*

○ *WOW!*

b. Every educator in my building is computer literate and incorporates technology effectively in the teaching of their discipline.

---

7. **Middle level educators advocate varied instructional strategies and alternative delivery systems for the teaching and learning of the curriculum.**

○ *Not Yet*

○ *Trying*

Sub points:

○ *OK*

a. Every educator in my building makes practical and effective use of the following instructional practices on a regular and consistent basis: Lecture, discussion, cooperative learning, learning stations, role plays, case studies, games, simulations, independent study projects, and other approved delivery systems.

○ *Almost There*

○ *WOW!*

b. Every educator in my building understands and applies varied instructional models in the design of their lesson plans, including Bloom's Taxonomy of Critical Thinking, Williams' Taxonomy of Creative Thinking, Gardner's Multiple Intelligences, deBono's Colored Thinking Hats, Johnson and Johnson's Cooperative Learning Model, and Riegle's Questioning Model.

c. Every educator in my building is able to differentiate instruction for students through manipulation of content, time, materials, complexity of learning tasks, expected outcomes, and assessment data.

d. Every educator in my building emphasizes active learning experiences over passive learning experiences in the teaching of academic content and skills to students.

Common Denominators of Successful Middle Schools
[rating scale]

8. Middle level educators encourage authentic assessment and evaluation tools and techniques that promote learning and that include portfolio, product, and performance assessment measures.

○ *Not Yet*

○ *Trying*

○ *OK*

Sub points:

a. Every educator in my building takes standardized and mandated state tests seriously.

○ *Almost There*

b. Every educator in my building is knowledgeable about the characteristics of authentic assessment measures.

○ *WOW!*

c. Every educator in my building incorporates portfolio, product, and performance assessment tools/techniques when evaluating student growth and development.

---

9. Middle level educators promote a full exploratory program that includes mini-classes, exploratory course options, service clubs, special interest activities, independent study projects, and field or community experiences.

○ *Not Yet*

○ *Trying*

○ *OK*

Sub points:

a. Every educator in my building promotes exploratory program as an integral part of our school's curricular offerings.

○ *Almost There*

b. Every educator in my building participates in one or more of the following exploratory options: mini-classes, service clubs, special interest activities, study projects, or field/community experiences.

○ *WOW!*

---

10. Middle level educators understand the need for positive adult-student relationships through a comprehensive advising and counseling program that recognizes teachers as student advocates and as members of an advisor-advisee or home-based advisor program.

○ *Not Yet*

○ *Trying*

○ *OK*

Sub points:

a. Every educator in my building has the opportunity to be an advisor to students.

○ *Almost There*

b. Every student in my building has a special adult advocate that he/she knows well.

○ *WOW!*

c. Every educator in my building sees themselves as an integral part of the guidance and counseling program in the school.

Common Denominators of Successful Middle Schools
[rating scale]

11. Middle level educators insist on strong parental involvement and community support through team conferences, student-led conferences, school advisory committees, learning communities for adults, community/business partnerships, shared decision-making, and community service programs.

○ *Not Yet*

○ *Trying*

○ *OK*

○ *Almost There*

○ *WOW!*

Sub points:

a. Educators in my building work diligently at encouraging parental involvement in their classrooms or programs.

b. Every educator in my building participates in team conferences and student-led conferences where appropriate to do so.

c. Every educator in my building uses communications such as memos, newsletters, telephone calls, home visits, e-mail, invitations, and/or message boards on a regular and consistent basis.

---

12. Middle level educators celebrate diversity among student, parent, and faculty/staff populations.

○ *Not Yet*

○ *Trying*

○ *OK*

○ *Almost There*

○ *WOW!*

Sub points:

a. Every educator in my building provides for cultural differences and alternative learning styles.

b. Every educator in my building promotes high expectations for students among all cultures.

---

13. Middle level educators place a high priority on violence and drug free schools as well as programs and policies that foster health and wellness, and safety.

○ *Not Yet*

○ *Trying*

○ *OK*

○ *Almost There*

○ *WOW!*

Sub points:

a. Every educator in my building works hard to keep the school safe from violence, drugs, and crime.

b. Every educator in my building fosters health, wellness, and safety within their domain.

Common Denominators of Successful Middle Schools
[rating scale]

4. **Middle level educators strive for high quality physical education and intramural programs that provide for differences in physical development.**

Sub points:

a. Every educator in my building is knowledgeable about the differences between intermural and intramural experiences for their students.

b. Every educator in my building is concerned with appropriate physical development of students, including availability of free and reduced lunch programs and other health-related services.

○ *Not Yet*

○ *Trying*

○ *OK*

○ *Almost There*

○ *WOW!*

---

5. **Middle level educators ensure a smooth transition from elementary to middle school and from middle school to high school.**

Sub points:

a. Every educator in my building recognizes that the middle school setting is different and unique from the elementary school setting and the high school setting.

b. Every educator in my building respects the need for a successful transition from the elementary school and to the high school, working hard towards that end.

○ *Not Yet*

○ *Trying*

○ *OK*

○ *Almost There*

○ *WOW!*

---

16. **Middle level educators value a rigorous and quality staff development program that is comprehensive, ongoing, lifelong, and that provides alternatives for its participants.**

Sub points:

a. Every educator in my building seeks out and willingly attends most staff development options available to them.

b. Every educator in my building has a personalized and individual staff development plan.

c. Every educator in my building supports the need for specially prepared, trained, and qualified teachers and administrators at the middle school level.

○ *Not Yet*

○ *Trying*

○ *OK*

○ *Almost There*

○ *WOW!*

10 PLUS 3 Major Distinctions Between The Middle School And The Junior High School

Middle School	Junior High School
1. Is student-centered	Is subject-centered
2. Fosters collaboration and empowerment of teachers and students	Fosters competition and empowerment of administrators
3. Focuses on creative exploration and experimentation of subject matter	Focuses on mastery of concepts and skills in separate disciplines
4. Allows for flexible scheduling with large blocks of time	Requires a regular six-period day of 50- to 55-minute periods
5. Varies length of time students are in courses	Offers subjects for one semester or one year
6. Encourages multi-materials approach to instruction	Depends on textbook-oriented instruction
7. Organizes teachers in interdisciplinary teams with common planning period	Organizes teachers in departments with no common planning period
8. Arranges workspaces of teamed teachers adjacent to one another	Arranges work spaces of teachers according to disciplines taught
9. Emphasizes both affective and cognitive development of student	Emphasizes only cognitive development of student
10. Offers advisor/advisee teacher-oriented guidance program	Offers study hall and access to counselor upon request
11. Provides high-interest "mini-courses" during school day	Provides highly-structured activity program after school
12. Uses varied delivery systems with high level of interaction among students and teachers	Uses lecture styles a majority of the time with high percentage of teacher talk time
13. Organizes athletics around intramural concept	Organizes athletics around interscholastic concept

10 Contributions To The Middle School From The Junior High School

1. The original goal of the junior high school was to provide a separate transition between the elementary school and the high school.

2. Another initial goal was to provide a basis for the scientific study of adolescence.

3. A new grade level pattern (7-8-9 in the case of junior high schools) was implemented to meet the social and physical needs of the age group.

4. The junior high school successfully expanded and enriched the curriculum for young adolescents.

5. A variety of exploratory programs became available to seventh and eighth graders.

6. Guidance-oriented homeroom programs were developed and put into operation.

7. Clubs and student activities based on special interests and needs were provided.

8. Junior high schools became centers for experimentation with curriculum and scheduling.

9. Opportunities for students to discover and explore special interests and aptitudes for future vocational decisions were provided.

10. The possibilities for careers in the major fields of learning were revealed to students.

10 PLUS 30

Needs/ Characteristics Of Young Adolescents

Physical Needs/Characteristics

1. Experience irregular growth spurts in physical development

2. Experience fluctuations in basal metabolism causing restlessness and listlessness

3. Have ravenous appetites

4. Mature at varying rates of speed

5. Are highly disturbed by body changes

6. Are highly physical

7. Are overly concerned with bodily changes and sexual development

8. Are lacking in good nutritional habits

Intellectual Needs/Characteristics

9. Are highly curious

10. Prefer active to passive learning experiences

11. Relate to real-life problems and situations

12. Are egocentric

13. Experience metacognition (the ability to analyze complex thought processes)

14. Enjoy human behaviors

15. Seek constant approval and reinforcement

16. Are intellectually curious about real world

Psychological Needs/Characteristics

17. Are often erratic and inconsistent in behavior

18. Are highly sensitive to criticism

19. Are moody, restless, and self-conscious

20. Are optimistic and hopeful

21. Are searching for identity and acceptance from peers

22. Experience mood swings

23. Seek independence

24. Are emotionally vulnerable

Social Needs/Characteristics

25. Are rebellious toward parents and authority figures

26. Are confused and frightened by new school/social settings

27. Are fiercely loyal to peer group values

28. Are often aggressive and argumentative

29. Need frequent affirmation of love from adults

30. Exhibit immature behavior

31. Tend to overreact when criticized or embarrassed

32. Experiment with new identities

Moral and Ethical Needs/Characteristics

33. Are idealistic

34. Have strong sense of fairness

35. Are reflective and introspective in thoughts and feelings

36. Confront moral and ethical questions head on

37. Ask large, ambiguous questions about the meaning of life

38. Show compassion for underdog situations and environmental issues

39. Are impatient with pace of change

40. Are slow to acknowledge own faults and flaws

10 PLUS 13

Indicators Of A Gifted/Talented Student

1. Is an avid reader

2. Is outstanding in science, math, or literature

3. Has a wide range of interests

4. Is anxious to try new things

5. Seems very alert and gives rapid answers

6. Is self-motivated and needs little outside control

7. Tends to dominate peers or situations

8. Has self-confidence

9. Is sensitive to situations and the feelings of others

10. Can solve problems ingeniously

11. Has creative thoughts, ideas, or innovations

12. Is anxious to complete tasks

13. Has a great desire to excel

14. Is very expressive verbally

15. Tells imaginative stories

16. Has a mature sense of humor

17. Is inquisitive; examines things closely

18. Can show relationships between apparently unrelated things or ideas

19. Shows excitement about discoveries and is eager to share them

20. Tends to lose awareness of time

21. Is adept with the art of visual expression

22. Exhibits very expressive body/facial gestures

23. Likes to work alone

 **Steps for Team/Site Based Implementation of Inclusion**

1. Conduct a survey or needs assessment of special services available on your team or in your school for target populations of students requiring special assistance. Collect and analyze the data so that it is both manageable and usable for the teachers to interpret and internalize.

2. Define the concept of "inclusion" for your team or school and develop a mission statement that clarifies its purpose and philosophy.

3. Plan and implement a series of focus groups or information sessions that involve administrators, teachers, students, and parents. Use these sessions to share data collected and to establish a set of goals for an inclusion program. Decide on the steps necessary to develop an inclusion program for the team or school.

4. Examine the options or the continuums of placement alternatives identified for inclusion programs and select a strategy that best fits your team or school setting. Develop a rationale for your choice.

5. Outline a staff development program for training educators who will be involved with the overall inclusion program. Be sure to include suggestions for curriculum modifications and varied active learning strategies that work best for inclusion teams. Determine what external or outside support services will also be necessary to make the program work effectively.

6. Clarify the role and job descriptions for all technological support resources that will be required by teams or the school to make the inclusion program a success as well as the processes for requesting such services on a need basis.

7. Formalize a written inclusion plan for implementation of the inclusion process on a team or in the school that identifies timetables, procedures, training requirements, and methods for obtaining feedback on how things are going.

8. Establish a comprehensive method for collecting both formative and summative data on the implementation of the inclusion program that includes observations, interviews, surveys, and self-reflective tools.

9. Determine ways to use the evaluation results for improving the inclusion plan making certain to consider both the benefits and the outcomes of inclusion on both student achievement and teacher performance.

10. Create multiple ways to celebrate the success of inclusion efforts that provide rewards for ALL who participate in the program.

10 Characteristics Of An At-Risk Student And Ten Characteristics Of Schools That Meet Needs Of At-Risk Students

Student Characteristics

An at-risk student:

1. . . . demonstrates academic learning and achievement problems.

2. . . . tends to be inattentive.

3. . . . is easily distracted.

4. . . . displays short attention span.

5. . . . has low self-esteem.

6. . . . lacks social skills.

7. . . . reflects narrow range of interests.

8. . . . fears failure.

9. . . . lacks structure and organization.

10. . . . avoids responsibility and independence.

School Characteristics

A school that meets needs of at-risk students:

1. . . . focuses on kids.

2. . . . challenges the regularities.

3. . . . collaborates with parents / guardians.

4. . . . avoids reforms that intensify or perpetuate impediments.

5. . . . decentralizes instructional decisions.

6. . . . promotes success.

7. . . . reduces negative effects of large school size.

8. . . . values differences in students.

9. . . . minimizes mistakes and failures.

10. . . . adopts a "whatever it takes" stance.

10 Traits Of Young Adolescents To Keep In Mind When Planning Lessons And Activities

As activities are planned, and lessons are developed and delivered the following points should be used as guidelines:

1. Young adolescents have unique interests and varied abilities. They need opportunities to express their creativity.

2. Young adolescents identify with their peers and want to belong to the group. They must have opportunities to form positive peer relationships.

3. Young adolescents reflect a willingness to learn new things they consider to be useful; therefore, they require occasions to use skills to solve real-life problems.

4. Young adolescents are curious about their world. They need varied situations for exploration and extension of knowledge.

5. Young adolescents experience rapid and sporadic physical development. They require varied activities and time to be themselves.

6. Young adolescents are self-conscious and susceptible to feelings of low self-esteem. They need opportunities for success and recognition.

7. Young adolescents are at a time in their lives when they need adults but do not want to admit it. They need caring adult role models and advisors who like and respect them.

8. Young adolescents want to make their own decisions. They need consistency and direction.

9. Young adolescents prefer active over passive learning activities. They need hands-on and cooperative learning experiences.

10. Young adolescents are idealistic and possess a strong sense of fairness; therefore, they require situations appropriate for sharing thoughts, feelings, and attitudes.

10 PLUS 8

Characteristics of Underachievers

Underachievers:

1. Harbor feelings of inferiority and failure

2. Feel rejected by family members

3. Take little responsibility for actions

4. Show hostility to authority figures

5. Resist adult influences

6. Feel victimized

7. Have negative feelings towards school and church

8. Appear rebellious

9. Lack academic skills and motivation

10. Demonstrate poor study habits

11. Tend to withdraw from classroom challenges

12. are less popular with peers

13. Demonstrate less mature behavior than achievers

14. Exhibit poor adjustment actions

15. have little interest in outside hobbies, sports, or activities

16. Tend to be test-phobic

17. Lack academic or vocational goals

18. Hold lower leadership status than peers

10 PLUS 4

Questions for Teachers of Ethnic and Language Minority Students to Ask Themselves

1. Do I have a clear and realistic sense of my own cultural and ethnic identity?

2. Do I firmly believe that all students can succeed regardless of their ethnic background?

3. Can I honestly bond with all types of students so that the "other" or the "we/they" perceptions do not exist?

4. Am I committed to achieving equity with all my students and not just a few?

5. Do I use culturally relevant materials that promote contributions and perspectives of various ethnic groups?

6. Do I maintain a balance in promoting the school culture with the maintenance of my students' sense of ethno-cultural pride and identity?

7. Do I maintain an academic and consistent interactive and collaborative learning environment?

8. Do I provide legitimate opportunities for students to work together in a wide variety of flexible social configurations and settings?

9. Do I use reality-based learning approaches with real purposes and real audiences?

10. Do I analyze students' learning styles or cultural preferences and accommodate these in designing and recommending complementary instructional methods and materials.

11. Do I promote home/school partnerships as essential elements in academic programs and in the overall development of the individual student?

12. Do I use varied and accelerated learning techniques that include consistent patterns of immediate rehearsal or application, numerous repetitions, and periodic reviews and recaps of materials learned?

13. Do I involve students actively, not passively, in most learning situations that nurture strategies that involve all types of students in leadership roles?

14. Do I identify and dispel prejudices, stereotypes, and inaccurate perceptions of individuals or groups as they are encountered in texts or other multi-media materials?

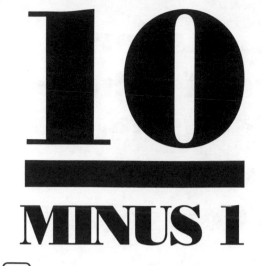

10 MINUS 1

Questions Concerning Instruction of Boys vs. Girls in the Classroom

Review each of these findings from the literature regarding the instructional tendencies and practices of teachers toward gender differences in the classroom. After each item, write down a suggestion for avoiding each of these discriminatory practices.

1. Did you know that teachers tend to punish boys more frequently and more harshly than they do girls, even in similar situations?

Suggestion: _____

_____

_____

_____

2. Did you know that teachers expect boys to be more active and assertive and girls to be more passive and unassertive in the classroom?

Suggestion: _____

_____

_____

_____

3. Did you know that teachers give boys more direct instruction as well as more attention and approval-oriented gestures?

Suggestion: _____

_____

_____

_____

4. Did you know that teachers ask boys to handle more physical and leadership activities in the classroom such as group facilitator, running of audiovisual equipment, moving furniture, or lifting boxes of materials?

Suggestion: _____

_____

_____

5. Did you know that teachers ask boys more factual, closed, or low level questions than girls?

Suggestion: _____

_____

_____

6. Did you know that teachers ask girls to assume more supportive and house-keeping chores such as watering plants and writing thank-you notes than boys?

Suggestion: _____

_____

_____

7. Did you know that teachers expect more from boys in mathematics and more from girls during reading/language arts instruction?

Suggestion: _____

_____

_____

8. Did you know that teachers criticize boys more for behavior problems and girls more for skill limitations or deficiencies?

Suggestion: _____

_____

_____

9. Did you know that teachers praise girls more for neatness and form in their work and boys more for their intellectual or academic thoughts?

Suggestion: _____

_____

_____

10 Important Needs Middle School Students Have While in School

Kids of all ages have several needs that must be met throughout the schooling process to be successful and productive. These needs impact both their behavior patterns and their academic achievements. As you read through these identified NEEDS, discuss and/or write down some classroom or school activities, events, experiences, policies, procedures, or programs that directly address each need as stated. Be specific in your comments.

1. Kids need to understand that they will be held responsible for their behaviors and their actions.

2. Kids need to understand that personal property and the rights of others must be respected at all times.

3. Kids need order, routine, structure, and fixed responsibility in their daily lives.

4. Kids need attention and expressions of caring or nurturing throughout the school experience.

5. Kids need an environment relatively free from anxiety, conflict, and unhealthy competition.

6. Kids need assistance in standing up to peer pressures that move them to conform to the behavioral norms of outside groups.

7. Kids need to realize that consequences follow behavior. This amounts to, "If I do THIS then THIS might happen."

8. Kids need sufficient rest, nourishment, and healthy practices.

9. Kids need protection from television and Internet violence, crime, and advertising hypocrisy.

10. Kids need the benefits of clear and positive communication between home and school.

10 Points To Consider When Developing A School Mission Statement

1. A school mission statement is a brief but essential sentence that clearly communicates the overall intent and focus for the schooling process in a given educational setting.

2. A school mission statement is important to a school because it very clearly communicates the teaching and learning priorities that a school has established for its "work."

3. A school mission statement is developed through the collaborative efforts of a team that includes representatives from the administrative staff, the faculty, the student population, the parents, and the business community it serves.

4. A school mission statement must reflect the diverse cultures, beliefs, values, and purposes of the entire school population.

5. A mission statement should evolve from a series of data-gathering activities that includes surveys or questionnaires, interviews, discussions, town meetings, and/or forums.

6. A mission statement draft should be written to reflect the input from the various stakeholders represented in the data-gathering process.

7. A mission statement draft should be circulated throughout the school community to elicit recommendations for revisions.

8. A final school mission statement should be written to represent the "best thinking" of all stakeholder groups in the school.

9. A sample middle school mission statement might read as follows:
"The mission of XYZ Middle School is to provide our students with the opportunities, resources, and environment to be lifelong learners and productive, responsible citizens in a changing, global society."

10. A school mission statement should be evaluated on a regular basis to determine the effect it is having on school practices and individual behavior of those associated with the school.

10 Suggestions For Facility Requirements For Middle Schools

1. Team classrooms should be in proximity to one another. This will make for instant communication and will cut down on time required for students to travel from one classroom to another.

2. These classrooms should adapt easily for grouping and regrouping of students. It may be necessary to vary class size, learning experiences, and delivery systems.

3. The environment at all times must be safe and secure for students and staff. This issue is of great concern to parents.

4. The furniture and equipment in classrooms should be functional, movable, and size-appropriate. Remember that flexibility is the *key* in middle school.

5. The media center should be the center of all curriculum and instruction, not just a library with books. The media specialist is the "expert" in curriculum, materials, equipment, and information.

6. The physical plant should be aesthetically pleasing and attractive. This enhances the setting for learning.

7. A large, well-lit group instruction/meeting area (with shades if necessary) should be made available for use by all teams. A good plan is to have a sign-up sheet posted at or near the entrance to the room and to ask team leaders to sign up in ink for no more than two consecutive days at a time.

8. It is recommended that teachers have an assigned team meeting room for their use. A round table, comfortable chairs, and a bulletin board with a calendar enhance team-meeting space.

9. Plan effective traffic patterns so that the minimum number of students is changing classes at one time. The environment (both inside and outside of classrooms) should reflect the physical needs of students.

10. If lockers are provided, consider height and size. Assign lockers to students whose team classrooms are in the same area.

10 PLUS 3 Suggestions For Developing A Positive Middle School Climate

1. Develop a school motto and logo and use them widely.

2. Develop a referral to the office for positive student recognition.

3. Reinforce good attendance at all school functions through individual and group incentives.

4. Display student work in all classrooms and throughout the building on a large scale.

5. Use marquees, school windows, and lobby showcases to convey positive messages.

6. Designate and maintain quality teacher, student, and parent lounges as "time in" rooms.

7. Take care when stating or promoting school rules so they take on a positive rather than a punitive flavor.

8. Support and encourage an active student council/ government and parent advisory groups.

9. Seize opportunities to augment school life with extracurricular activities.

10. Form an "academic boosters" group to promote academics within the school.

11. Issue many invitations and encourage people to visit your school.

12. Draw attention to personal and professional growth of staff members.

13. Develop a positive marketing plan for your school that includes a multi-media presentation, regular newspaper/radio/television promotions, and parent communications.

# 10

MINUS 4

Tasks to Develop Understanding of Full Service Schools

It has been documented that maximizing the involvement of schools with community services can serve a major purpose in enhancing the potential for addressing myriad and complex teenager need. Use these activities to explore the potential of FULL SERVICE SCHOOLS in your community. In essence, full-service schools, also called community schools and full-service community schools, are arguably the most popular examples of the transformation of the public school.

1. **KNOWLEDGE LEVEL TASK:** A full service school can be defined as "a school center in which health, mental health, social, and/or family service may be co-located depending on the needs of the particular school and community." Make a list of potential health, mental health, social, and/or family services that might be included in such a concept.

2. **COMPREHENSION LEVEL TASK:** In your own words, explain how grouping a number of support services in one place, such as school, makes these services more accessible to the public and promotes coordination of services.

3. **APPLICATION LEVEL TASK:** Generate a list of questions that one might ask schools who have implemented the full service concept to determine both their process for development and their effectiveness to date.

4. **ANALYSIS LEVEL TASK:** Create a chart that shows the advantages and disadvantages of a full service school for the student, teacher, and family as compared to a traditional public school that is not a full service institution.

5. **SYNTHESIS LEVEL TASK:** Create a promotional tool (commercial, poster, flyer, advertisement, or billboard) highlighting the many benefits of the full service school for educators, social service agencies, and families of a community.

6. **EVALUATION LEVEL TASK:** The Coalition for Community Schools has identified the following operating principles of an ideal community school. On a rating scale of 1 to 5 (with one being least important and 5 being most important) rank each one of these areas in terms of their importance to you.

ONE: Quality Education—All of the community's assets serve as resources for learning.

TWO: Youth Development—All young people develop their assets and talents and serve as resources to their communities.

THREE: Family Support—All family resource centers, early childhood development programs, coordinated health and social services, counseling, and other supports enhance family life.

FOUR: Family and Community Engagement—All family members and other residents actively participating in designing, supporting, monitoring, and advocating quality programs and activities in school and community.

FIVE: Community Development—All participants focus on strengthening the social networks, economic viability, and physical infrastructure of the surrounding community.

10 High-Priority Areas To Consider When Setting Up A Master Schedule

1. Build in an advisory program for 20–30 minutes daily.

2. Provide common planning time for interdisciplinary teams.

3. Place all core teachers on a single academic team with no cross teaming.

4. Maintain a student-teacher ratio of 150 students per four-person team.

5. Allow students to have options in choosing exploratory classes.

6. Offer a co-curricular program.

7. Plan for multi-age groupings in electives and mini-classes.

8. Organize electives and academic classes on a trimester schedule.

9. Program reasonable times for lunch periods.

10. Encourage a "school within a school" concept or a multi-age pilot team.

10 MINUS 1 Things To Think About When Putting Together A Middle School's Master Schedule

1. Every schedule for every school is unique because the demographics of every school vary.

2. Set priorities for scheduling and accept the fact that every schedule has its share of trade-offs or compromises.

3. With more single or special classes/programs, more conflicts will surface during the scheduling process.

4. Limit or, if possible, eliminate prerequisite courses in the exploratory areas.

5. Don't depend on computer services and/or scheduling software packages to solve scheduling problems.

6. The master schedule must serve the students first, the teachers second, and the administrators third.

7. One must have the courage to try new paradigms when setting up the schedule. Try something different.

8. One must live a master schedule to realize its limitations, advantages, and possibilities.

9. Keep a sense of humor.

10 PLUS 20

Rules to Consider for Establishing a Successful Middle Grades Setting

Read through these classroom rules carefully and evaluate each one in terms of the guidelines for establishing rules in a successful middle school setting. It should be noted that all of these rules have been taken from existing classrooms throughout the country.

1. Always strive to be on time for classes or other engagements.

2. Keep your hands and feet to yourself.

3. Use appropriate voices when inside.

4. Treat everyone with respect.

5. Be prepared with books, pencils, and papers.

6. Respect other people and their property.

7. Be prepared to participate in activities, projects, and group projects.

8. Make sure to bring all learning materials with you to class.

9. You may tell others when you are angry, and you may give yourself time to calm down, but you may not hit, yell, act out, or use profanity.

10. Wait to talk until you are called upon.

11. Complete all assignments in a timely manner.

12. Use common sense—if you think there's a chance you or someone else might get hurt, do not do it.

13. Use only kind words when speaking of others.

14. Strive to do your best work at all times.

15. Come to class prepared to succeed.

16. Support others when they need it; let others support you.

17. When others are speaking, listen.

18. Walk, do not run, in halls and classroom.

19. If it is not yours, do not touch it.

20. Refrain from eating or chewing gum in class.

21. Clean up your own workspaces.

22. Avoid profanity, teasing, or disrespectful behavior at all times.

23. Sit in your seat, ready for class, when the bell rings.

24. Raise your hand for permission to speak.

25. Ask for restroom passes during instruction time only in cases of emergency.

26. Treat others as you would like to be treated.

27. Laugh *with* anyone when there is something to laugh about; do not laugh *at* anyone under any circumstances.

28. Assume responsibility for your own learning.

29. Avoid behavior that would disturb people who are working.

30. Prepare and hand in assignments on time.

10 Starter Statements To Assess Classroom Climate

Your teacher wants to know what you think about the way your classroom looks and feels and what you think could be done to make it a better place to work and learn. Please complete the following statements as honestly as possible; your feedback is important.

1. The most exciting part of this classroom is . . .

2. The most comfortable aspect of this classroom is. . .

3. The arrangement of the furniture is . . .

4. The characteristic I find most distracting is . . .

5. A classroom object that is difficult or inconvenient to use is . . .

6. An aspect of this room that is boring is . . .

7. Another classroom in this school that looks interesting and attractive appeals to me because . . .

8. One change I think could be made to make this room a better environment for learning is . . .

9. The one characteristic I would most like to change is . . .

10. One other characteristic I would like to say about this room is . . .

10 Ways to Maximize Space in a School Setting

Each of these suggestions for better meeting the space needs of students to improve the delivery of content and instruction is relatively simple and inexpensive to implement. They do, however, require some creative thinking and openness to new ways of doing things.

1. Extend the school day by keeping the media center open for student and family use before school, after school, in the evenings, or on weekends. Use this time and space for special study sessions, tutoring sessions, remediation sessions, or enrichment sessions.

2. Decorate school hallways, corridors, auditorium stage areas, or cafeteria spaces and use foldout tables and stackable chairs as furniture.

3. Place television sets on school buses or in the cafeteria areas for teaching enrichment classes such as foreign language and extended art, drama, and music topics.

4. Use bulletin boards, bookshelves, hanging posters, and clotheslines for learning stations within the regular classroom.

5. Use outdoor courtyards or picnic tables or gazebos as extensions of classroom instructional spaces.

6. Use color as the foundation for separating room areas designated as learning spaces.

7. Use an empty conference room or classroom as a student lounge for enrichment activities or as an audiovisual room for showing movies or videos using a sign-up schedule and a volunteer to run the equipment.

8. Encourage students to help reorganize classroom learning spaces and table or desk arrangements on a regular and consistent basis.

9. Provide a supply table where students can quickly replenish forgotten or broken pencils and misplaced or depleted packages of notebook paper without disruption of other students.

10. Use magnets to clip teacher notes and lecture outlines on the chalkboard during instruction. This helps to avoid misplaced papers and to give quick references to ideas while keeping teacher's hands free for instruction.

10 Creative Approaches To A Positive Classroom Climate

1. Ask students to discuss how they have handled the tantrums or inappropriate behavior of younger siblings or of children who have been in their care.

2. If students are having a hard time "settling down," give them five minutes of writing time during which they are permitted to write anything they want. No one will see what they write, and when the designated time is over, papers will be torn up and thrown away. Then it's time for work!

3. If a student criticizes you, smile (even when you don't feel like smiling) and respond positively to the criticism. If you agree, say something like "In fact, I am probably more _____ than you realize." If you don't feel the criticism is warranted, you might say, "Do you think so? I wasn't aware of that." Either way, continue with the lesson.

4. Try to leave your "anger response" outside of the classroom. If students see they are unable to goad you into anger, this takes away some of their perceived power to disrupt.

5. Call on your sense of humor to defuse a tense situation or elicit group support for an unpopular cause. You will be amazed at how effective a good laugh or even a big grin can be.

6. The use of group approval or focusing on a child who is doing well may be effective when maintaining discipline with young children, but public approval or disapproval may backfire with your middle schoolers. Try speaking privately with a student who misbehaves or needs extra support, using a foundation of previously developed rapport to guide the conference.

7. Inappropriate behavior may stem from boredom or frustration. If the entire class is exhibiting behavior problems, reconsider your instructional material or teaching strategy. More interestingly appropriate materials and presentations may automatically eliminate many behavior problems.

8. Provide choices. For example, if your class is working in cooperative groups and one group appears to be finding it difficult to stay on task, give that group the choice of continuing to work as a group, or of splitting up to complete the assignment individually.

9. Arrange for older students to work as tutors or group leaders with your students and to serve as role models.

10. Allow students 30 minutes every Friday to engage in a free-time activity of their choice (even if it involves being "loud and silly") as a privilege earned by behaving with decorum during the week.

10 Questions To Use To Assess Creativity In Your School

How does your school feel about innovation and creativity in the curriculum and in the assessment process that drives the curriculum? Use this list of questions to determine your school's Creativity Quotient, or C.Q.

1. Is creativity highly regarded by your school's administration and faculty members?

2. Is creativity included in your school's mission statement, goals, and objectives?

3. Are creative ideas implemented quickly in your school setting?

4. Does your school encourage brainstorming sessions as part of its agenda for in-service days?

5. Do you have staff meetings to discuss opportunities and challenges as frequently as those to discuss problems and procedures?

6. Is your school's student assessment program designed to generate qualitative as well as quantitative information about your students?

7. Do you combine creative enterprises and innovative programs with your best and brightest teachers?

8. Do you maintain the notion that faculty is here first and foremost to meet the creative and critical thinking skill needs of the students?

9. Do you celebrate creativity in your school with ceremony, traditions, and rewards?

10. Are innovators in your school treated like heroes?

Ways To Use Questions To Develop Higher-Level Thinking Skills

1. **Knowledge Questions:** Who, what, when, where, why, and how _____ ?
Recite, recall, record, or reproduce _____ .
Locate, label, or list _____ .

2. **Comprehension Questions:** Retell _____ in your own words.
Describe, summarize, discuss, or explain the main idea of _____ .
Give examples of _____ .

3. **Application Questions:** How is _____ an example of or related to_____ ?
Distinguish between _____ and _____ .
Illustrate the workings of a _____ .

4. **Analysis Questions:** What are the parts or features of_____ ?
Compare and contrast _____ with _____ .
Outline, diagram, or web _____ .
Draw conclusions or make inferences about _____ .

5. **Synthesis Questions:** What would you predict or propose about _____ ?
What might happen if you combined _____ with _____ ?
How would you improve a _____ ?
What creative solutions would you suggest for _____ ?

6. **Evaluation Questions:** Rank order _____ according to_____ .
What criteria would you use to assess or evaluate _____ ?
Defend or validate this idea/statement:_____ .

7. **Personal Questions:** How do you feel about _____ ? Do you
think _____ ? Where do you stand on the issue of_____ ?

8. **Observation Questions:** What seems to be happening in this picture ___ ?
What might you infer from your observations of _____ ?

9. **Cause/Effect Questions:** Why did _____ ?
What would happen if _____ ?

10. **Viewpoint Questions:** How would this look to a _____ ?
What would a _____ mean from the viewpoint of a _____ ?
How would _____ view this?

10 MINUS 7

Important Decisions to Make for Effective Classroom Management

1. Establish rules and procedures for each of the following:

a. beginning the class period
b. handling tardy and absent students
c. assigning initial bell work
d. distributing supplies
e. returning student class work/homework
f. deciding how students are to contact you
g. deciding when and how students leave their seats
h. deciding when and how students leave the room (bathroom, media center, office)
i. getting students' attention
j. ending the class period

2. Consider guidelines for each of the following:

a. headings for papers
b. asking for teacher help/assistance
c. talking during seatwork
d. how to handle fast workers who finish tasks or assignments early
e. distributing tests and assignments
f. picking up tests and assignments
g. making transitions from one task to another
h. turning in completed assignments

3. Determine academic feedback for each of the following:

a. handling incomplete work
b. formulating grading
c. monitoring student work periods
d. maintaining a record of student grades
e. student procedures for self-grading and reflection
f. evaluation practices for long-term projects
g. maintenance of student portfolios

Student Self-Assessment of
Classroom Management Attitudes

Directions: Please read and assign a number from 1 to 4 (with 1 being All the Time, 2 being Much of the Time, 3 being Some of the Time, and 4 being Little of the Time) for each of the items listed below. Be honest in your self-assessment efforts.

_____ I get to class on time

_____ I have my class materials with me and come prepared to learn.

_____ I turn in my assignments meeting the required deadlines.

_____ I do my homework.

_____ I participate in class discussions and activities.

_____ I listen to the teacher during instructional sessions.

_____ I listen to my peers during instructional sessions.

_____ I follow directions well.

_____ I ask questions when I do not understand something.

_____ I make good use of class time for working on assigned tasks.

Now . . . look back over your ten items and write down three things you could do to improve one or more of the behaviors for which you scored only a 3 or a 4.

1. _____

_____

_____

2. _____

_____

_____

3. _____

_____

_____

10 PLUS 13

Rewards to Consider for Good Behavior

Experts stress that providing students with a wide variety of rewards or positive consequences for consistently good behavior is essential to the long-term management of a productive classroom. Below you will find some suggested incentives to encourage positive student behavior.

1. Good Newsletters, notes, or telephone calls to parents

2. Citizen of the Day or Week award

3. Special "free time" allotment

4. Extra media center time

5. Homework exemption pass

6. Special treats such as snacks or drinks

7. Opportunities to visit other classrooms and work with friends

8. Freedom to work on a special project with a peer

9. Special seat in class, at lunch, or on the bus

10. Opportunity to sit and/or work at the teacher's desk

11. Donated gift certificates or passes to local retail outlets or movie theaters

12. Special recognition certificate

13. Serve as assistant to school secretary, media specialist, or principal

14. Serve as discussion leader or teacher's aide

15. Special comments on report card

16. Provide extra time in the computer lab

17. Have a games period and allow students to bring their own games

18. Exempt rewarded students from a question or two on an assignment

19. Arrange for excellent work of students to appear in the newspaper or some other source of public display complete with photograph and/or short biography of the student

20. Host of gym, library, or computer night at the school for students and parents.

21. Provide free tickets to school sporting or performance events

22. Allow a student to run errands for the teacher

23. Surprise the student with a teacher note of appreciation

10 MINUS 3

Guidelines to Consider When Establishing a Set of Classroom Rules

Rules, much like laws, define acceptable and unacceptable behavior in a community setting. Although possible, it is undesirable to establish hundreds of rules in order to cover every anticipated behavior problem; therefore, the teacher should define only those rules that are most important to running a safe environment that is conducive to learning. Some guidelines to consider when establishing rules for a classroom of students are listed below. Review them and record the reactions you have to each point.

1. Guidelines must be clear and specific. That is, they must be short and simple in syntax.

YOUR REACTION: _____

_____

_____

2. One must always be able to determine if the rule is broken or followed; rules must not be ambiguous.

YOUR REACTION: _____

_____

_____

3. Rules must make sense to the people who enforce and follow them; they are best agreed upon by both student and teacher alike.

YOUR REACTION: _____

_____

_____

4. They must state what is allowed as well as what is not allowed. Rules should be explainable through both examples and non-examples.

YOUR REACTION: _____

_____

_____

5. Rules must be stated simply and demonstrated so that all can understand; they should be taught, discussed, and/or role-played before implementation.

YOUR REACTION: _____

_____

_____

6. Guidelines should state positive expectations rather than focus on unacceptable behaviors.

YOUR REACTION: _____

_____

_____

7. Guidelines should be fundamental and non-negotiable.

YOUR REACTION: _____

_____

_____

10 PLUS 28

Behavior Problems that Occur Most Often in the Classroom

____ **1.** Arguments among students who quarrel with each other or the teacher

____ **2.** Assignments not turned in by students who cannot do them, will not do them, or refuse to do them as a means of control

____ **3.** Students who bother their classmates disrupt learning for the entire classroom.

____ **4.** Behavior on a bus that is negative because of disrespect for adults or because of a need to draw attention to oneself

____ **5.** Cheating among students who care either too much or too little

____ **6.** Cleanup, whether it be one's desk, work station, locker, or room that is kept in order

____ **7.** Disorganization that can have an impact on a student's performance

____ **8.** Disrespectful behavior by a student who has little self-respect, or few positive role models to imitate

____ **9.** Enthusiasm that is lacking due to a sense of powerlessness in today's world

____ **10.** Energy in the wrong way causing the student to seek negative reinforcement rather than positive feedback for behaviors displayed

___ **11.** Profanity that has become a "way of life" for even the best students, due to social norms and influences

___ **12.** Friendship problems and peer pressures which all too often impact on a student's attitude toward the schooling process

___ **13.** Gangs that fill a student's need to belong to a group in order to avoid isolation

___ **14.** Gum chewing that not only interferes with oral communication tasks, but also finds itself attached to desks, sidewalks, and other inappropriate places

___ **15.** Holidays causing students to be absent from class or to become distracted from academics

___ **16.** Hurrying through assigned tasks often leading to poor quality work and wasted time

___ **17.** Interruptions by students who are poor listeners, are egocentric learners, or are lacking in social skill

___ **18.** Isolation or withdrawal by students who lack confidence in their ability to learn

___ **19.** Jurisdiction disputed and disparities that lead students to play one adult against another

___ **20.** Jealousy among students who compete for attention from peers, parents, and persons in charge

___ **21.** Kicks that come from the wrong sources such as tobacco, drugs, or breaking school rules

___ **22.** Kissing or other forms of sexual expression that lead to promiscuity or other forms of undesirable behavior

___ **23.** Lying by students who are confronted with discrepancies between what they say and do

___ **24.** Limits which students refuse to acknowledge or honor in their daily activities

___ **25.** Manipulation by students who are discouraged or disillusioned about the world in which they learn and live

___ **26.** Motivation levels demonstrated by many students who approach the school setting without goals, skills, resources, or family support

___ **27.** Note writing between students, which often takes priority over attention to classroom instruction

___ **28.** Nonsense fads, fashions, or behaviors among students that are self-initiated distractions from the "business" of school

___ **29.** Procrastination by some students who do not know how to set priorities or budget their time

___ **30.** Put downs which are used all too often by students when referring to their peers

___ **31.** Rigidity among students who are unable to see the "gray" areas of life and the time and place for negotiation

___ **32.** Rigor in the curriculum that is often undervalued by students in the courses they choose to take

___ **33.** Skipping school or cutting classes leading to student suspensions and dropouts

___ **34.** Sportsmanship that is lacking in many types of competition, whether it be academic or athletic in context

___ **35.** Taking turns which requires students to be more patient and tolerant of others

___ **36.** Tardiness as students often fail to appreciate time on task opportunities and responsibilities

___ **37.** Understanding prejudices and stereotypes among school populations that value diversity and differences within the student body

___ **38.** Undertaking responsibility for one's own learning as an alternative to a top-down approach to learning content and skills

10 PLUS 2

Guidelines for Handling Inappropriate Behaviors

1. Place an emphasis on prevention through classroom rules and regulations that are clear, consistent, fair, and understood by all students.

2. Try to quickly "size up" the situation in order to determine if the behavior is indeed interfering with instruction or whether it is merely annoying to you as the teacher.

3. Be certain to attack the behavior problem or classroom interruption and not the student.

4. Whenever possible, count to ten before attacking the problem in order to minimize your reaction and to keep yourself cool, calm, and collected.

5. Deal specifically with the infraction at hand and not references to previous incidents or misconducts.

6. Always focus on orchestrating a win/win situation rather than a win/lose situation for all parties involved.

7. Remember and remind yourself that you, and you alone, are responsible for your words and your actions, so keep the discipline constructive and productive at all times.

8. Be fair in assigning consequences that fit the crime, and apply those consequences as soon as possible after the misbehavior.

9. Provide the student who is being disciplined the opportunity and privilege of rejoining the ongoing classroom activities as soon as possible to avoid undue delay and limitations on task time.

10. If the student is out of control and unable to rejoin the group, isolate him/her in some way, but emphasize when the privilege of class participation will be allowed again.

11. Emphasize to the student that you will offer support, feedback, guidelines, and limits to the student at any time, but that the ultimate responsibility for exercising proper behavior always rests with the student.

12. If certain misbehaviors are chronic among students, arrange for ongoing instruction and assistance that will involve the class in their solution.

10 MINUS 7

Approaches to Conflict Mediation

APPROACH ONE: Employ the following nine steps to resolve conflict situations:

1. Identify and define the problem or conflict.

2. Determine the circumstances, situations, and behaviors that led up to the problem or conflict.

3. Examine the feelings experienced by those involved.

4. Ask yourself, "Have I dealt with a problem/conflict such as this before? What did I do? Did it work? What would I do differently next time?"

5. List and reflect on many different alternatives for handling the problem.

6. Select one alternative and develop a plan of action.

7. Implement and monitor the plan.

8. Evaluate the plan to determine if it is working and, if not, what other alternatives need to be considered.

APPROACH TWO: Design a Conflict Mediation Form similar to the sample given here and use this with a group of student-trained mediators who follow these ground rules for mediating a conflict:

1. Get the conflicting parties to agree to solve the problem with the help of the mediator. This requires a voluntary "yes" from the involved parties.

2. Instruct disputants that they cannot engage in name-calling, but must be considerate and respectful of one another.

3. Inform disputants that they will each have an opportunity to state his/her views of the conflict including what they want, how they feel, and what would be an acceptable solution.

4. Encourage disputants to be both honest and accurate in their descriptions of the conflict including what they want, how they feel, and what would be an acceptable solution.

5. Stress to the disputants that they must agree to abide by the agreement or resolution.

6. Emphasize to disputants the importance of confidentiality and that all discussion at this meeting is confidential and will not be reported to authorities unless it involves weapons, drugs, or alcohol-related incidents. It is important that the mediator listens closely to all disputants, finds out the facts causing the conflict, exhibits patience, and respects all parties.

SAMPLE INFORMATION GATHERING FORM
FOR MEDIATION MEETING

1. What is the basic conflict and who is involved?

_____

_____

_____

2. What did you want that caused the conflict?

_____

_____

_____

3. What did the other person(s) want that caused the conflict?

_____

_____

_____

4. What are three possible solutions/agreements to the conflict that would satisfy you?

_____

_____

_____

5. What are two things you might do if this conflict surfaces again?

_____

_____

_____

6. What would you like to say to the other person(s) involved in this conflict?

_____

_____

_____

APPROACH THREE: Organize a problem-solving team of teachers at each grade level to handle the difficult conflict situations that arise during the school year. These problem-solving teams should consider the following guidelines:

1. Teams should be composed of volunteers or participants who believe in the effectiveness of systematic, collaborative troubleshooting. Teams should include regular classroom teachers, an administrator, a support staff person (such as a school counselor, a psychologist, a social worker), parents, and possibly students.

2. School administrators must provide resources and support to facilitate team functioning including such possibilities as release time, financial compensation, relief from other duties, and paperwork assistance.

3. Training in trust building, collaboration, interventions, and consultation should be provided for all team members.

4. Teams should be enabled to make use of their collective expertise and be encouraged to bring individual perspectives to the decision-making and problem-solving sessions.

5. Behavior contracts for use with students should be developed and used as part of this process. A sample is included on the following page.

6. Teams should consider a wide variety of interventions for improving student behavior because different students respond to different interventions based on their needs and the causes of their behavior.

   Some possible interventions include:
   a. Opportunities to be a leader and contribute
   b. A behavior management contract
   c. A mentor or buddy
   d. An opportunity to "let off steam" via a physical outlet
   e. A good role model
   f. More one-to-one attention from volunteer, aide, peer, or tutor
   g. Shorter or modified classroom assignments
   h. More choices regarding classroom assignments and activities
   i. More rigorous consequences
   j. Parental support or involvement
   k. More tangible rewards
   l. Some quiet times or places
   m. Conflict resolution skills training

SAMPLE BEHAVIOR CONTRACT

Student Name: _____ Date: _____

I, _____ , agree to do the following things

during the time span from _____ to _____ .

   1. _____

     _____

   2. _____

     _____

   3. _____

     _____

I can expect the following help from others in the school:

   1. _____

     _____

   2. _____

     _____

   3. _____

     _____

When others and I have done the above, the following will happen:

   1. _____

     _____

   2. _____

     _____

   3. _____

     _____

Signed by: _____

Witnessed by: _____

Activities to Help Students Think Through and Classify Appropriate Behaviors

ACTIVITY ONE:
"Dear Ann Landers" Discussion Groups

Introduce this activity to students by having them bring copies of the advice columns from their local newspaper including Ann Landers or Dear Abby columns. Discuss their purpose, format, and how they are used as a tool for problem solving. Next, instruct each student to write his/ her own version of an advice column focusing on a behavior problem or situation that he/s he finds inappropriate for the classroom or school setting. Divide the class into small cooperative learning groups and have them respond to the questions generated by members of their group by writing a response to each behavior problem area.

ACTIVITY TWO:
"Acting Out Problem Situations"

Create a set of scenarios that describe common behavior problems that are encountered by students of this age group. (See the example.) Assign students to cooperative learning groups and have each group create a skit, role play, or case study to act out the solution or alternative solutions to their assigned problem.

ACTIVITY THREE:
"A Picture is Worth a Thousand Words"

Collect a series of magazine pictures that feature groups of people in various settings—families, sporting events, work groups, social settings, etc. Give each student a picture and ask them to describe the various behaviors and feelings they detect in the picture by writing a paragraph about it. Mix up finished paragraphs and pictures and ask students to match them correctly.

ACTIVITY FOUR:
"Inside and Outside Circle"

Prepare a list of discipline or behavior-problem issues that are concerns in today's classroom and post these on the chalkboard, the overhead projector, or a large chart stand with newsprint. Divide students in the classroom into two circles—one circle inside the other circle—with partners facing each other. Each pair of partners will discuss the first item on the list of problem areas with one another. After several minutes of discussion, play some taped music for a few seconds and have students move their circles in opposite directions until the music stops. Facing a different person, students now discuss the second item on this list. The process repeats itself until the items on the list have been exhausted. Some possible discussion topics might be:

1. Why do some students cheat on class assignments and what should be done about it?
2. How can the teacher better motivate kids to perform and/or do better work in school?
3. Why do so many kids your age smoke?
4. How do you feel about in and out-of-school suspensions?
5. What classroom rules are hardest for you to follow and why?

ACTIVITY FIVE:
"A Century from Now"

Divide the class into small cooperative learning groups and ask each group to create a time capsule for future generations of students that will tell them as much as possible about the norms, feelings, attitudes, lifestyles, and behavior patterns/preferences of today's young teenager. In your time capsule, include such items as the following (although others can be added as well):

1. A musical tape
2. Two newspaper articles of current events
3. A series of journal entries about the day in the life of each group member
4. Photographs or drawings of special places in the community where kids hang out
5. A restaurant menu from a favorite fast food outlet
6. A list of teenage heroes
7. A book review or book cover
8. An artifact from the school
9. A series of magazine pictures showing what the lifestyle is like
10. A movie advertisement

ACTIVITY SIX:
"The Gossip Danger"

Choose six students to send out of the room for a short period of time. Select a student from the remaining class members and tell him or her a short story or anecdote. Call in one of the students from the removed group and ask the in-class student to repeat the story. Call in another student and have the first student called in repeat the story as he or she heard it. Repeat this process several times so that the previously returning student tells each returning student the same story. Ask the rest of the class take notes on where and when the original story takes on new details. End the activity with a discussion of "gossip" and how it can hurt others and become distorted over time.

ACTIVITY SEVEN:
"The School Banner"

Distribute a large piece of drawing paper to students and have them draw and cut out a large banner. Instruct students to divide the banner into six parts and cut out a large banner. Instruct students to divide the banner into six parts and draw each one of the following elements—one per section.

Section One: A symbol that best depicts the school climate.

Section Two: A symbol that best depicts a favorite subject area or course taught at school.

Section Three: A symbol depicting a special and positive happening or event at school.

Section Four: A symbol depicting a favorite place in school.

Section Five: A symbol depicting a favorite place in the school.

Section Six: A symbol depicting a favorite adult in the school.

ACTIVITY EIGHT:
"Name Tag"

Have students create a king-sized, and tent-shaped name/place card out of poster board or oak tag to stand in the center of their desk. Instruct students to write their names on one side of the tent card and to locate pictures ad words/phrases/captions out of magazines and newspapers to decorate and paste on the other side of the tent card. These cutout graphics should represent the personality, behavior patterns, and interests of the person they represent. Use these to identify students for a parent event such as an open house.

ACTIVITY NINE:
"There Are Always Two Sides to A Person"

Have students write a short, one page essay describing themselves - their physical appearance, their personality and behavior traits, their personal strengths, and their weaknesses. Then, have these same students write a short, one page essay describing how they think others in the class perceive their appearance, traits, strengths, and weaknesses. Ask each student to share these two perspectives with one another in small groups and discuss their accuracy.

ACTIVITY TEN:
"You Are What You Wear"

Set aside one day in a given week where students are asked to wear to class a special outfit or pieces of apparel that best represents who they think they are or want to be. Discuss how clothes can tell a great deal about a person and the way he/she behaves. Ask students to design a new school uniform that they would wear if given the chance. Discuss how school uniforms often influence how a student behaves in school.

10 MINUS 2

Ways to Head Off Potential Discipline Problems Before They Become Major Disruptions

1. Provide consistent and meaningful positive reinforcement for students who behave appropriately that includes a combination of sincere praise, creative awards, group rewards, and informative phone calls or notes to home.

2. Develop a discipline plan or "ladder" of discipline offenses that correlates minor infractions with minor consequences and major infractions with major consequences. These might include listing student names on the board that serve as warnings, conducting private talks with students, contacting parents for assistance, and scheduling conferences established by the teacher.

3. Experiment with alternative methods of classroom control such as Time-Out Tables that last approximately 15 minutes, one-on-one talks with a student taken aside, or providing options for students to decide on their own punishment or fate based on predetermined behaviors established by the teacher.

4. "Walk the talk" by circulating around the room while teaching a lesson, pausing or stopping by problem students on a need basis.

5. Draw up a formal contract that specifies desired student behavior and that lays out timelines and penalties. Have the contract cosigned by student, teacher, and parent alike.

6. In cooperative or small group work sessions or settings, pull out misbehaving students and have them work in a group with the teacher as the leader for that class period or until they are ready to join their peers.

7. In extreme cases, invite a parent monitor to class and have them spend the entire day sitting and working with the student in a "monitoring" and not a "friendly" capacity.

8. Maintain a discipline log with each student's name listed in it. When a problem occurs, have the student sign the log next to or under his/her name. The student then completes a discipline sheet answering the following questions: What did I do? Why did this cause a problem? What can I do to prevent this problem from happening again? The discipline sheets are kept in a folder with the log and both serve as a method of accountability for anecdotal records and parent/guardian conferences.

10 PLUS 8

Teaching Tips and Tidbits

Below is a collection of assorted "tips and tidbits" for teachers who would like new ideas for improving their classroom management and instructional efforts. They are not organized in any significant way, but are recorded as "random ideas" to select for use or discard if not appropriate for a given situation.

1. Prepare more material than you think you will need for any given lesson plan. This not only ensures that you will have adequate material for the time allowed, but that you will have options within the time frame to pick and choose what activities or experiences seem most appropriate as the lesson progresses.

2. Divide the chalkboard according to your lesson plans with colored rubber tape. Use one section for Schedule/Date, another for the day's assignments, a third section for notes and reminders, and a fourth section for homework assignments.

3. Maintain an "IN BOX" and an "OUT BOX" on or near your desk for students to hand in their work as it is completed, and for corrected papers that are ready to be handed back. Assign a student to check the OUT BOX each day and to take responsibility for distributing papers, placing those papers without names with the "NO NAME CLIP" suggested below.

4. Use a large magnetic clip to hold all student work that does not have a name. Attach it to your desk or the chalkboard so students know where to look if they do not get an assignment back.

5. When handing out new worksheets or assignments, put the name of each absent student at the top of any of the papers and place in a strategic location or the "OUT BOX" if you have one to be distributed upon their return.

6. When collecting assignments and papers from the entire class, call for them in alphabetical order to save time during the grading and recording processes.

7. Speed up the attendance process by having students check off their names on a standard attendance sheet when entering the classroom or ask the first student who comes in to serve as the attendance taker for the day.

8. Use special school (if school will allow you to do so) letterhead or classroom (design you own) letterhead for all official communications to the home; this signals their importance to parents/guardians immediately.

9. Organize your filing cabinet with drawers for each subject area or a drawer for each marking period of topics/themes or drawers for each cluster of skill/concept areas.

10. Design a standard "Meetings" form on which you record notes from all meetings whether they be school staff, team meetings, district curriculum, or planning meetings. On this form include such information as: Type of Meeting, Date/Time of Meeting, Leader of Meeting, Members Present at Meeting, Topics/Points Covered at Meeting, and Notes to Myself As Follow-Up to Meeting.

11. Create a Student Participation Log to keep track of student interaction during a class discussion. List the names of students in the class and check off a space every time you call on a student. This is a good way to note who has or has not been called upon to participate in a group discussion. It would look something like:

Class or Course _____ Date From _____ To _____	
Student's Name _____	
Called Upon ( ) ( ) ( ) ( ) ( ) ( ) ( ) ( ) ( ) ( ) ( ) ( ) ( ) ( ) ( ) ( )	

Another strategy for keeping track of student participation in a group discussion or activity is to write each student's name on a file card, and as you call on a student, put aside his/her file card until all names have been used.

Another strategy to consider for this purpose is a Stick Jar. Print student's name on a Popsicle stick or tongue depressor and place the sticks in a glass jar. Draw names from the jar as the student is called upon or volunteers a response.

12. Arrange student desks in islands of two, three, or four as opposed to straight rows. This makes walking around the room easier for the teacher and when the teacher is working with a student at one of the islands, he/she is also influencing the other close by. This idea also encourages peers to help one another in their small group and to be less influenced by others working outside their group.

13. Establish a reward program within the school, team, department, or classroom that focuses on the idea of "Catch' em Doing Good." When a teacher, staff member, parent, or other adult in the setting after that kid is awarded a predetermined "Catch' em Doing Good" certificate that reads something like: "This is to certify that _____ performed a kind act on _____ as observed or witnessed by _____ ."

14. When establishing due dates for assignments, consider giving students a requirement that is not limited to one day such as Monday but one of three days such as Monday, Tuesday, or Wednesday. This allows for individual student differences, reduces the number of late hand-ins, and spreads the teacher's time for grading papers.

15. Prepare a Team Homework Sheet for each day of the week that lists the homework assignments for each class period/teacher that is distributed and briefly reviewed by the last teacher of the day with the students. Use this strategy also as a planning tool so that students do not have to study for more than one test on any given day.

16. Use students as facilitators and presenters at the annual Open House to share their experiences and perceptions of the assigned work and classroom expectations. They can serve as assistant to the teacher and can make the time as student-centered as it is teacher-centered.

17. Prepare a special "Follow-Up Activity Book" for students to do when their regular classroom work is completed. This activity book should contain related puzzles, riddles, games, and other fun tasks related to content or subject matter being taught. This can be used as an incentive to finish early or for extra credit.

18. When students work in cooperative learning groups or one-group projects, have each one initial those parts or pages that they worked on and were responsible for to ensure equal participation and contributions.

10 MINUS 2

Ways to Build A Good Parent Communication Program

(Williams' Taxonomy of Creative Thinking)

1. **FLUENCY ACTIVITY:** List as many communication products and performances as you can think of that your school develops and/or deliver in any given year to its families of students as a means of communicating information.

2. **FLEXIBILITY ACTIVITY:** Group or classify each of these products and performances from the fluency list in one of the following categories: Very Effective, Somewhat Effective, Not Effective, or Unknown.

3. **ORIGINALITY ACTIVITY:** Create an idea for a very unusual and unique product or performance that a school might implement to improve parent/student/teacher partnerships.

4. **ELABORATION ACTIVITY**: Elaborate on the good or poor qualities of each of the following products and performances offered yearly at your school: Monthly Newsletter, Open House, Parent/Teacher Conferences, Student Handbook, Parent Programs, Home Visits, Parenting Workshops, PTA/PTO Meetings, Parent Lounges/Resource Rooms, Parent Social Events, etc.

5. **RISK-TAKING ACTIVITY:** Write a mock letter as a teacher, student, or parent outlining your fear or concerns that could occur in either a school conference, an open house, or a home visit.

6. **COMPLEXITY ACTIVITY:** Discuss the desired role of parents as collaborators, advisers, and decision-makers in the school.

7. **CURIOSITY ACTIVITY:** Design a survey to administer to parents and other adults in the community who serve as volunteers in the school. Use the results to develop a recruitment campaign, a thank-you celebration, or a training session for volunteers.

8. **IMAGINATION ACTIVITY:** Pretend you are in charge of scheduling a conference for absent parents. As an alternative for family members who simply cannot arrange their schedules to attend a conference at the school, plan to send home a videotape of a student-teacher conference. The conference is taped just as if the parent were there. Prior to the conference, the student and affected teachers outline what the conference will cover. While the tape rolls, the student reviews samples of his/her work, answers relevant questions asked by the teachers, discusses individual progress and problems, and shares special interests and accomplishments. Follow the video-conference with a personal telephone call for parent reactions.

10 PLUS 3

Ways To Inform Parents And Caregivers And Involve Them In Their Middle Grader's School Progress

1. Parent-teacher conferences on a regularly scheduled basis as well as for special needs.

2. Notes home: often, informative, and always open-ended with provision for response.

3. Parents' Night with ample opportunity for group discussion and question-and-answer sessions.

4. A strong parent-teacher organization founded on meaningful goals and clear channels of communication, with regularly-scheduled meetings, including at least one opportunity early in the school year for a potluck meal or other social opportunity.

5. A standing invitation to join the class for lunch in the school cafeteria (if school rules permit).

6. Book lists for suggested family readings, with short response sheets for opinions or extensions to be returned to the teacher.

7. A meaningful grading and report system including provision for explanation of grades, anecdotal records, and explanatory notes.

8. School and/or class newspaper, journal, or newsletter.

9. Student work sent home regularly with teacher comments attached.

10. A clear, concise, and complete student handbook explaining school philosophy, calendar, rules of conduct, grading systems, administration and faculty responsibilities, and other pertinent information, delivered at the beginning of the school year.

11. Published schedules for the year, quarter, and month, including all extracurricular and before-and-after school activities, made available as far in advance as possible.

12. Intramurals and other extracurricular activities planned to allow parent participation without undue stress or interruption of normal work schedules.

13. Invitation to assist with classroom projects and special events such as science fairs, field days, plays, off-campus field trips, etc.

10 Steps For An Effective Parent Conference

1. Document academic or behavior problems through use of observation checklists, anecdotal records, test scores, work samples, and teacher reports. Try to include positive as well as negative evidence in your portfolio.

2. Arrange the conference time and place so that both are convenient for parents and team members. Encourage parents/guardians and student to attend.

3. Approach the conference with a positive "can do" attitude. Discuss the student's strengths and successes before discussing problem areas.

4. Encourage the parents/guardians to talk and share their perceptions while you listen carefully to what is being said. Take notes and ask clarifying questions.

5. Allow ample time for parents/guardians to air their frustrations and concerns without getting defensive or interrupting a train of thought. Try to use body language and verbal comments that are reassuring.

6. Make certain that all team members provide input at all stages of the conference, including preparation, implementation, and follow-up.

7. Develop an action plan that focuses on specific strategies and responsibilities for improving problem areas. Record who is to do what, when, and how.

8. Keep all team members and parents/guardians focused on the problem areas identified for resolving at this conference. Try to discourage digression from the task at hand.

9. Dismiss parents/guardians in a positive way so that they feel their time and energy have been well spent and so that they know exactly what has to be done to help the student.

10. Above all else, make certain to follow the established plan of action in a timely fashion and arrange for a follow-up conference or discussion. Monitor the plan of action strategies in a consistent manner.

10 Things to Consider When Planning Student-Led Conferences

1. Compose a letter to parents that informs them how you are enhancing the role of students in the conference process. Emphasize the fact that in student led conferences, students take ownership of their work, accomplishment, and plans for remediation, improvement, or enrichment. Also stress that the teacher plays an important role by providing students with the knowledge and strategies that will allow them to be self-sufficient on the day of their conference.

2. Talk with students about the multiple purposes of the student-led conference:
   a. It empowers students to take charge of their own progress and the reporting of that progress to parents.
   b. It provides leadership and communication skill practice for students.
   c. It demonstrates collaboration among student, teachers, and parents so that all hear the same message at the same time.
   d. It encourages students to be involved in the planning and selection process for what is to be discussed and displayed.
   e. It often provides extra incentive for parents to attend the conference.

3. Work with the students to prepare them for this activity by teaching the basic steps for conducting the conference, using an outline such as the following:
   a. Welcome parent to conference.
   b. Share portfolio of artifacts that represent student progress.
   c. Describe strengths, successes, and accomplishments.
   d. Talk about areas that need improvement.
   e. Ask parents for input, reactions, or questions.
   f. Write down any follow-up steps that need to be taken by student, parent, or teacher.
   g. Give parent the post-conference reflection later and ask them to complete it as directed.
   h. Thank parent for coming.

4. Work with students as a group or individually to select items for inclusion in the conference portfolio. Consider worksheets, homework assignments, tests or quizzes, creative writing samples, journal entries, product or performance rubrics, artwork, etc.

5. Give students an opportunity to role-play a mock conference where one student is the parent and the other student conducts the conference and then reverse roles. Do this only after a demonstration has been done with the teacher playing the part of the student and a student volunteer playing the part of the parent.

6. A few days before the conference, sit down with each student and go over their portfolio of artifacts and the outline they are to follow during the conference itself.

7. Prepare a classroom Parent Post-Conference Reflection Sheet that asks parents to write a note commenting on such things as:
   a. I think you did a great job leading the conference because . . .
   b. I noticed that you are doing well in . . .
   c. I especially liked the work you did on . . .
   d. Something I would like you to work on or improve for next time is . . .
   e. I would like to help you with . . .
   f. I can see that you enjoy . . .
   g. The thing that surprised me most was . . .
   h. You could improve the conference by . . .
Ask the parent to return this reflection sheet within one week
of the conference.

8. Prepare a Student Post-Conference Reflection Sheet that requires students to give feedback on the conference process they conducted using such starter statements as:
   a. I think things went well today (or did not go well today) because . . .
   b. The best part of the conference for me was . . .
   c. Things might have gone better if I . . .
   d. Something I would do differently next time is . . .
   e. I think my parents enjoyed the conference most because . . .
   f. One thing I wish I had talked about at the conference was . . .

9. If one or more parents still feel a need to meet with the teacher privately, be sure to set up a time and place to do so.

10. Student-Led conferences can be conducted one-on-one with the teacher as a close observer, or they can be conducted at a series of conference stations established around the room as the teacher facilitates the process.

10 PLUS 3 Things to Consider When Establishing Classroom Homework Policies

Homework issues continue to be a "headache" for many students, teachers, and parents alike. It is critical that a set of Homework Procedures be established and communicated to all stakeholder groups early in the school year. To begin this process, a group of teachers (and even a student and parent or two) should sit down and develop some guidelines for each of these homework-related situations. After each item, write down a tentative rule or strategy that you think might work in a classroom setting.

1. Planning Student Homework Tasks

_____

_____

2. Assigning Student Homework

_____

_____

3. Making Up Homework After Student Absence

_____

_____

4. Collecting Student Homework

_____

_____

5. Dealing with the Missing Homework Paper

_____

_____

6. Providing Incentives for Completing Homework

_____

_____

7. Copying Other Student's Homework

_____

_____

8. Refusing to Do or Hand in Homework

_____

_____

9. Grading of Student Homework

_____

_____

10. Dealing with Students Unable to Do Homework

_____

_____

11. Giving Back Student Homework

_____

_____

12. Contacting the Home About Homework

_____

_____

13. Checking Student Progress in Homework

_____

_____

10 PLUS 10

Things to Include in A Classroom Handbook

One way to get a new year started off on the right track is to prepare a Classroom Handbook for Parents/Guardians that is sent home the first month of school and that contains relevant information about the operation of a particular classroom/teacher/team. A sign-off sheet for parents to complete indicating they have received and read the information provided should accompany this handbook. Some possible items for the handbook are:

1. Teaching philosophy of teacher or team of teachers

2. Homework policy

3. Behavior expectations and consequences for infractions

4. Schedules for core curricular tests in math, science, English, and social studies

5. Explanations of policies on work quality

6. Descriptions of grading policies and procedures

7. Procedures of making up work due to tardiness or absenteeism

8. Library or media center schedule

9. Important dates for open house, parent/teacher meetings, field trips, performances

10. Sample newsletter

11. Holiday and birthday celebration policies

12. List of supplies/materials required for class

13. Classroom roster

14. Information on available school tutors or community tutoring services

15. Information about community learning resources that correlates to curriculum, such as concerts, museums, tourist attractions, parks, etc.

16. Description of volunteer needs/resources

17. Parent request form for a parent/teacher/student conference

18. Biographical information of teacher or team of teachers

19. Interest Inventory to be completed collaboratively by parent and student

20. Background Information Sheet on special parent skills, hobbies, or interests

10 MINUS 3

Measures for Gauging Benefits and Barriers for Family Involvement
(Multiple Intelligences)

1. **VERBAL/LINGUISTIC INTELLIGENCE:**
Write a short position paper or essay on one of the following topics:

1. Improved student academic performance results from family involvement.

2. Family members grow closer to their children as school becomes a "family" effort.

3. Relationships between home and school, as well as between the school and community, improve.

4. The variety of skills family members possess help students in the classroom and out, both academically and socially.

2. **LOGICAL/MATHEMATICAL INTELLIGENCE:**
Construct a parent participation profile of a classroom setting in the school that shows these five major types of involvement outlines in the work of Joyce Epstein:

1. Building positive home conditions to support school learning.

2. Communicating to the home concerning children's progress and school programs.

3. Involving families in school-sponsored events, programs, performances, and PTA meetings.

4. Involving families in home learning activities coordinated with class work.

5. Involving families in school decision-making, governance, or advocacy.

3. **VISUAL/SPATIAL INTELLIGENCE:**
Construct a poster that depicts these three major barriers that discourage parent and family involvement in school programs.

    1. Many adults perceive school as a "negative or threatening" place, based on their own memories of unpleasant experiences.

    2. Many adults face barriers that relate to their work schedules, health status, and/or conflicting family commitments.

    3. Many adults find the knowledge, attitudes, and skill levels of teachers and administrators inadequate or lacking in making families full partners in the educational process.

4. **PHYSICAL/KINESTHETIC INTELLIGENCE:**
Create a chant, slogan, or rap that promotes parent/teacher/student partnerships. Create a logo to go with it.

5. **INTERPERSONAL INTELLIGENCE:**
Organize a "welcome wagon" program to greet new families to the school. Like the national program for newcomers in a community, include a packet of information about various groups (scouts), organizations (little league), clubs, community (YMCA) and child care facilities (after school programs) that could be helpful to new families of the school. You might also want to include coupons that could be cashed in for free items donated by local merchants or donated by the school PTA (personalized pencils). Finally, you might want to develop a directory of favorite haunts for kids and families such as special restaurants, malls, hobby shops, or video arcades.

6. **INTRAPERSONAL INTELLIGENCE:**
Maintain a log or journal that records entries for each time someone in your family interacts with the school through meetings, performances, telephone calls, conferences, or classroom visits over a marking period. Determine the level of involvement based on these entries.

7. **NATURALISTIC INTELLIGENCE:**
Determine how the concepts of "indoor classroom climate" and the "outdoor natural environment" both need parent support and involvement to protect their integrity.

10 PLUS 12

Teacher Planning Strategies for Classroom Success

1. Buy and use the best lesson plan book available.

2. Make long-range plans (well in advance) that lend themselves to constant revision and transition to manageable short-range plans.

3. Divide large projects into classroom-relevant smaller sections.

4. Delegate tasks when appropriate and possible.

5. Consult other people for answers, help, or input.

6. Make use of classroom-ready" commercial materials when they fit into learning goals and developmental objectives.

7. Upgrade and downgrade priorities as needed.

8. Set out daily goals in order of priority.

9. Make a list of "TO DOs" every day.

10. Unless absolutely necessary, refuse to make decisions under stress.

11. Carefully select a time and place free of interruptions for completing paperwork.

12. Allow a reasonable amount of time for interaction on a one-on-one basis with students and do not allow less important tasks to take precedent over this important time.

13. Keep a list/copy of class work and homework in a notebook for reference for students who have been absent.

14. Have presentation materials ready and accessible beforehand. Organize in folders by topic or instructional objective.

15. Capitalize on the use of student "experts" in the classroom whenever possible.

16. Utilize color as a classroom organizer. Color-code instructional areas with materials and supplies for easy access and return.

17. Color-code subject area notebooks (i.e., green for math, red for science, etc.) for quick reference and easy identification.

18. Color-code your grade book using different colors for daily, test, or failing grades so it is easy to spot problems and average grades.

19. Keep a small pad of paper and a pen in your school mailbox for instant replies and on-the-spot notes.

20. Show a scheduled video or film only once, to the entire team, at the same time freeing the remaining class periods for instruction instead of viewing.

21. Utilize uniform team timesaving procedures: conference form, substitute form, and team meeting agenda form.

22. Share and exchange teaching ideas, lesson plans, and creative activities with peers.

10

Findings from the Published Literature About Needs and Characteristics of Early Adolescence and Adolescent Programs

1. FINDING:

NMSA's 1995 update of ***This We Believe*** states that the developmentally responsive middle schools are those that have:

. . . Educators committed to young adolescents

. . . A shared vision

. . High expectations for all

. . . An adult advocate for every student

. . . Family and community partnerships

. . . A positive school climate

. . . Curriculum that is challenging, integrative, and exploratory

. . . Varied teaching and learning experiences

. . . Assessment and evaluation that promote learning

. . . Flexible organizational structures

. . . Programs and policies that foster health, wellness, and safety

. . . Comprehensive guidance and support services

Reference: (1995). This We Believe: A position paper of National Middle School Association. Columbus, OH: National Middle School Association.

2. FINDING:

James A. Beane points out:

I want to reiterate my claim that the middle school concept is "under siege." There are many reasons why middle school advocates are having difficulty defending their concept, but three are particularly worth noting. First, our society does not particularly like its young adolescents and does not know what to do about their demands for independence, fairness, and truth, to say nothing of their proximity to the physical event of puberty. In this sense, as middle schools try to respond in a humane fashion to what the rest of society does not like, their advocates seem to become disliked as well. Second, as tensions with authority figures heighten for many young adolescents, the public can think of little else to do except crack down on them, or shut down the middle school and send them back to K-8 elementary schools where they will presumably be compliant little children.

Third, middle schools still suffer from a lack of clear identity. The reasons for establishing them are still a mystery to many people who consequently must see little reasons for establishing them are still a mystery to many people who consequently must see little reason to preserve them. Clearly the oft-used phrase "caught in the middle" applies not only to young adolescents, but to their schools as well.

Reference: Beane, J. (1999, March). Middle schools under siege: Points of attack. Middle School Journal 30(4).

3. FINDING:
Donald G. Hackman and Jerry W. Valentine write:

The following factors provide guidance to school faculties as they consider scheduling alternatives:

. . . The schedule should support interdisciplinary team organization. In middle level research, the worth of interdisciplinary teaming has been so thoroughly documented that the issue has become a "given" when speaking of organizational expectations of a quality middle level program (Dickinson & Erb, 1997).

. . . The schedule should support an appropriate curriculum. The schedule should allow teachers to develop a curriculum that is responsive to the needs of their students and ensures that all students "have equal access to curriculum offerings" (Williamson, 1993).

. . . The schedule should support quality instruction in the disciplines through the expanded and flexible uses of time. The schedule must provide adequate periods of time to effectively implement active learning experience. The effective schedule is defined by instructional responsiveness, allowing teachers to vary the time devoted to different subjects on different days, avoiding the necessity of giving equal time to unequal subjects (George & Alexander, 1993).

. . . The schedule should promote student development and supportive relationships. The quality schedule should achieve a balance between daily stability and creative variety that is developmentally responsive to young adolescents (Schurr, Thomason, & Thompson, 1995).

. . . The schedule should promote quality teacher collaboration. Research studies have found three organizational characteristics that correlated significantly with teacher collaboration. Those were the extent of teaming in the middle school, the degree of flexibility of the schedule, and the presence of common planning times for the team member (Clark & Clark, 1994 and Steffes & Valentine, 1995).

. . . The schedule should promote teacher empowerment. The greater the degree of teacher autonomy for making decisions about their students and the team, the greater the degree of three variables: (a) teacher innovation and creativity; (b) varied instructional strategies and techniques, and (c) ability to identify and address student needs and behavior (Steffes & Valentine, 1995).

Reference: Hackmann, D., & Valentine, J. (1998, May). Designing an effective middle level school. Middle School Journal 29(5).

4. FINDING:

John Arnold and Chris Stevenson state:

We believe that "small partner teams" consisting of two or three teachers and forty to seventy-five students have some distinct advantages over larger groupings. With larger teams there is a marked tendency for such teams to divide the day into periods of less than an hour and to teach their subjects separately, thus replicating the junior high school departmental format that deters curriculum integration. With partner teams virtually all of the potential advantages of teaming are magnified. In these smaller teams people get to know each other better and find agreement more easily. Because a two-teacher team has on average half as many students as a four-teacher team, there is a greater potential to create a strong spirit of belonging and community. Curriculum can be more easily attuned to students' interests and needs. Comprehensive student-centered assessment appears to be more easily accomplished. Occurrences of student self-government are notably more frequent and more highly developed among smaller teams, and students appear to take initiative and accept responsibilities more easily in these groupings. Discipline is also less external, rule-bound, and adversarial, and student advising appears to occur more naturally throughout the day. From the teacher's standpoint, partner teaming brings the advantage of more efficient communication between adults and more ease in flexing the schedule to accommodate the irregular time requirements of a more integrated curriculum.

Although multiple years, multi-age, and multi-grade teams do not characterize teaming at the middle level, we are increasingly encountering this arrangement. In some versions students are age- and grade-mixed in classes; in other versions they may be separated into team classes by grade level for particular activities or subjects. Chief among the many benefits of these team groups is that teachers have fewer new students each year than do teachers in grade-level teams. The potential for maintaining continuous progress is a particularly attractive advantage of this arrangement as well.

Finally, a little-used but interesting version of multi-year teacher-student relationships at the middle level is known as "student-teacher team progression" or "looping," whereby a team of teachers "moves up" with the same students, teaching them a second, and sometimes third, year in order to build on already established relationships and maintaining curriculum and assessment continuity. After the first year, looped teachers would have no new students other than the occasional transfer student.

Reference: Arnold, J. & Stevenson, C. (1998). Teachers' teaming handbook: A middle level planning guide. Orlando, FL: Harcourt Brace College Publishers.

5. FINDING:
It is inappropriate to judge the success of the middle level school solely on the basis of how well students do in high school. Success in further education is important, of course, but a good middle level experience is its own reward. School effectiveness at any level should be measured in terms of how well students deal with current life tasks. At the middle level, some include: negotiating puberty with a minimum of stress, acquiring a lifelong love of learning, developing interpersonal skills, establishing values as a guide for living, and the like. The well-being of young people at this critical age demands nothing less from all of us who care about them.

Reference: Lipka, R. & others. (1998). The eight-year study revisited: Lessons from the past for the present. Columbus, OH: National Middle School Association.

6. FINDING:
Diane Chelsom Gossen points out:
Let us look at the word "discipline." It is derived from the Latin word *disciplina*, which means learning. The verb discipline comes from the same root as the word disciple. The original meaning of this word connotes the self-discipline of the students of Socrates and Plato, of the competitive athlete. Self-discipline allows a person to harness his potential toward a goal, toward what he values. In our culture we have transformed the meaning of discipline into something one does to another to encourage conformity. We tend to associate the word *discipline* with discomfort, not with what we value.

Source: Gossen, D.C. (1997). Restitution: Restructuring school discipline. Chapel Hill, NC: New View Publications. Xv.

7. FINDING:
Successfully teaching English Language Learners at the middle level decreases the very real risk of their becoming high-school drop outs. Try these effective strategies:

- Establish a caring environment in the classroom
- Learn about the language and culture of all students
- Use an integrated, thematic approach to learning
- Activate prior knowledge
- Teach academic vocabulary
- Use visuals as often as possible
- Lessons should be relevant, meaningful, active, and varied
- Employ creative assessment measures

Reference: NMSA (2001, August). Classroom Connection, Volume 4, Number 1.

8. **F**INDING:
As explained by Dr. Neila Connors:
"Creating the Ambiance" of a school has seven key components:

   a. Ensure the physical, intellectual, emotional, and social safety of all teachers, students, and administrators

   b. Embrace change and remain open to the notion that change enriches personal and professional lives.

   c. School leaders must project a positive attitude daily

   d. Clear communication school-wide through the process of listening, speaking, reading, writing, thinking, and providing feedback

   e. Practice good human relation skills - "Positive and caring relationships are the heart of what makes a school extraordinary."

   f. Active participation by all directs the focus on what needs to be done, how to do it, and what outcomes will be celebrated

   g. Positive public relations creates a school where community members feel welcomed and supported by educators

Reference: Neila Connors (2000) If You Don't Feed the Teacher's They Eat the Students!, Nashville, TN: Incentive Publications

9. **F**INDING:
Students should be taught to have ownership of the classroom, that they are responsible for themselves and for their own self-discipline.

Terri Breeden and Emalie Egan assert that:
"When students share the responsibility for the development of the rules and expectations that guide classroom activities, they are far more likely to understand the necessary limits on their behavior." Holding a constitutional convention to create a classroom constitution is an effective method to involve students in creating the tone of a positive classroom and serves as a preventative against improper behavior.

Reference: Terri Breeden and Emalie Egan (1997) Positive Classroom Management, Nashville, TN: Incentive Publications

10. FINDING:

Turning Points 2000 makes the seven following recommendations for schools:

1. Curriculum is based on rigorous, public academic standards for student knowledge and performance, is relevant to adolescents, and is centered on how students learn most effectively.

2. Use teaching methods aimed at preparing students to reach higher levels of achievement and become lifelong learners.

3. Middle grade teachers must excel at teaching young adolescents, and be provided with various and continuing professional development opportunities.

4. Cultivate relationships for learning that lead to a climate of intellectual development and a cohesive community of common educational purpose.

5. Govern democratically, through participation by all school staff members.

6. Create and ensure a safe and healthy environment, which leads to better academic performance and fosters supportive and ethical citizens.

7. Involve parents and communities in reinforcing student learning and positive development.

Reference: Jackson, Anthony W. & Davis, Gayle A. Turning Points 2000, Educating Adolescents in the 21st Century, Teachers College Press, Teachers College, Columbia University, New York, NY. Copyright 2000.

Structures That Successfully Meet the Needs of Early Adolescents

KNOWLEDGE

List at least three unique needs and characteristics of the early adolescent in each of the following categories: Intellectual Development, Moral Development, Physical Development, Emotional/Psychological Development, and Social Development.

COMPREHENSION

Summarize the needs and characteristics of underachievers and the needs and characteristics of gifted students. Compare and contrast the two as determined by your summaries.

APPLICATION

If you were to interview the principal of an exemplary middle school, compile a list of questions you would want to ask him /her about the factors that make that school a successful one.

ANALYSIS

It has been said that all middle level students are at risk. Determine why this statement is likely to be true.

SYNTHESIS

Create an observation checklist or anecdotal record form that a teacher could use in the classroom to identify and document special needs and characteristics of students in the class.

EVALUATION

Use the Common Denominators of Successful Middle School to judge the effectiveness of a middle school in your community. Justify your results.

INTERDISCIPLINARY TEAMING AND BLOCK SCHEDULING

Interdisciplinary Teaming and Block Scheduling Overview

INTERDISCIPLINARY TEAMING ENCOURAGES:
- Conservation of time and space in an ever-expanding curriculum.
- Elimination of overlap in varied subject areas.
- Promotion of collaboration among students and teachers.
- Coordination of assignments.
- Reduction of fragmentation of learning from one discipline to another.
- Relevance of motivational and enrichment projects.
- Multiple use of resources, teaching tools, and instructional techniques.
- Recognition of interrelationships among different subjects.
- Promotion of critical and creative thinking through the application of skills and concepts across subject area lines.

TEACHERS ADVANTAGES INCLUDE:
- Improved intellectual stimulation provided by closer association with colleagues.
- Improved discipline through use of varied teacher personalities, styles, and strategies.
- Improved delivery system provided through flexible schedules and group sizes.
- Improved colleague support through shared goals, esprit de corps, and communication.
- Improved evaluation through team input and assessment techniques.
- Improved time management through team meetings and common planning periods.
- Improved instruction through diversity in teacher talents, styles, and interests.
- Improved coordination of curriculum through interdisciplinary instruction and joint planning in areas such as homework, texts, grades, and field trips.

STUDENTS ADVANTAGES INCLUDE:
- Improved student/teacher relationships through sense of belonging to established team or school family with special identity, customs, and rituals.
- Improved motivation and enthusiasm for learning through varied instructional materials, techniques, and personalities.
- Improved attendance and behavior because of consistent environment with common rules, guidelines, and procedures.
- Improved attitudes toward school through sharing of excellent teachers and not-so-excellent teachers.
- Improved opportunity for achievement through flexible grouping and scheduling options.
- Improved self-concept through team-initiated advisory groups.
- Improved chances for matching teaching styles with learning styles.

# 10 PLUS 6 Important Questions To Find Answers For Related to Interdisciplinary Teaming and Block Scheduling

How would you respond to each of these questions or tasks?

1. What is the single most important reason for teaming in the middle school?

2. What are advantages and potential disadvantages of the teaming process for teachers?

3. What are advantages and potential disadvantages of the teaming process for students?

4. How does block scheduling contribute to the effectiveness of interdisciplinary teams?

5. What are the advantages of block scheduling for teachers?

6. What are the advantages of block scheduling for students?

7. How is student achievement affected by interdisciplinary instruction?

8. What are some things administrators and teachers can do to "sell" the concept of interdisciplinary teaming and block scheduling to parents or guardians.

9. What are two different tools or techniques that might be used to place teachers on a team?

10. What are some things that team members can do to support the concept of interdisciplinary teaming?

11. What are some major factors that can create friction and cause a team to be unsuccessful in meeting goals set by the team?

12. What are some good reasons for a joint team planning period?

13. What are some things team members can do to create a team identity?

14. What is the key role of the team leader?

15. How can teachers determine their own readiness for interdisciplinary teaming?

16. How does research support interdisciplinary and block schedule teaming in the middle school setting?

10 PLUS 7 Terms Important to Interdisciplinary Teaming and Block Scheduling

1. **Collaboration:** Collaboration implies a relationship between individual or organizations that enables the participants to accomplish goals more successfully than they could have separately. Educators are finding that they must collaborate with teachers to deal with increasingly complex issues.

2. **Common Planning Time:** Interdisciplinary teaming works best when teachers on the same team have a common planning period during which they can meet together on a daily basis to hold team meetings, student/parent conferences, and plan interdisciplinary instruction.

3. **Conflict Resolution:** Core concepts of conflict resolution include recognizing that conflict exists and is a pathway to personal growth, learning skills to solve problems effectively, and understanding that there are alternative solutions to a problem.

4. **Databased Decision-Making:** This type of decision-making involves the analysis of existing sources of information (class and school attendance, grades, tests) and new data (portfolios, surveys, interviews) to make decisions about the school. The process involves organizing and interpreting the data and creating action steps.

5. **Empowerment:** Empowerment means enabling teachers to manage themselves in pursuit of organizational goals.

6. **Goals:** These represent the expected end results of education as described by individual schools, districts, states, or other agencies.

7. **Interdisciplinary Instruction:** Teams of teachers combine their expertise and course content to integrate the disciplines and interface common areas of the curriculum.

8. **Interdisciplinary Teaming:** The interdisciplinary team requires that the same group of teachers share the same group of students for an uninterrupted block of instructional time. Teams vary in size from two to four teachers and serve students ranging from 70 to 150 in number.

9. **Norm:** A norm is a system of shared beliefs. These beliefs produce patterns of behavior within a group of people, organizational structures, and control systems. A norm is to a group what a habit is to an individual.

10. **Participative Leadership:** This type of leadership creates interdependency among its team members by empowering, freeing up, and serving others.

11. **Shared Responsibility:** This type of responsibility establishes an environment in which all team members feel as responsible as the administrator for the performance of the work unit.

12. **Synergism:** This phenomenon is the simultaneous actions of separate entities that together have greater total effect than the sum of their individual efforts.

13. **Team Handbook:** An effective interdisciplinary team develops a handbook for the students and parents they serve. The purpose of this handbook is to share the team's philosophy, goals, policies, procedures, expectations, and plans for the school year.

14. **Team Leader:** Every interdisciplinary team has a team leader who facilitates the teaming process for its members by coordinating the team's meetings, activities, budget decisions, and communications with the school's administrative team.

15. **Team Meeting:** An interdisciplinary team holds daily team meetings during its common planning time in order to carry on the assigned duties and responsibilities of the team itself.

16. **Team Rules and Discipline Plan:** Interdisciplinary teams place a high priority on establishing a meaningful set of team rules and discipline procedures that are consistent throughout the school day regardless of the varied teacher personalities, styles, and disciplines.

17. A **flexible block schedule** is a "chunk" of uninterrupted teaching time allocated to a given group of students and teachers on an interdisciplinary team.

It allows the team to do one of several things:

1. Vary size of instructional groups of classes

2. Vary frequency or number of times a group or class meets

3. Vary length of instructional time for a group or class

4. Vary order or sequence of meeting times

5. Vary number of groups or classes that meet within an established block of time

In short, flexible block scheduling is a way of better responding to the needs of young adolescents. It allows the students and teachers to master the master schedule.

10 PLUS 4

Things To Remember When Developing Teams

1. Team development is evolutionary. It does not happen quickly.

2. Team members must be trained in the "art and science" of teaming so they share the same vision and understanding of what teaming is all about.

3. Team effectiveness and team activities will vary from site to site because implementation of interdisciplinary teams is unique to each location.

4. Not every team member will embrace the teaming concept and the empowerment that goes with it to the same degree.

5. All team members must be assured that the teaming concept will improve work life and the performance of students.

6. Team development will not follow a straight path but will encounter ups and downs in its evolution.

7. Team leaders and administrators must model the behavior they want their team members to display.

8. Teams are often highly motivated at the beginning of their teaming experience, but they require constant guidance, training, and support from leaders.

9. Team members should complement, not clone, one another's styles, temperament, skills, talents, and interests.

10. Team members who do not work well together should have procedures or provisions for changing work assignments.

11. Teams should begin making easy decisions before they are faced with difficult decisions.

12. As teams develop operating policies, procedures, and systems, they will need to be changed to allow for continued growth and empowerment.

13. Teams should emphasize communication as the "soul" of their existence both within the team and outside the team.

14. Teams must be rewarded for their successes.

10 Questions To Ask When Forming Teams

When forming teams, each teacher should be asked the following:

1. What subjects are you certified to teach?

2. What subjects would you like to teach? Please list in priority order.

3. What grades would you like to teach? Please list in priority order.

4. What special interests/talents/hobbies do you have?

5. What special skills do you bring to the team?

6. How would you describe your basic teaching style?

7. Who are some staff members you would like to work with on a team?

8. Who are some staff members you would prefer not to work with on a team?

9. Where do you see yourself professionally in three to five years?

10. What else would you want your team members to know about you?

10 Possible Team Member Traits To Consider

Directions: Form a small group of three or four members. Suppose your group has been given the responsibility of selecting four persons to serve on an interdisciplinary team in a middle level school for the next year. First, read through the descriptions of potential team members. Next, choose your ideal coworkers and record the appropriate numbers in the spaces provided below. Finally, work with your group to reach a consensus on who should be on the team. Be prepared to defend your choices!

1. Helen Humorous: Helen is the funniest character in the group. She often makes everyone laugh with her keen sense of humor. When things get dull, you can count on Helen to liven things up. She always makes the best of a situation and helps others to do so as well.

2. Tom Truthful: Tom always tells what he feels. He never lies to the group or hides things from them. He will always tell team members the truth (and always with tact) when asked a direct question.

3. Laura Leader: Laura is a natural leader. She is well respected and most people listen to her. She's careful to include other points of view when trying to make a group decision.

4. Carl Creative: Carl is the most creative teacher on the staff. He will stop at nothing to promote his innovative ideas and materials with the team. He tends to motivate both staff and students.

5. Ida Informed: Ida knows all about middle schools. She has a wealth of knowledge and experience in all areas of interdisciplinary teaming and instruction and will provide the group with information about every important middle school issue.

6. Frank Favorite: Frank knows the principal very well and can get special favors. He is very dedicated to the teaching profession and knows how to arrange his priorities when asking for budgetary support from the administration.

7. Mary Motivation: Mary knows the secret to inspiring both teachers and students. She is constantly using original tools and techniques for keeping her colleagues on task and getting the tough jobs done.

8. **Wanda Worker:** Wanda is a workaholic and never minds going the extra mile to complete a project or an assignment. She truly enjoys doing "more than her share" and will often bail out a teammate when necessary.

9. **Ernie Energetic:** Ernie is a beginning teacher who has more energy than ten teachers put together. He did his student teaching in an exemplary middle school setting that serves as a training ground for some of the best middle school teachers in the country. What he lacks in experience, he makes up for with enthusiasm.

10. **Polly Professional:** Polly is a highly experienced elementary teacher with a desire to become the best middle school teacher in the district. She received the "Best Teacher of the Year Award" for her ability to develop interdisciplinary units. She has expert knowledge of ways to vary delivery systems and grouping of students for optimal learning conditions.

My four choices for Team Members are:

Number	Name	Because
_____	_____	_____
_____	_____	_____
_____	_____	_____
_____	_____	_____

Our Group's four choices for Team Members are:

Number	Name	Because
_____	_____	_____
_____	_____	_____
_____	_____	_____
_____	_____	_____

10 PLUS 15

Criteria To Determine How Well You Would Fit Into The Teaming Concept

Directions: Use this self-check quiz to determine your potential as a middle school teacher working on an interdisciplinary team. Place a mark in the appropriate column on the left and remember to give yourself the benefit of the doubt!

Yes	No	DO YOU . . .
___	___	**1.** Understand your own strengths and weaknesses as a person?
___	___	**2.** Understand your own strengths and weaknesses as a teacher?
___	___	**3.** Interact constructively with other adults?
___	___	**4.** Interact constructively with young adolescents?
___	___	**5.** Feel as a teacher you are approachable, responsive, and supportive to your peers and colleagues?
___	___	**6.** Feel as a teacher you are approachable, responsive, and supportive to your students?
___	___	**7.** Readily acknowledge the physical, intellectual, social, and emotional needs/characteristics of early adolescence?
___	___	**8.** Regularly apply different and varied methods/activities in the teaching/learning process?
___	___	**9.** Regularly use group processes and group learning techniques?
___	___	**10.** Organize your curriculum in a way that facilitates the interdisciplinary approach to instruction?
___	___	**11.** Willingly counsel an individual student with an identifiable need?
___	___	**12.** Design and conduct group activities that capitalize on individual differences and learning styles of students?

Criteria To Determine Fitting Into The Teaming Concept

Yes | No | DO YOU . . .

13. Have the skills required to work in cooperative teaching situations with other teachers, paraprofessionals, and resource persons?

14. Accept the responsibility of multidisciplinary instruction in planning thematic and coordinated studies with other teachers?

15. Seek out and enjoy teaching subjects outside of your own area of specialization?

16. Readily acknowledge there are many ways—not just "my way"—of teaching students?

17. Recognize that team members will have differences, disagreements, and conflicts, but also understand that these can and should be resolved?

18. Believe in weekly team plans and meetings?

19. Display a tactful honesty and willingness to work and plan together with team members?

20. Demonstrate a willingness to utilize differences between, as well as similarities among, team members?

21. Demonstrate a realization that your subject area is of no more or less importance than other subjects?

22. Demonstrate a realization that ability grouping may not be compatible with interdisciplinary team teaching?

23. Agree that team members ought to be flexible in individual scheduling to meet a particular student's needs?

24. Display an interest in (not necessarily an understanding of) the other academic subjects?

25. Show sensitivity to the feelings of the other team members? (Can you eliminate petty and/or personal complaints that may interfere with the primary objectives of interdisciplinary team teaching?)

(Totals)

yes   no

Scoring: Give yourself one point for every YES response.

20–25 You are definitely a middle school person.
15–19 You are definitely leaning towards a middle school commitment.
10–14 You are mildly interested in learning more about middle schools.
0–10 You are really an elementary or high school teacher at heart.

10 Ways To Rate Yourself As An Effective Team Builder

Directions: On a scale of one to seven (1–7), how would you rate yourself as a team builder?

___ 1. I spend sufficient time selecting team members with the appropriate skills and attitudes required to make the teaming concept work.

___ 2. I encourage ownership among team members by allowing them considerable independence and autonomy in goal setting, problem solving, and delivery of instruction.

___ 3. I nurture and practice the spirit of teamwork throughout the school setting.

___ 4. I insist on open and honest communication at all times.

___ 5. I keep my word, my agreements, and my promises to people.

___ 6. I respect the personality differences and cultural diversities of others.

___ 7. I provide quality staff development opportunities for enhancing the teaming process.

___ 8. I value constructive criticism.

___ 9. I believe that teaming and collaboration will maximize the learning that takes place.

___ 10. I will coach and counsel team members who are not able to meet reasonable standards and expectations.

Scoring:
- A score of 60-70 means you are well aware of what it takes to be an effective team builder.
- A score of 40-59 is acceptable, although you need to sharpen your team-building skills and attitudes.
- A score below 40 means you aren't really a team player yet, but you may be willing to give it a try!

10 PLUS 4

Roles And Responsibilities Of A Team Leader

1. Functions as a liaison between the administration and team

2. Coordinates instructional programs within the team

3. Coordinates practices and procedures between leader's team and other teams

4. Serves on and/or appoints team members to various school or district committees

5. Schedules and coordinates administration of criterion-referenced and standardized tests

6. Prepares and submits the team budget for supplies, textbooks, audio-visuals, and equipment needs

7. Familiarizes new teachers and substitute teachers with the school program and the team practices and procedures

8. Disseminates trends, new approaches, and research findings to team members

9. Schedules and conducts team meetings

10. Assists in the selection of personnel that affects team activities including aides, volunteers, team members, substitute teachers, and support staff

11. Promotes public relations between team members and parent/school community

12. Facilitates communication among team members

13. Coordinates interdisciplinary instruction efforts

14. Maintains a high level of morale among team members

10 Things To Consider When Selecting A Team Leader

Directions: Prepare a mock application form that could be filled out by each team member who is interested in being considered for the team leader position. Encourage applicants to be as honest as possible in their responses. Use these questions to select the "best" person for the job, given the circumstances. Ten possible items are suggested below.

1. What would appeal to you most about being the team leader?

2. What bothers you most about the team leader position?

3. How do you think a leader influences a team?

4. What would be most stressful to you about being a leader of this particular team?

5. Why do you think the team would want to follow you?

6. What do you see as your leadership strengths?

Your leadership weaknesses?

7. How would you describe your leadership style?

8. What key tasks should be the responsibilities of the team leader?

9. How would you want the team members to evaluate your performance as the team leader at the end of the school year?

10. Who would make a good leader for your team and why?

BONUS ACTIVITY: As a potential team leader, think of several metaphors that could be used as the springboard for constructing a logo, creating a slogan, or inventing a cheer. Try these for starters:

A team that has a vision is like a superhighway because . . .

_____

_____

_____

_____

A team that works well together is like a symphony because . . .

_____

_____

_____

_____

A team that is student-centered is like a rain forest because . . .

_____

_____

_____

_____

10 MINUS 1

Responsibilities for Team Members

As in any cooperative learning or collaborative group setting, team members must be assigned legitimate roles and responsibilities if they are to function as a quality and interdependent group of team players. Depending upon the size of the team, individuals may need to assume more than one job. Some possible options are:

1. **TEAM LEADER:** Schedules and facilitates meetings, coordinates items for agendas, manages conflicts, and provides leadership for team activities.

2. **TEAM RECORDER:** Keeps a record of actions and decisions made by the team and serves as historian of the team's operations.

3. **TEAM TIMEKEEPER AND GATEKEEPER:** Nurtures team relationships and keeps team members on task in a timely fashion.

4. **TEAM GOPHER OF RESOURCE PERSON:** Locates and manages the multiple resources needed to plan, implement, and evaluate team activities.

5. **PR OR MARKETING PERSON:** Prepares reports, news releases, and information flyers or memos that keep other faculty members, administrators, and parents aware of the team's accomplishments and actions.

6. **ENCOURAGER:** Provides ongoing support, and praise to team members during team meetings, events, and activities.

7. **SOCIAL CHAIRMAN:** Organizes social and celebrating functions for students and teachers on the team.

8. **LIAISON LINK:** Communicates with other teams, administrators, and support staff to encourage two-way communication between and among various groups and stakeholders of the school.

9. **ACTION RESEARCHER:** Maintains records of student growth and achievement levels for purposes of documenting team's impact on the teaching and learning process.

BONUS IDEA: Prepare a set of role cards for each of the jobs above. Write a description of each role on a single card. Have each person randomly draw a card for a meeting and play that role during the meeting. At the end of the meeting, redistribute the cards so that every member will play another role at the next meeting. Repeat this procedure until everyone has had a chance to play every role as well as a chance to decide who best fits what role. Encourage members to play the "best fit" role on the team for a year.

10 PLUS 1

Things On Which Team Members Should Agree

Team members should meet during the pre-school planning days. It is essential that the team members agree on . . .

1. Times for regular team meetings.

2. The ways to schedule students into classes.

3. The continual sharing of curriculum objectives leading to the development of interdisciplinary units.

4. Selecting and securing textbooks and other needed resources.

5. How and when to meet with parents and students.

6. A team classroom-management plan.

7. Ways to communicate in writing to parents.

8. A homework policy.

9. Field trip plans to extend classroom experiences.

10. Team assignments.

11. The importance of a professional approach to all team and school efforts to educate the children.

10 PLUS 2

Causes of Team Failure

1. Information does not flow freely in all directions, but tends to flow from the top down.

2. Relationships among team members tend to be viewed as partisan and suspicious.

3. Conflict that focuses on persons and not issues.

4. The atmosphere is not participative and open, but fragments members and compartmentalizes ideas.

5. Decisions emphasize manipulation and dissonance rather than consensus and compromise.

6. Team structure is compatible with the hierarchical organizational structure of the administration.

7. Team members lack self-discipline and are unwilling to recognize the patterns and stages of the team process.

8. Teams reward individual achievements and hold little value for group rewards.

9. The institution has failed to use team efforts in any meaningful way.

10. Teams have received insufficient training.

11. Appraisals are too often subjective and arbitrary rather than collective and self-initiated.

12. Teams have focused on task activities to the exclusion of work on team member relationships.

10 PLUS 20 Tools For Building A Team Identity

1. Team Name/Logo/Mascot/Colors/Slogan
2. Team Decorations for Door, Hallways, Rooms
3. Team Newspaper/Newsletter
4. Team Rules/Codes of Conduct
5. Team Rewards
6. Team Intramurals
7. Team Birthday Celebrations
8. Team Government
9. Team Recognition Days
10. Team Meals
11. Team Assemblies
12. Team Display of Student Work
13. Team T-Shirts
14. Team Bulletin Boards
15. Team Handbooks
16. Team Student Conference
17. Team Contests
18. Team Field Trips
19. Team Song
20. Team Parties
21. Team Scrapbook
22. Team Name Tags for Special Events
23. Team Honor Rolls
24. Team Calendar
25. Team Special Events and Activities
26. Talent Shows, Spirit Days, Dress-Up Days
27. Clean-Up Days, Community Projects
28. Academic Brain Bowls, Open House, Holiday Parties
29. Team Cheers/Songs/Choral Readings
30. Team Rituals

10 Things That Great Teams Do

1. Build a strong team identity, but be certain that the team's identity is compatible with and supportive of the school's overall identity.

2. Conduct regular team meetings with predetermined agendas and follow-up minutes. Appoint a team historian to maintain records of the team's progress throughout the year.

3. Hold regular parent and student conferences. Do not let a week go by without inviting some student(s) or parent(s) to become the focus of a productive discussion or action plan. Try to have conferences that "celebrate" an individual's success as well as those that are scheduled for solving problems.

4. Maintain a team calendar. Distribute this weekly or monthly calendar to both students and parents. Include as many important dates, events, and deadlines as you can to communicate team member schedules.

5. Maintain and use a flexible block schedule. Spend considerable time grouping and regrouping students for instruction and scheduling and rescheduling blocks of time for that instruction. Take full advantage of the opportunity to expand or reduce predetermined blocks of time for the academic subject areas in order to maximize the learning process.

6. Celebrate team successes. Do not let a day go by without taking time to review the high spots of the day or the high points of the week for yourselves, your students, or your parent community. Remember that a string of minor successes can lead to sensational ones!

7. Integrate subject matter. Look for ways to interface the different academic subjects every chance you get. Do not assume that students will automatically see the connections from class to class; you must help them understand the links between one content area and another.

8. Forget mistakes, but learn from them. All team members should feel comfortable in taking risks to tease their minds and stretch their imaginations. Some of your ideas or activities will falter, but develop the attitude that a group learns more from its failures than from its successes.

9. Plan "play" into the work week. It is all right to allow some free time in a weekly schedule for both teachers and students. Use this time for reflection and refocusing so that the week becomes both enjoyable and productive.

10. Hold team "professional reading/learning" sessions. Try to build a professional library of resources for the team so that team members can continue to grow in their careers. Do not limit the materials to educational themes, but include books, pamphlets, tapes, and journals in areas of business, economics, and politics.

10 More Things That Great Teams Do

1. Develop common discipline procedures. Be certain that all team members enforce the same rules in the same way so that students can't "play one teacher against another."

2. Establish common grading guidelines. Agree on a grading system that will be used by the team and develop a specific set of descriptors for each point on the grading scale to avoid discrepancies from one team member to another.

3. Coordinate homework. Communicate daily to determine types of homework to be required in the core content areas. Avoid overloading students with unrealistic homework tasks on any given day.

4. Coordinate the administration of quizzes and tests. Create a plan for assessing student achievement in the core subject areas so that no student is required to study for more than one major quiz or test at any one time.

5. Encourage a standard paper heading. Although this may seem like a minor point, the students do not find it so. It can minimize the frustration of a student who has to remember if the name and date go in the upper right hand corner for one class and in the lower left hand corner for another class.

6. Hold team detentions. Handling student discipline problems within the structure of the team is a goal of the teaming process; therefore, time and procedures for dealing with student detentions must be built into the team's schedule.

7. Conduct team "help sessions" for students. It is important that the team try to build into the weekly and monthly schedule of team activities time for helping, tutoring, or coaching students in the academic areas. These sessions could vary according to the schedule, with time blocks set-aside before school, after school, and within the school day.

8. Provide students with opportunities for extra credit work. A written team policy should encourage any student to complete extra credit work for enrichment or remedial purposes, regardless of that student's ability level.

9. Give frequent student academic and personal progress reports. A bank of tools and techniques for recognizing cognitive and affective achievements in the classroom should become an integral part of the teaming process. Progress charts, awards assemblies, recognition banners, personal badges/buttons, and happy-grams to the home can all be parts of this celebration.

10. Monitor student academic and personal progress. Student folders, portfolios, notebooks, and anecdotal records should all be considered parts of the accountability process for keeping track of where students stand both academically and personally. Learning logs, journals, and projects can all be parts of this data-collecting effort.

10 Barriers For Effective Teams To Overcome

1.
PERSONALITY CONFLICTS
Recognize and appreciate diversity and make allowances for different needs, characteristics, moods, and personalities within the team.

2. **INCONSISTENCY IN STUDENT EXPECTATIONS**
Recognize that team members all view the teaching and learning process differently and that it is the team's responsibility to synthesize these expectations when making decisions.

3. **INCONSISTENCY IN TEACHER EXPECTATIONS**
Recognize the individuality of team members when setting personal goals and objectives for the school year and work to reach consensus on goals and objectives, in keeping with teacher talents.

4. **POOR PLANNING, ORGANIZATION, AND PREPARATION**
Recognize that teams often take shortcuts in planning or goal setting for the school year, organizing resources, and preparing students and parents for the teaming process. It is critical that an effort be made in the opening weeks of school to set the tone for the next nine months.

5. **LACK OF SUPPORT FOR ONE ANOTHER OR DISLOYALTY**
Recognize that there will be times when team members do not offer one another the degree of support or loyalty required for making interdisciplinary teams successful. This is often due to teacher stress and/or burnout. Remember that when team members begin to experience these difficulties, time must be set aside immediately to resolve the divisive issues and get back on track.

6. **POOR COMMUNICATION**
Recognize that two-way communication is the very heart and soul of effective teaming and should become the first priority when dealing with the various members of the teaming process.

7. **REFUSAL TO SHARE IDEAS AND MATERIALS**
Recognize that in the past many teachers have been programmed to hoard materials and hide ideas rather than share resources and exchange information. Teaming requires collaboration on a daily basis to maximize learning and growing for students and for teachers.

8. **DIFFICULTY WITH INDIVIDUAL TEAM MEMBERS**
Recognize that on some teams there will be teachers who don't want to be there for reasons ranging from individual feelings of inadequacy to ignorance of the teaming concept. For the good of the students, each team member must accept individual strengths and weaknesses within the team.

9. **INABILITY TO VARY DELIVERY SYSTEMS**
Recognize that it is not enough to recognize the grouping of teachers and students into teams, but that the restructuring of instructional time and techniques is also critical to the redesign of middle-level classrooms.

10. **POOR PUBLIC RELATIONS**
Recognize that teachers must do a better job of "tooting their own horns" and letting the public know the advantages that teaming brings to the schooling process. Teaming is compatible with today's workplace with its emphasis on quality teams, shared decision-making, and empowerment of workers. Let the world know that today's middle school classrooms now represent a more realistic training ground for tomorrow's business settings.

Ideas For Developing A Team Handbook

It is suggested that each interdisciplinary team develop a team handbook for use by both students and parents. The purpose of the handbook is to provide relevant information about the team to which a given student is assigned. Possible contents of a teaming handbook are given below.

1. **PROFILE OF TEAM MEMBERS**
Start with short biographical sketches of each teacher on the team. This information can be written in an essay, outline, or short paragraph format. Teachers might want to tell something about their childhoods, families, hobbies, special interests, travels, pet peeves, previous teaching experiences, and future goals.

2. **TEAM IDENTITY SHEET**
An outline of the team's unique characteristics and plans for the year should be included. Briefly describe the team's name, color, logo, slogan, cheers, secret handshake, traditions, rituals, and celebrations.

3. **TEAM GUIDELINES AND PROCEDURES**
An overview of the team's rules for student grades, for absences, for homework, for make-up work, and for discipline should also be a part of the teaming handbook.

4. **TEAM SCHEDULE OF CLASSES**
A brief explanation of how the students spend their time in school is appropriate for the teaming handbook. A block schedule might also be part of this section.

5. **STUDENT/PARENT CONFERENCE PLANNING SHEET**
A sample of the student/parent conference-planning sheet should be part of the handbook so that students know what to expect when they attend a teacher/student conference. It should be noted that all teachers on the team should be present for a student/parent conference, which is generally held during the team's common planning period.

6. **PARENT CONFERENCE PLANNING SHEET**
A sample telephone report form should be part of the handbook so that parents can see that team teachers keep records of telephone contacts with the home.

7. **TEAM MEETING AGENDA**
It is useful to include a sample team meeting agenda in the handbook as a reminder to both students and parents that much school-day time is spent planning and evaluating the team's instructional program.

8. **TEAM MEETING MINUTES**
A sample of minutes from a typical team meeting can be a useful tool in showing students and parents the kinds of tasks completed during the team's common planning periods.

9. **TEAM CALENDAR OF SPECIAL DATES AND EVENTS**
Students and parents will appreciate a list of the planned rituals, celebrations, traditions, events, and special dates that will have an impact on their time and energies during the school year. This calendar can be used as a vehicle for planning both short-term and long-term activities.

10. **STUDY HINTS**
The teaming handbook is a good place in which to remind students and parents of the importance of cultivating good study habits while in school. This section might include everything from hints on how to study for a test to suggestions for writing an effective research paper or book report.

10 PLUS 2

Ways To Use Common Planning Time

1. Hold formal and informal team meetings to discuss students, parents, schedules, curriculum issues, school business, and team policies and procedures.

2. Plan grade level/departmental meetings or sessions with administrators and/or colleagues to foster communication and an appropriate level of shared decision-making.

3. Offer special staff development activities or a mini-workshop for self-improvement, including short audio/visual training tapes, lectures by district personnel, or programmed texts/workbooks.

4. Develop interdisciplinary approaches or units. This could be a high priority for common planning time get-togethers. Try integrating a concept, skill, or topic on a daily basis in at least some small way to help students understand the correlation between their teachers, subject areas, and skills development.

5. Reward students. Celebrating student success should be a regular occurrence and should vary from appreciation roles and verbal praise to student work displays.

6. Conduct student and parent conferences. It is important to build "talking" time into the weekly schedule for dealing with both student and parent problems as they arise. Remember, "an ounce of prevention is worth a pound of cure."

7. Share teacher ideas, concerns, worries, failures, and success to foster morale, emotional health, and well being by providing outlets for sharing "war stories" or brainstorming creative ideas.

8. Update team records. Documenting team events, discussions, and decisions is important to team success. This includes everything from student records to team minutes so that paperwork does not become a burden at any given time.

9. Organize team events, celebrations, or field trips. Building a strong team identity depends upon a team's ability to plan and implement a wide variety of special happenings for all teachers and student members of the team.

10. Update team calendar to coordinate course requirements, test dates, class excursions, and special lesson plans. Avoiding duplicate or conflicting class requirements or regulations can pave the way for considerable academic achievement.

11. Brainstorm solutions to problems or alternatives for decisions. Holding short stand-up team meetings during the day can help solve short-term problems or aid in making short-term decisions as they come up.

12. Enjoy a social time with special treats or a potluck lunch. Take time for fun and socializing among you.

10 PLUS 2

Characteristics Of Effective Teaming

1. Teams should be balanced and should include team members who have varied teaching and learning styles. Learning style inventories can be used to identify modalities, right/left brain tendencies, and preferred instructional modes.

2. Teams should include team members with the appropriate subject matter competencies. A four-member team should include the specialties of math, science, social studies, and language arts/English/reading. A three-member team should include any three of these areas with a strong backup in the fourth area. A two-member team should include experiences/training/degrees in a science/math combination and a language arts/social studies combination.

3. Teams should be assigned or housed in specific team areas with adjacent classrooms. School floor plans can be adapted to the teaming process by designating sections of the building for trade/team assignments and reassigning space to accommodate those teachers working together.

4. Teams should have a common planning space so that team members can meet daily for team meetings, house shared materials for mutual accessibility, hold student or parent conferences in close proximity to one another, and store team records or files.

5. Teams should have a common planning time to facilitate daily meetings which are needed to: (a) determine schedules; (b) discuss students; (c) develop interdisciplinary units; (d) plan goals and objectives; (e) design special team events/activities; and (f) evaluate programs.

6. Teams should designate a team leader as well as key roles and responsibilities for both the team leader and team members.

7. Teams should hold regular team meetings with predetermined agendas and concise minutes.

8. Teams should strive to preserve team autonomy and flexibility in planning, implementing, and evaluating instructional practices for team members and their students.

9. Teams should share decision-making tasks with the administration whenever and wherever possible to do so. This requires both a mutual commitment and respect among all parties involved.

10. A team should be accountable for its own budget and supplies whenever possible. This encourages both wise spending and maximum use of resources by the team.

11. Teams should include specialists and other support staff members in team decisions and activities. Exploratory teachers and guidance counselors, for example, can add a great deal of valuable input when dealing with issues ranging from student behavior to interdisciplinary units.

12. Teams should respect the similarities and differences that exist among team members and practice the art of compromise or negotiation to accomplish team goals and objectives.

A List Of Advantages And Disadvantages Of Varying Team Sizes

An important decision one must make in setting up an interdisciplinary team organization for a given school setting is the size or sizes of teams servicing the students and teachers in the school. There are both distinct advantages and disadvantages for teams ranging from two-person teams to five-person teams.

Two-Person Team

ADVANTAGES

1. Fewer students—teachers know each student better
2. Variety of subjects may be taught
3. Ease of integrating the disciplines
4. Ease of getting together for meetings
5. Fewer personality conflicts
6. No "odd man out"
7. More secure environment
8. Good transition from single teacher at 5th grade level to two-person team at 6th grade level

DISADVANTAGES

1. Students deal with a limited number of teaching personalities
2. May burden teachers with too much preparation
3. Not as much backup for absenteeism
4. Limited diversity in teaching styles

Three-Person Team

ADVANTAGES

1. Diversity of instructional materials and methods (three heads are better than one)
2. Group will usually teach one subject in common and may integrate subject areas easily
3. Diversity in teaching styles
4. More opportunity to group students according to ability

DISADVANTAGES

1. Sometimes difficult to find a common subject to teach
2. Increased likelihood of "two against one"

Four-Person Team

ADVANTAGES

1. Usually one major subject per teacher (requiring one preparation)

2. Good transition to high school

3. Teacher may specialize if so desired

4. More opportunity to ability-group students within a team

5. Greater diversity of instructional materials and methods (four heads are better than one)

6. Greater diversity in teaching styles

DISADVANTAGES

1. Sometimes more difficult for members to meet

2. Greater potential for personality conflicts

3. May be more difficult to gain and maintain consistency in program

4. Teachers may specialize too much and become departmentalized

Five-Person Team

ADVANTAGES

1. Usually one major subject per teacher (requiring one preparation)

2. Good transition to high school

3. Teacher may specialize if so desired

4. More opportunity to ability-group students within a team

5. Greater diversity of instructional materials and methods (five heads are better than one)

6. Greater diversity in teaching styles

7. Possibility of using one individual as remedial teacher with smaller groups of students

DISADVANTAGES

1. Sometimes more difficult for members to meet

2. Greater potential for personality conflicts

3. May be more difficult to gain and maintain consistency in program

4. Teachers may specialize too much and become departmentalized

Sample Interdisciplinary Team Assignment Data Sheet

Directions: Complete this information for the administrator to consider in assigning you to a team.

1. Name _____

2. Current Assignment

   A. Building _____

   B. Subject or Position_____

   C. Grade Level_____

   D. Certification Area(s) _____

3. Learning Modalities *(Rank order from 1–3 with 1 being your dominant learning style.)*

   _____ Visual _____ Auditory _____ Kinesthetic

4. Right Brain/Left Brain Dominance: Score _____

5. Results of Gregoric _____

   _____

   _____

   _____

6. Results of LSI Inventory_____

   _____

   _____

   _____

7. Other information you feel is relevant_____

   _____

   _____

   _____

10 PLUS 10

Techniques For Effective Team Meetings

1. Plan the meeting cooperatively.

2. Acknowledge the schedules of others.

3. Provide ample lead-time.

4. Keep a portion of the agenda open.

5. Stay on task.

6. Keep presentations/discussions short and to the point.

7. Make space ready and presentable for the meeting.

8. Eliminate distractions.

9. Schedule time to socialize if possible.

10. Feed the troops.

11. Value humor.

12. Learn to read silence.

13. Manage hostility.

14. Respect differences.

15. Protect confidentiality.

16. Stretch for closure.

17. Invite participant feedback.

18. Retire useless practices.

19. Establish priorities.

20. Evaluate results.

10 PLUS 10

Ways to Spend Team Meeting Time

1. Grouping and regrouping of students for instruction

2. Sharing major curricular thrusts with one another

3. Building a team schedule or calendar for the semester or year

4. Preparing for "teachable moments"

5. Integrating two or more of the discipline areas

6. Planning outside field experience or in-class speakers

7. Discussing problematic students and/or parents

8. Holding collaborative student and/or parent conferences

9. Setting consistent behavioral expectations for students

10. Engaging in self-renewal and/or staff development tasks

11. Discussing educational philosophies, hot issues, or national trends

12. Playing an active role in school policy making

13. Coordinating lesson plans to reinforce one another's subject areas

14. Brainstorming or bouncing ideas off of one another

15. Planning to reinforce an academic skill across several subject areas

16. Sharing successful teaching experiences with team members

17. Teaching team members a new active learning strategy

18. Engaging in a problem-solving or decision-making session

19. Working to build team unity or team identity

20. Planning team celebrations

Time Wasters at Team Meetings

1. No purpose, agenda, or follow-up to the meeting

2. Too few people or too many people at the meeting

3. Key people or leadership missing from the meeting

4. Starting late, ending late, or no time limits to the meeting

5. People not interested, prepared, or willing to take an active part in the meeting

6. Redundant, rambling discussions that do not lead to decisions or solutions at the meeting

7. Hidden agendas introduced with side issues that dominate the meeting

8. Too many interruptions at the meeting

9. Participants who do not know what is expected or what procedures to follow at the meeting

10. Agenda topics at the meeting not relevant to one's personal, professional, or work needs

11. Short notice or lead time for meeting

10 PLUS 2

Difficult Situations in Meetings and/or Teaming Situations

Directions: Use the following situations as springboards for discussing conflict or problem situations that sometimes arise during team discussions or team meetings. Try to role-play and determine what could be done to remedy the problem setting.

1. A person who tends to dominate the discussion

Solution: _____

_____

2. A person who wants to argue

Solution: _____

_____

3. A person who attacks the messenger and not the message

Solution: _____

_____

4. A person who starts another side meeting with a fellow teammate

Solution: _____

_____

5. A person who comes unprepared or is disinterested

Solution: _____

_____

6. A person who lacks interest in or shows little concern for the Ideas of others

Solution: _____

_____

7. A person who fails to participate in or contribute to group discussions or decision making

Solution: _____

_____

8. A person who is lazy, careless, or fails to follow up on agreed upon tasks

Solution: _____

_____

9. A person who is antagonistic

Solution: _____

_____

10. A person who is extremely opinionated and strongly defends own opinions

Solution: _____

_____

11. A person who lacks tact or finesse

Solution: _____

_____

12. A person who resists change of any nature

Solution: _____

_____

Guidelines For Setting Team Discipline Rules

Classroom rules, regulations, rewards, and penalties should be established early in the school year. It is also important to involve students in the making process. Here are some factors to consider when developing a set of team rules for the classroom.

1. Rules should be limited to four or five simple reminders or behaviors.

2. Rules should be written in clearly stated sentences.

3. Penalties should be specific, fair, and consistently enforced by all team members.

4. Rules and penalties should be posted in each team and classroom area.

5. The administration should approve the "last resort" or "bottom line" clause in the list of penalties.

6. A longer list of rewards to reinforce acceptable behavior should also be developed and posted in each team and classroom area.

7. Parents should have copies of the team classroom management system of rules.

10 PLUS 5 Tools for Team Decision-Making and Problem Solving

1. **BRAINWRITING**
Divide the class into team 4-6 students. Pass out a piece of paper with a question or issue for debate written on the top to each team member. Have each member write down three ideas and put the paper in a center pool. Ask each member to draw a new paper from the pool and add yet three more ideas that are either completely new or extensions of ideas a team member has already put on the form. Papers are exchanged until each member's form is nearly full. Finally, ask teams to read aloud in a round robin the ideas on the forms while other teams simultaneously cross out ideas that are repeated on their own forms. Note that 10 minutes of "brainwriting" usually generates from 75 to 100 ideas.

2. **DECISION CHART**
The Decision Chart is helpful when you have to make a decision and you don't know quite where to begin. In the DECISION rectangle at the top of the page, write a brief statement that describes the nature of the decision you must make. Then, in the ALTERNATIVE IDEAS column, list a number of alternative ideas that could resolve your dilemma. Then decide on a set of criteria to be used in judging the worth of each alternative idea and list these in the slanted boxes labeled CRITERIA. Rate each individual criterion according to the scoring scale as shown. Finally, compile the total score for each alternative idea. The best decision is probably the idea that has the highest point value.

3. **PLANNING TREE**
Use the Planning Tree as a tool for planning and completing a project that has a major goal and sub goals to accomplish through a variety of sequential tasks. Write your major goal in the large box. Finally, organize the sequence of tasks for the implementation of the goals in the smaller boxes. It is important that each set of tasks be grouped with the appropriate sub goal in the diagram.

4. **CAUSE AND EFFECT CHAIN**
Use the Appropriate sections of the Cause and Effect Chain to record a series of cause-and-effect relationships learned from a topic of study. Be sure that each CAUSE produces a related EFFECT.

5. COMPARE AND CONTRAST DIAGRAM

Use the Compare and Contrast Diagram when you want to relate a new concept you are researching or learning to knowledge you already have on a related concept. Concept 1 and Concept 2 should be recorded in the two rectangles at the top of the page. Comparison Step: Write how the two concepts are similar in the HOW ALIKE? Box. Comparison Step: Note the differences between the two concepts in the HOW DIFFERENT? Columns.

6. FISHBONE MODEL

The Fishbone Model is helpful when investigating the causes of a research problem that involves a cause-and-effect situation. The effect is written in the rectangle at the HEAD of the fish and various categories are written in the rectangles at the ends of the major BONES of the fish. Possible causes of the effect are recorded on the SMALLER BONES under the most appropriate category names.

7. FLOWCHARTS

Flowcharts are used to organize sequences of events, actions, or decisions. A standard set of symbols is used when designing flowcharts so that all can understand them. The arrangement of the symbols will vary according to the type of sequence depicted. The symbols and how each one is used are explained. Use a blank piece of paper to create your flowchart.

8. ISSUE IDENTIFICATION AND CLASSIFICATION DIAGRAM

The Issue Identification and Classification Diagram is especially helpful when a small group of students is analyzing a large or complex issue in social studies, current events, or science classes (such as prejudice, crime, or pollution). It is a good way to organize and understand thoughts and ideas related to issues that may be difficult to grasp.

9. OPPOSING FORCES CHART

The Opposing Forces Chart is best used in small groups. Use it when you are trying to identify potential causes of and solutions for a problem or important challenges/opportunities. At the top of the chart, write the situation to be resolved or challenge/opportunity goal to be reached. In the arrows under the DRIVING FORCES heading, record as many forces as you can that you think would move you toward your goal or problem solution. (Driving forces are defined as positive actions, skills, people, tools, and procedures available to you at this time.) In the arrows under the OPPOSING FORCES heading, record as many forces as you can that you think are keeping you from reaching your goal or solving your problem. (Opposing forces can be any restraining actions, skills, people, tools, and procedures that are interfering with your attempts to resolve your situation.) Once the forces have been identified, it is up to you to prioritize the driving and opposing forces and to begin eliminating the problem areas and capitalizing on the positive areas.

10. ORGANIZING TREE

Use the Organizing Tree to organize information and structure your ideas on a topic in any content area. Write the major topic in the oval at the top of the tree, subheadings in other ovals, and information on diagonals extending from the subheadings.

11. DISCUSSION GUIDE

For each of the given statements, choose a response from the scale as shown. Share your thoughts by discussing them with a partner. After you have finished, revise your ratings as needed and be prepared to discuss your responses with the entire team.

12. DELPHI METHOD

Each team member independently and anonymously writes down comments and suggestions about ways to deal with a problem, issue, or decision. Ideas are then compiled, reproduced, and distributed to team members for observation and reaction. Next, each member provides feedback to the entire team concerning each of the comments and proposed solutions or decisions. Finally, the members reach consensus on which solution or decision is most acceptable to the team as a whole.

13. MULTIVOTING

Each person on the team votes for as many ideas as he or she likes. The ideas that get the most votes are circles. The remaining votes are consolidated where possible to do so. Each person then votes again, but this time for only half the number of ideas that are circled. Multi-voting continues until the list is down to no more than three to five ideas.

14. NOMINAL GROUP VOTING

Use this technique as a good alternative to multi-voting, or use it to further reduce and prioritize the discussion options. Assume that the multi-voting exercise resulted in six items remaining, and there is not time enough to discuss for consensus. The facilitator then asks each team member to rate the remaining items from "1" to "6" on a 3 x 5 card or a self-stick note. The "6" represents the item they most favor and "1" the least favored. These ratings are then tabulated on a flip chart by the recorder. The highest-scored item represents the team's greatest support. After discussion, the team is asked if it can fully support this item.

15. THE DOT TECHNIQUE

The group brainstorms a number of items. Each member of the group received three sticky dots—one red, one yellow, and one green. A red dot equals 3 points; a yellow dot equals 2 points; and a green dot equals 1 point. Team members then "spend" their three dots by placing them on the master list of brainstormed items. If a person feels strongly about one item, all three dots can be placed on that item, but if a person prefers to spread their feelings around then he/she can spread dots over three different items. The value of the dots is then tallied for each item and the results of the tally are discussed. The "dot procedure" can be repeated to reduce the number of items necessary. All items receiving at least one red dot (someone's highest ranking) should remain on the list for further discussion and voting.

10 PLUS 5 — Questions to Answer When Observing a Team Meeting or Problem-Solving Session

To obtain an objective opinion about how a team is functioning, recruit an outside observer to sit in on a team meeting or problem-solving session. The following questions can be used to record the behaviors of the group members and the group processing outcomes.

1. Did the team get started on time, and, if so, how was this accomplished?

2. How well did the team set up its agenda and structure for the meeting?

3. How did the team establish their rules and/or follow their predetermined procedures?

4. How did the team share information and explore different perspectives or points of view?

5. How did the team handle conflict?

6. How did the team stay on task?

7. How were ideas accepted, rejected, and/or recorded?

8. How were decisions made?

9. How was consensus achieved?

10. How active and widespread was the participation of team members?

11. How did the team reflect on its own functioning?

12. How did the team leader or facilitator maintain order, control, and/or time on task?

13. What type of climate emerged?

14. What types of minutes or records were kept?

15. How were follow-up tasks and timelines delegated or handled?

10
PLUS 1

Questions To Use During A Team Interview

These questions are to be used when a person who is not a member of a given team is called in to interview selected team members regarding the effectiveness of the team duty time and member's feelings about interdisciplinary team organization. Responses should be recorded on a separate piece of paper.

1. How do you generally feel about being a member of an interdisciplinary team?

2. What is the best thing about being a member of your team?

3. What is the most difficult thing about being a member of your team?

4. How do you feel about the effectiveness of your team meetings?

5. Tell me something about the face-to-face parent conferences conducted by your team.

6. Tell me something about the student conferences conducted by your team.

7. Explain how your team used the services of resource personnel in your building, such as counselors, house leaders, psychologists, and special education teachers.

8. Tell me about the coordination of instruction and scheduling in your team.

9. State three things that your team is doing to help meet the needs of your students.

10. State three things that your team is doing to help meet the needs of the adult team members.

11. State three things that your team has done to help build team identity with your students.

From *How To Evaluate Your Middle School* by Sandra Schurr. Columbus, OH: National Middle School Association, ©1992. Used by permission.

10 PLUS 5

Ways to Determine If You Are A Good Team Player

Determine whether or not you are a good team player by rating yourself on the following behavior tasks:

1. I am well aware of my team role and the functions of the team.

Never   1   2   3   4   5   6   7   Always

2. I express my willingness to cooperate with other group members and my expectation that they will also be cooperative with me.

Never   1   2   3   4   5   6   7   Always

3. I support the efforts of the team leader and other team members.

Never   1   2   3   4   5   6   7   Always

4. I follow the guidelines for gaining consensus and participate equally in making team decisions.

Never   1   2   3   4   5   6   7   Always

5. I am open and candid in my dealings with the team.

Never   1   2   3   4   5   6   7   Always

6. I recognize the relationship of planning periods to the effectiveness of the team's activities.

Never   1   2   3   4   5   6   7   Always

7. I respond to the needs of students through the teaming process.

Never   1   2   3   4   5   6   7   *Always*

8. I do my part in helping to resolve conflicts among team members.

Never   1   2   3   4   5   6   7   *Always*

9. I share materials, books, sources of information, or other resources with other team members to promote the success of the entire group.

Never   1   2   3   4   5   6   7   *Always*

10. I collect and use data for purposes of improving the team's effectiveness and for developing the overall instructional program.

Never   1   2   3   4   5   6   7   *Always*

11. I stick to agenda items at team meetings wherever possible to do so.

Never   1   2   3   4   5   6   7   *Always*

12. I complete team paperwork and tasks in a timely fashion.

Never   1   2   3   4   5   6   7   *Always*

13. I actively participate in parent and/or student conferences.

Never   1   2   3   4   5   6   7   *Always*

14. I communicate effectively with team members, parents, administration, and other support staff.

Never   1   2   3   4   5   6   7   *Always*

15. I regularly participate in staff development activities.

Never   1   2   3   4   5   6   7   *Always*

A Sample Team
Self-Evaluation Checklist

School _____ Team Number _____

Name _____ Grade Level _____

This checklist should be completed individually by all members of an interdisciplinary team. Afterwards the team leader should facilitate a meeting where responses
are shared and consensus is reached. The agreed-upon answers should be recorded on
a master sheet, kept in the team master notebook, and reviewed on a regular basis.

	Always	Frequently	Infrequently	Never	Comments
1. Our team meets on a regular basis.					
2. All team members are present at our team meetings.					
3. All team members come to our meetings on time.					
4. All team members stay for the duration of our meetings.					
5. Our team talks about ways to best meet the needs of students.					
6. Our team works effectively with resource personnel such as our counselor and our house leader.					
7. The members of our team support the efforts of our team leader.					

Self-Evaluation Checklist

		Always	Frequently	Infrequently	Never	Comments
8.	Every member of our team participates in the decision-making process.					
9.	The team's decisions are implemented.					
10.	Our team keeps a team notebook that includes agenda, minutes, parent conference forms, student conference forms, and other information pertaining to our team.					
11.	Our team has goals and objectives for the school year.					
12.	Our team periodically evaluates its goals and objectives.					
13.	Our team members use team duty time to correlate subject matter and to plan for interdisciplinary instruction.					
14.	Our team members conduct face-to-face parent conferences during team duty time.					
15.	Our team members use team duty time to conduct student conferences.					
16.	Our team discusses ways to use our block time effectively.					
17.	Our team groups and regroups students for instruction within our team.					
18.	Our team changes our "regular" schedule to accommodate teacher and student needs.					
19.	Our team has an agenda for all team meetings.					

Self-Evaluation Checklist

	Always	Frequently	Infrequently	Never	Comments
20. Our team follows the agenda at our meetings.					
21. Our team planning time is kept strictly for team business.					
22. The team paces itself and allows for "ups" and "downs," cycles of hard work and relaxation.					
23. The team regularly takes time to provide outlets for members to share ideas and frustrations.					
24. Our team members inform the exploratory teachers about decisions reached at our team meetings.					
25. Our team coordinates the amount of homework given to students so that it is spread throughout the week.					
26. Our team coordinates test days so that students do not have more than one test on a given day.					
27. Our team has established team procedures and policies for our students.					
28. Our team has established a team identity through the use of a team name, team logo, team assemblies, etc.					
29. Our team plans, implements, and evaluates at least two interdisciplinary units a year.					

10 MINUS 7

Ways to Assess Team Progress

Directions: Once a month, try using the simple form outlined below to record the team's progress toward team goals and objectives established for the year. You might want to reproduce the three columns on a large piece of chart paper and do this as part of a team meeting, or you may want to have individual team members record their responses on individual forms. The team may want to brainstorm responses to columns one and two and decide together how to celebrate the items listed in column one.

Great Things We Have Done As A Team This Month	Things We Have Done That We Wish We Had Not	Things We Have Not Yet Done But Would Like To Do
1. _____	1. _____	1. _____
2. _____	2. _____	2. _____
3. _____	3. _____	3. _____
4. _____	4. _____	4. _____
5. _____	5. _____	5. _____
6. _____	6. _____	6. _____
7. _____	7. _____	7. _____
8. _____	8. _____	8. _____
9. _____	9. _____	9. _____
10. _____	10. _____	10. _____

10 PLUS 10 Ways to Document Student Growth and Achievement on Individual Teams

It is important for teams to have a plan for documenting student growth, performance, and achievement levels during the school year, especially because there is growing evidence that the teaming concept does indeed enhance the teaching and learning process in the classroom. Some worthy goals to consider and document might be:

By at least _____ percent (insert a realistic figure here), our team plans to . . .

1. Decrease student tardiness and/or attendance rates.

2. Increase parent involvement through participation in school functions.

3. Increase student participation in extracurricular academic clubs or activities.

4. Increase student attendance at school sporting or social events.

5. Increase student achievement on standardized test scores for a given subject area.

6. Increase student achievement on criterion-referenced test scores in a given subject area.

7. Increase averages of report card letter grades.

8. Increase number of community service projects.

9. Increase number of elective field experiences.

10. Increase number of positive parent contacts by telephone calls, e-mails, or conferences.

11. Increase number of communications sent home to parents and/or guardians.

12. Increase number of interdisciplinary units implemented during a semester.

13. Increase number of student-generated or student-led activities within the classroom.

14. Decrease number of discipline referrals.

15. Decrease number of in- or out-of-school suspensions.

16. Decrease number of drug and alcohol referrals.

17. Decrease number of violent acts or acts of vandalism.

18. Decrease number of missing homework assignments.

19. Decrease number of in-class assignments.

20. Decrease number of disruptive behaviors within the classroom setting.

10 PLUS 5

Key Benefits of Teams

1. Improved work climate through a highly motivated environment

2. Shared ownership and responsibility for tasks

3. Conservation of time and space in an ever-expanding curriculum

4. Coordination of assignments, testing schedule, rules, guidelines, and classroom procedures

5. Common commitment to goals and values as result of complete buy-in

6. Reduction of fragmentation of learning from one discipline to another

7. Proactive approach to problems due to innovative and effective problem solving

8. Multiple uses of resources, teaching tools, technology, and instructional techniques

9. Better decisions and implementation and support of those decisions

10. Intellectual stimulation provided by closer association with colleagues

11. Skill development of staff via cross-training in roles and responsibilities

12. Delivery system improved through the use of varied teacher personalities, styles, talents, and strategies

13. Early warning system for problems

14. Effective delegation of work load and flexibility in task assignments

15. Improved time management through team meetings and common planning periods

10 PLUS 5

Drawbacks to Teaming

1. Can be time-consuming, especially in the beginning months

2. Sometimes results in personality conflicts, which lead to lack of support or disloyalty to one another

3. Requires people to change and reconceptualize their teaching roles

4. Inconsistency in teacher expectations as team members all view the teaching and learning process differently

5. Requires a long time to produce significant results in attendance, discipline, achievement, and motivation of students

6. Inability or reluctance to share ideas and materials freely

7. Are viewed negatively by "old school" colleagues and parents who like order, control, and authority levels

8. Difficulty with individual team members who feel inadequate or uncomfortable with the teaming concept

9. Can cause role confusion as members have difficulty leaving "traditional hats" at the door

10. Inability to vary delivery systems due to inexperience with the restructuring of instructional groups, times, and techniques

11. Can appear confused, disorganized, and ineffective to the outside observer

12. Poor communication due to time constraints, lack of commitment, or poor listening skills

13. Poor public relations as team members reluctant to "toot their own horns" and point out the compatibility of teams in school with teams in the workplace

14. Lack of consistent problem-solving or decision-making model to apply as needed

15. Lack of comprehensive team evaluation and reflection process

10 PLUS 10

Important Questions to Find Answers for Related to Block Scheduling

1. Will students retain more or less with the block schedule?

2. Will the curriculum have to be changed?

3. How will yearlong, sequential courses be handled, such as foreign language courses and Advanced Placement courses in U.S. History or Government?

4. Will students make the most of these extended classes?

5. Will teachers be able to adapt their instructional delivery systems for these longer blocks of time?

6. Will more intense schedules help students develop better decision-making, problem-solving, and creative-thinking skills than in a traditional 180-day schedule?

7. What impact does a block system have on class size?

8. Will absent students have a more difficult time catching up on missed assignments?

9. Will students be able to earn more credits under the block system?

10. How will retention rates of students be affected when there is a gap in sequential courses?

11. Is early graduation still a possibility with the block schedule?

12. How is content coverage affected by the block schedule?

13. What impact is the block schedule likely to have on the school climate?

14. What results have been reported by schools using the block schedule?

15. What is the major negative factor to overcome when implementing the block schedule?

16. What assurances do we have that students will be able to function effectively in these "macro classes" of two hours?

17. Will teachers suffer "burnout" from the drain of teaching two-hour sessions?

18. What impact will the block schedule have on electives?

19. What type of staff development is essential to make the block schedule successful?

20. How can the community best be informed about the benefits of the block schedule?

10 Terms Important to Time as it Relates to the Block Schedule

It is important to equate the concept of block scheduling with the concept of time. The primary focus of the block schedule is to make the best use of classroom time for impacting positively on the achievement and performance of students.

1. Classroom Time:
Block scheduling encourages interaction and individualization of instruction between the teacher and the student. In many high schools, students enter into a contract and/or an individual educational plan to ensure both student and teacher accountability.

2. Prime Time:
Block scheduling allows for periods of "prime time" teaching, which is generally the first thirty minutes at the beginning of the period followed by a "down time" during the middle of the period and ending with another "prime time" block of minutes at the end of the period. It is important that the teacher directs instruction during the first "prime time" period, provides interesting and motivating practice or application during the "down time" period, and provides a creative and challenging summary during the final "prime time" period.

3. Transition Time:
Block scheduling provides for a smooth transition between the "prime" and "down" time periods by emphasizing understanding and application of material learned rather than on content coverage.

4. **Reflection Time:**
Block scheduling demands that teachers spend part of their prep or planning time reflecting on what happened in class and how well the established lesson plan went over with the students.

5. **Personal Time:**
Block scheduling also demands that teachers take some part of their prep or planning time to regroup their own personal thoughts and energies so that it becomes the "pause that refreshes."

6. **Preparation Time:**
Block scheduling promotes the idea of varied delivery systems and the alternative instructional strategies that meet the diverse needs, interests, abilities and learning styles of students. Quality lesson plans are essential to this process.

7. **Consulting Time:**
Block scheduling has built-in time for teachers to consult with students who are at risk and who need special attention and academic assistance.

8. **Facilitating Time:**
Block scheduling argues the fact that teachers must reconceptualize their roles in the classroom from "sage on the stage" to "guide on the side."

9. **Team Time:**
Block scheduling builds a time in the school day for teams of teachers to meet and talk to one another about curriculum, about individual students, and about interdisciplinary options.

10. **Professional Growth Time:**
Block scheduling encourages teachers to pursue professional growth experiences on school time. This can be done as part of the Preparation Time, Prime Time, and/or Team Time and should involve anything from observing colleagues in action (during Prime Time) to discussing professional journal articles (during Team Time) and critiquing one another's lesson plans (during Prep Time).

10 Musts to Consider as Change Agents when Promoting the Block Schedule

1. Conduct a needs assessment with teachers, students, and parents prior to the implementation of the block schedule.

2. Include teachers, students, and parents in the planning and decision-making activities and action steps.

3. Make the transition from the traditional to the block schedule for the right reason, which is to facilitate instruction and improve student performance.

4. Work to improve assessment measures that will enhance and not detract from the improved delivery systems for instruction.

5. Modify the curriculum to support the new block scheduling structure.

6. Alter teachers, parents, and students that many trial and error experiences are inevitable when making a major change, such as that represented by implementing the block schedule.

7. Create a school climate and environment that values change, promotes collaboration, and encourages risk taking to improve the schooling process for students.

8. Remember and remind others that it takes time and resources to make a major transition in the restructuring of any organization.

9. Keep in mind that whatever scheduling pattern you foster, it must promote the skills you are trying to teach and the concepts that are most important for your students to grasp.

10. Never forget that the workload and union issues must always be addressed throughout the change process!

10 Potential Hindrances to Block Scheduling

1. Moving to a block schedule does not insure that teachers will improve their instructional delivery systems and that students will learn more. Changing the schedule alone is not enough.

2. Many scheduling changes are done to benefit the administrative needs of the adults in the school rather than the academic needs of the students. Both must benefit.

3. Too many block schedules are developed around existing or established models rather than an honest diagnosis of problems embedded in the current scheduling system. Don't throw out the baby with the bath water!

4. A significant number of faculty members think that the schedule should drive the instructional and assessment process, rather than the other way around. It is imperative that curriculum, instruction, and assessment determine what schedule is most appropriate in any given situation.

5. Block schedules rarely involve representatives from all major stakeholder groups. Students must be involved in the decision-making process.

6. Decisions on what to do with student transfers from school without the block schedule must be considered. Options need to be considered for alternative enrollment problems.

7. Students still find an over dependence on the lecture in classrooms and too much independent study needed outside the class with the block schedule. Teachers need to become the facilitators of the learning process rather than the dictators of learning content.

8. Faculty and staff show reluctance to provide direct input and feedback into the planning and implementation process for the move to the block schedule.

9. District personnel are not willing or able to provide adequate training options and opportunities for teachers in the instructional areas of effective pacing and alternative delivery systems.

10. Teachers are not effective in applying either adequate pacing skills or active learning strategies within the block schedule primarily because course material does not contain suggested lesson plans or pacing guides for doing so.

10 Reasons To Flex The Block

A flexible block schedule can have the following beneficial results.

1. The total team can test during the same time period to accommodate best testing time and better use of class time.

2. A film/video can be shown to a total team to make better use of instructional time.

3. A teacher can be relieved so that he or she can attend to the development of an interdisciplinary unit, conferencing, team teaching, or visitations.

4. Total team activities (such as a guest speaker, field trip, assembly, field day, or intramurals) can be arranged.

5. An extra period once or twice a week can be created for extended advisory periods, silent sustained reading, study skills, etc.

6. An extra period can be created for a guest teacher.

7. The schedule can be rotated within the block so that each teacher sees each group at different times of the day.

8. The schedule can be shortened to provide time for mini-courses.

9. Home-base, mini-, or maxi-classes can be created to accommodate an interdisciplinary unit.

10. A maxi-class period can be created to accommodate an extended period for science labs, projects, research, presentations, etc.

10 MINUS 1

Ways To Flex A Block Schedule

The block schedule is at the heart of the middle school. It is designed to accommodate a program that meets the needs and characteristics of the middle grade youngster. It has three main parts: advisory, basic skills, and physical education/exploratory classes. The basic skills interdisciplinary team of teachers has a block of time for academic instruction that can be manipulated to meet the teachers' needs and the needs of their students.

The following ideas are based on a block of time consisting of five 45-minute "periods" for a total of 225 minutes.

1. Use one hour for a total team guest speaker experience, which leaves 165 minutes for:

   a. Five 33-minute mini-periods

   b. Four 41-minute periods

2. Create seven 32-minute mini-periods.

   a. Each regular block teacher teaches his or her normal class, while two guests teach additional classes.

   b. All regular block teachers plus two guests teach interest classes.

3. Create a 75-minute bonus-class.

75	Science	Social Studies	Mathematics	Language Arts	Reading
37	Social Studies	Mathematics	Language Arts	Reading	Science
37	Mathematics	Language Arts	Reading	Science	Social Studies
37	Language Arts	Reading	Science	Social Studies	Mathematics
37	Reading	Science	Social Studies	Mathematics	Language Arts

4. Use the entire block of time for a combination large group/small group experience.

    A. Team Meeting
    B. Guest Speakers
    C. Mini-Conference
    D. Drama Presentation
    E. Advisory Skit Presentations
    F. Team Awards Assembly
    G. Team Movie
    H. Trivia Bowl
    I. Jeopardy Bowl
    J. Field Trip
    K. Career Day
    L. Team Students Work at Elementary School
    M. Science Fair Project Displays and Presentations
    N. Interdisciplinary Unit Group Activity
    O. Team Intramurals

5. Create an extra period one day per week (six 37-minute "periods").

    A. Sustained Silent Reading
    B. Introduction of Skill of the Week
    C. Introduction of Vocabulary of the Week
    D. Team Meeting
    E. Current Events
    F. Teaching Skills for Standardized Testing
    G. Study and Organization Skills
    H. Mini-Interest Classes
    I. Any Team Unity/Identity Activity

6. Rotate schedule within the block.

    Week One 1-2-3-4-5

    Week Two 5-1-2-3-4

    Week Three .... 4-5-1-2-3 etc.

7. Implement a drop schedule within the block.

A.	Week 1	Week 2	Week 3	etc.
	##	1	1	
	2	##	2	
	3	3	##	
	4	4	4	
	5	5	5	

B. Periodically, run four classes instead of five to allow a team member to be engaged in one or more of the following activities:
   1) Team Teaching
   2) Student Remediation
   3) Student Enrichment
   4) Planning Future Team Activities
   5) Staff Development Activities
   6) Parent Conferences
   7) Planning an IDU (Interdisciplinary Unit)

8. Switch teachers within the block! Periodically, without telling the students beforehand, the team teachers should switch teaching assignments for a day.

9. Place half of the class and two teachers with a guest speaker for half of the block time (112 minutes), while the other three teachers are teaching the other half of the class in 37-minute periods. After the 112-minute time interval, switch the two groups.

Example: Upon completing a two-person IDU, the language arts teacher and the reading teacher may wish to culminate the activity with a speaker.

SAMPLE SCHEDULE: FLEXING THE BLOCK

(Common Flexible Schedule For All Teams)

Grade 6

9:15–9:37	9:40–10:20	10:23–11:03	11:03–11:33	11:35–12:05	12:56–1:26	3:30
Advisory	P.E. or EXPLORATORY		Team A Team B Team C Lunch	Team D Team E ½ Lunch	Team E ½ Lunch	

Grade 7

9:15–9:37	10:30–11:00	11:35–12:05	2:07–2:47	2:50–3:30
Advisory	Team A Team B Team C Lunch	Team D Team E	P.E. or EXPLORATORY	

Grade 8

9:15–9:37	11:33–12:13	12:16–12:53	12:56–1:26
Advisory	EXPLORATORY / P.E.	Team A Team B Team C Lunch / EXPLORATORY	P.E. / Team D Team E Lunch

Note option of splitting a team for separate lunch times if necessary (shown on Grade 6 schedule).

153

10 PLUS 8

Ways to Use the Time Block Constructively

Using instructional strategies that are active, varied, motivating, and relevant for students is the key to making the block schedule effective. Here are twenty tools and techniques that should be an integral part of the high school program regardless of the discipline being taught or the diversity of students being challenged. These are discussed in more detail in Module Five.

1. An interactive lecture than includes one or more of the following variables:

    a. Feedback Lecture   e. Pause Procedure Lecture
    b. Guided Lecture   f. Think/Write/Discuss Lecture
    c. Responsive Lecture   g. Bingo Lecture
    d. Demonstration Lecture

2. A class discussion that is led first by the teacher and then by a student or group of students.

3. A media-based lesson that replaces verbal information with one or more aids to learning such as a video, chart, transparency, pictures, artifacts, records, audiotapes, or a set of objects with manipulability.

4. A demonstration and hands-on lesson that actually shows students how to perform a new skill or apply a new concept.

5. A directed textbook/reading lesson in which the teacher guides the reading and learning experience by pre-teaching key vocabulary, asking questions, and checking for understanding.

6. A writing lesson in which the teacher directs the writing experience by giving a series of directives on how to proceed and the students engage in a sustained writing task.

7. A field experience where the students learn directly from an outside expert or resource through observation of objects and situations.

8. A visit by a guest speaker in which a resource person uses one or more teaching techniques to share directly information or personal experiences not possessed by the teacher.

9. A cooperative learning small group activity, which can take any of the following formats:

a. Think/Pair/Share
b. Three Step Interview
c. Jigsaw
d. Round Table

e. Team Learning
f. Circle of Knowledge
g. Numbered Heads Together
h. Co-op Co-op

10. A skills practice lesson in which the teacher provides instruction and materials so that the student can practice a previously learned skill in a context different from the one in which it was taught.

11. An industrial arts or construction lesson in which the teacher provides instructions and materials for the students to reproduce a product, construct an artifact, or engage in a work activity for an industrial process.

12. A role-play or case study lesson in which the teacher sets up a scenario for students to play the assigned parts and situations, which can either be prescribed by the teacher or left up to the creative interpretations of the students.

13. A simulation experience provided by the teacher that requires the students to engage in a situation that closely resembles a real-life scenario. The teacher provides directions and materials, monitors the simulation activity, and conducts a follow-up discussion or debriefing.

14. An action research lesson in which the teacher works with the students to design an experiment or hypothesis, collect data, record and tabulate data, and share their subsequent findings or results.

15. A series of learning stations in which the teacher develops a number of learning tasks around a central theme and sets up small group sites for these tasks to be completed by students on a rotating schedule.

16. A debate or panel discussion lesson whose topic and guidelines are provided by the teacher so that students can argue the pros and cons of an issue or controversial idea.

17. A survey, interview, or questionnaire lesson that provides students with the tools and techniques for developing and using an original instrument to collect and interpret data on a given topic.

18. A game-based lesson that models a popular game show or format such as Tic-Tac-Toe, Jeopardy, or Concentration to review learned information.

10 Statements to Use in a Teacher Survey about the Block Schedule

Directions: Please use the five point scale to answer each of the following questions about your teaching under the block-scheduling plan. The results of this survey will help us evaluate the effectiveness of the block schedule to date.

1 = Strongly Agree   2 = Agree   3 = Not Sure Yet   4 = Somewhat Disagree   5 = Strongly Disagree

___ **1.** I feel the students are learning and retaining more about my subject area.

___ **2.** I feel that I know the students better.

___ **3.** I have been able to upgrade and vary my teaching strategies.

___ **4.** I think fewer class changes have improved student behavior and attendance.

___ **5.** I find the students to be more interactive, motivated, and responsive to my teaching.

___ **6.** I feel more involved in the curriculum and the decision-making process.

___ **7.** I am more comfortable with active learning techniques.

___ **8.** I am less dependent upon the lecture and textbook.

___ **9.** I have seen improvement in the quality of work and grades my students produce.

___ **10.** I am better able to meet the different needs and learning styles of my students.

Please complete these two statements:

1. The thing I like most about the block schedule is . . .

2. This thing I like least about the block schedule is . . .

10 Statements to Use in a Student Survey about the Block Schedule

Directions: Please use the five-point scale to answer each of the following questions about your learning under the new block-scheduling plan. The results of this survey will be used to help evaluate the effectiveness of the block schedule to date.

1 = Strongly Agree   2 = Agree   3 = Not Sure Yet   4 = Somewhat Disagree   5 = Strongly Disagree

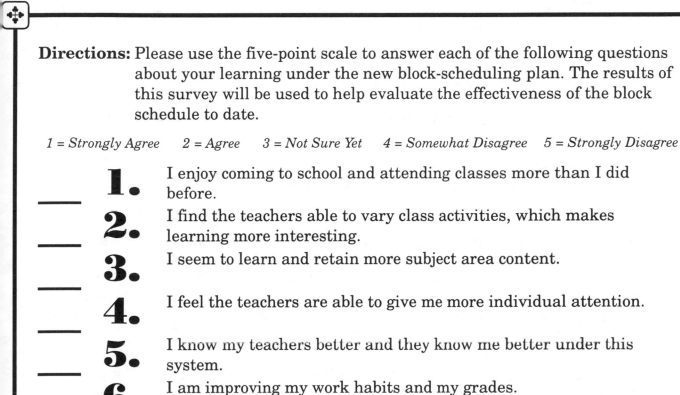

___ **1.** I enjoy coming to school and attending classes more than I did before.

___ **2.** I find the teachers able to vary class activities, which makes learning more interesting.

___ **3.** I seem to learn and retain more subject area content.

___ **4.** I feel the teachers are able to give me more individual attention.

___ **5.** I know my teachers better and they know me better under this system.

___ **6.** I am improving my work habits and my grades.

___ **7.** I find school more challenging and responsive to my needs.

___ **8.** I understand more because the teachers are able to cover the material more thoroughly.

___ **9.** I find the time in classes to be more productive and to move by more quickly.

___ **10.** I feel the teachers are better able to plan and teach their subject areas more effectively.

Please complete these two statements:

1. The thing I like most about the block schedule is . . .

2. This thing I like least about the block schedule is . . .

10 Advantages of the Block Schedule for Teachers

1. Teachers are required to teach only three courses with one of the four daily periods used as a planning period.

2. Teachers see only 90 students per day, rather than 150 students per day.

3. Teachers are in control of the learning time, which allows for extended teaching periods and team teaching with colleagues.

4. Teachers have opportunities to develop varied instructional techniques that are more compatible with individual learning styles and needs of students.

5. Teachers can use the extra teaching time within a class for more complex lab experiences, more in-depth class discussions, more extended field trips and quality resource speakers, more effective use of technology, and more efficient cooperative learning group activities.

6. Teachers can better monitor at-risk students since they have fewer students in all.

7. Teachers can engage in more authentic kids assessment due to reasonable time periods and student numbers for evaluation purposes.

8. Teachers will experience fewer attendance and discipline problems because students find it harder to skip a class now because they miss so much.

9. Teachers experience little or no negative impact on school budget allocations since block scheduling does not require significant dollar amounts to implement.

10. Teachers experience a more relaxed and "user friendly" classroom climate, and the reduction in passing periods means increased time for instruction.

10 Advantages of the Block Schedule for Students

1. Students of all abilities and special needs can meet graduation requirements in three years.

2. Students can complete college courses during their last two years of high school.

3. Students have only four teachers and only four classes to prepare for each day, instead of the traditional six or seven. Students have homework for four classes each night rather than for seven or eight.

4. Students have a greater range of classes from which to select.

5. Students develop more of a team spirit, rather than an isolated or competitive spirit.

6. Students often report a better understanding of the lessons and are more likely to apply the new concepts learned.

7. Students often report a better understanding of the lessons and are more likely to apply the new concepts learned.

8. Students often report higher Advanced Placement scores.

9. Students often report that the day is much less frantic and stressful because it is free of distractions, arbitrary time constraints, and student conflicts.

10. Students are more likely to experience varied instructional methods that better accommodate their individual learning styles.

Findings from the Published Literature about Teaming and Block Scheduling in the Middle School

1. FINDING:
Jon R. Katzenbach and Douglas K. Smith write:

The best way to understand teams is to look at teams themselves. Their own stories reveal their accomplishments, skills, emotions, and commitment better than any abstract commentary or logical presentation. Real teams are deeply committed to their purpose, goals, and approach. High-performance team members are also very committed to one another. Both understand that the wisdom of teams comes with a focus on collective work-products, personal growth, and performance results. However meaningful, "team" is always a result of pursuing a demanding challenge.

Source: Katzenbach, J. R., & Smith, D. K. (1993). The wisdom of teams. New York: Harper Collins.

2. FINDING:
John Arnold points out:

As compared to conventional departmentalized arrangements, well-functioning teams enjoy the following potential advantages relative to curriculum:

- Teams can create a more personal, positive climate where risk taking, initiative, and responsibility on the part of teachers and students can be cultivated.
- Teachers know student needs, interests, and abilities better and thus can tailor activities to meet individual and group concerns.
- Teachers have greater flexibility in the use of time and the grouping of students.
- Teachers have colleagues with whom they can develop curriculum, share ideas and responsibilities, learn new skills, and receive support.
- Integrative and interdisciplinary curriculum as well as special events are more easily facilitated.

Source: Arnold, J. (1997). Teams and curriculum. In Dickinson, T. S., & Erb, T. O. (Eds.). We gain more than we give: Teaming in middle schools. Columbus, OH: National Middle School Association.

3. FINDING:

Elliot Y. Merenbloom summarizes:

Every team is unique. No other team has the same teachers or same students. As a result, each team will have its own personality, strengths, and limitations. Each team must develop its own structure to accomplish it goals and purposes. As a result, every team should have a measure of local autonomy. Although there are regulations and guidelines for each school or department of instruction, teams are able to make many decisions within the framework or guidelines. Each team is responsible, in its own way, to respond to the needs of its students and deliver the prescribed program of studies.

Source: Merenbloom, E. Y. (1991). The team process: A handbook for teachers. Columbus, OH: National Middle School Association.

4. FINDING:

Clay Carr states:

The most effective form of team power, when the organization can support it, is the fully self-managing, or self-directing, or semi-autonomous work team. Almost without exception, fully self-managing work teams produce higher quality products and services, and they generally have a much higher rate of production, than organizations with traditional work organization. What characterizes a fully self-managing team? It takes responsibility for its own operation and output. When such a team is fully developed, it assumes most of the tasks normally associated with supervision: setting goals, measuring output, insuring that members perform effectively - even hiring, appraising, disciplining members, and selecting its own team leader.

Source: Carr, C. (1992). Teampower: Lessons from America's top companies on putting teampower to work. Englewood Cliffs, NJ: Prentice Hall.

5. FINDING:

Paul George and Bill Alexander tell us:

During the period from 1981 through 1991, we have assembled the collective wisdom of hundreds of experienced middle school educators into what we might describe as the "ten commandments of interdisciplinary team organization at its very best." Here they are: (1) interpersonal compatibility among team members; (2) balance of subject strengths, personality styles, ethnic backgrounds, sexes, ages, certifications, etc.; (3) planning time together; (4) skillful team leadership; (5) personal characteristics of members that include patience, tolerance, optimism, and enjoyment of teaming concept; (6) pro-attitudes towards students where kids are treated like "customers"; (7) attitudes towards teammates where members fit the expression "diverse but unified"; (8) relative autonomy for their own policies, schedules, performance; (9) principal involvement who are able to "keep a tight grip on loose reins"; and (10) continuing education aimed at team member interests and concerns.

Source: George, P. S., & Alexander, W. M. (1993). The exemplary middle school. Orlando, FL: Harcourt Brace Jovanovich College Publishers.

6. FINDING:
Lou Romano and Nicholas P. Georgiady write:

Even though team teaching is advocated herein, one must keep in mind that some effective teachers rightly belong in a self-contained or departmental classroom situation. Teachers should not be forced into teaming. Individuals should be permitted to teach in the situation of their strength. Many effective classroom teachers are often collaborating and planning with their colleagues, thereby gaining some of the advantages that a teaming organizational pattern provides. It is hoped that within a short time, these teachers will volunteer to try team teaching.

Source: Romano, L. G., & Georgiady, N. P. (1994). Building an effective middle school. Madison, WI: Brown & Benchmark.

7. FINDING:
Deborah Harrington-Mackin summarizes:

The results of extensive research indicate that collective decision-making is a more productive process than individual decision-making. Benefits of team decision making are: (1) new and different ideas emerge; (2) understanding and support increase; (3) individual points of view are aired and reconciled; (4) self-interests surface and are incorporated into decisions; (5) strong commitment to the decision develops; (6) increased learning and personal growth occur; (7) intellectual competence is enhanced; (8) increased awareness and empathy for the decision-making process are created; (9) no winners or losers emerge, so there is greater unity among team members; (10) team members are persuaded rather than coerced; (11) more opinions and viewpoints are expressed; (12) the importance of each member's view is confirmed; (13) backroom politics are discouraged; and (14) more thought and energy are required than for a simple vote.

Source: Harrington-Mackin, D. (1994). The team building tool kit: Tips, tactics, and rules for effective workplace teams. New York: American Management Association.

8. FINDING:
What is wrong with the single-period schedule? In traditional schedules, students generally attend six or seven different classes daily and teachers teach four to six different classes. Teachers are asked to do the impossible—address the intellectual and personal needs of approximately 150 young adults daily. Equally challenging is the task facing students—to adjust to the academic standards, behavior codes, teaching styles, homework assignments, and tests/exams of these multiple teachers daily. If schools are ever to improve, critics say, teachers must work with fewer students and students must work with fewer teachers.

Reference: Rettig, M., & Cannizzaro, J. (1996). Block scheduling: An introduction. Prentice Hall Social Studies Educators' Handbook. Upper Saddle River, NJ, 4.

9. FINDING:

A collaborative approach to school reform emerges when parents, students, administrators, and above all teachers creatively design and implement a block schedule. In 1992, the literature on alternative scheduling configurations was not extensive and we made a few mistakes along the way. To borrow a phrase from "Getting Reform Right" (Fullan and Miles 1992), we learned that "change is a journey, not a blueprint." To help other teachers and administrators wind their way through the complexities of block scheduling, I offer the following 10 guidelines.

- Employ a systems thinking approach.
- Secure the support of your superiors.
- Understand the change process.
- Involve all stakeholders.
- Consult sources outside the school.
- Brainstorm creative alternatives.
- Examine the budgetary implications.
- Plan faculty in-services.
- Include an evaluation component.
- Share and celebrate your successes.

Reference: Hackman, D.G. (1995, November). Ten guidelines for implementing block scheduling. Educational Leadership, 24-27.

10. FINDING:

Educators are besieged by a multiplicity of demands that preclude adequate time for planning, reflecting, collaborating, researching, and assessing. The shortage of time is a problem in all schools and is one of the most complex and challenging problems teachers face every day. These time limitations impact the working lives of teachers and other school employees, causing frustration and inhibiting change. The primary dilemma is that school personnel require "time" to restructure, "while" restructuring time. Unlike other enterprises that shut down to redesign, retool, and re-inventory, schools must continue in pedagogy, curriculum, and organization while being constructed, implemented, and assessed.

Reference: Dalheim, M. (Ed.) (1994). It's about time. TIME Strategies, National Education Association, NEA Special Committee on Time Resources, 9.

Interdisciplinary Teaming and Block Scheduling Teacher's Wrap-Up, à la Bloom

KNOWLEDGE
List the advantages of interdisciplinary teaming and of the block schedule.

COMPREHENSION
Give examples of how a school can implement interdisciplinary teaming and block scheduling.

APPLICATION
Describe how you would accommodate individual learning styles within the block schedule.

ANALYSIS
Compare and contrast interdisciplinary instruction, including the block schedule, with the traditional school schedule.

SYNTHESIS
Create a sample block schedule lesson for one day.

EVALUATION
Support the use of interdisciplinary teaming and block scheduling to a parent who is critical.

CURRICULUM AND INSTRUCTION

Curriculum and Instruction Overview

Important points to consider when planning and/or evaluating curriculum and instruction appropriate for the middle school student include the following:

- The overriding goals of the complete curriculum must be based on the learner's acquisition of in-depth knowledge and understanding of skills, concepts and meaning, must be designed to develop higher order thinking skills and to foster the quest for continued self-motivated learning.

- A motivated learner learns more readily than one who is not motivated but moderate motivation is preferable to intense motivation that can be accompanied by distracting emotional states, as well as damaging burn out.

- Active learning experiences result in more meaningful and lasting learning than content delivered by the teacher.

- Learning under intrinsic motivation is preferable to learning under extrinsic motivation.

- Learning under the control of reward is preferable to learning under control of punishment.

- No school subject or discipline is superior to another for strengthening a student's intellectual prowess. A balanced curriculum takes into account and makes room for each component.

- Learners need consistent practice in setting and achieving both long and short-range realistic goals for themselves.

- Transfer of learning from one task or subject to another occurs more readily when students can discover relationships for themselves.

- The level of difficulty for learning tasks must be carefully evaluated so that they are challenging, yet not threatening to students.

- Students must have skills and concepts presented to them in varied yet specific objective-based situations.

- There is no substitute for repetitive practice in and recall of previously learned knowledge in the over learning of important concepts and skills.

- Textbooks play an important role in the student's cognitive learning experience. It is imperative that each textbook's strength and weaknesses be considered and their integration into the total curriculum is carefully planned.

- Students learn a great deal from one another and especially from those they know well. Cooperative learning, peer tutoring, and shared reading are examples of invaluable venues for student support one for the other.

- Opportunities for formulating and asking questions that foster creative and critical thinking skills are essential components of a sound curriculum plan.

- Constructive and consistent feedback is essential to a learner's progress. It must be planned for, considered an important part of lesson planning, and never left to chance.

- Authentic Assessment and bench-marking at regularly planned intervals is a must for lesson planning and differentiated instruction to meet individual student needs.

Terms Important to Curriculum and Instruction

ACTIVE LEARNING:
Learning activities and experiences that have these characteristics:

(1) Students are involved in more than listening;

(2) Less emphasis is placed on transmitting information and more on developing students' skills;

(3) Students are involved in higher-order creative and critical thinking skills;

(4) Students are engaged in hands-on and learning-by-doing tasks or activities;

(5) Greater emphasis is placed on students' exploration of their own attitudes, values, and interests.

AUTHENTIC LEARNING:
Learning experiences that have real-life application and value so that learning is used to solve problems and complete open-ended tasks.

COLLABORATIVE LEARNING:
Learning that allows teams or groups of students at the same location to learn together as opposed to highly individualistic modes of learning.

CONTEXTUAL LEARNING:
Learning that occurs in an environment that makes the learning relevant to the experience and expectations of the learner.

CORE CURRICULUM:
Curriculum that focuses on content and skills considered to be basic for all students, especially in the disciplines of reading/language arts, social studies, science, and mathematics.

CURRICULUM:
A set of predetermined work plans developed by or for teachers to use in classrooms by which the content, scope, and sequence of that content, and the skills taught through that content are defined and configured.

CURRICULUM ALIGNMENT:
Alignment refers to the "match" or fit between the curriculum and the tests to be used to assess learners and measure what these learners know and can do.

CURRICULUM MAP:
A diagram that lays out the sequence of topics and concepts that will be studied in each subject through the grades.

EXPLORATORY AND ELECTIVE CURRICULUM:
Curriculum that provides for essential, but less structured learning experiences (exploratory courses) and student-selected enrichment, participatory experiences (elective courses/activities).

FORMAL CURRICULUM:
Predetermined and structures curriculum of the school that appears in curriculum guides, state regulations, or officially sanctioned scope and sequence charts.

HIDDEN CURRICULUM:
Curriculum that is taught without formal recognition but includes lessons that are powerful conventions and norms at work in the schools although not formally recognized as such.

INFORMAL CURRICULUM:
Curriculum that represents the unrecognized and unofficial aspects of designing or delivering the curriculum such as issues of tracking, passing on of values, and personality variables of the teachers.

INSTRUCTION:
Systematized teaching that uses a variety of delivery systems and active learning strategies to teach the predetermined curriculum.

10 Important Questions to Find Answers for Related to Curriculum and Instruction

1. What is the academic purpose of schooling in the middle grades? How does this differ from the academic purpose of schooling in the elementary and high school grades?

2. How are high expectations for all students defined?

3. How are desired academic outcomes established and what factors are considered when determining academic outcomes for all students?

4. What steps can be taken to assure that realistic outcomes are established so that all students can achieve these outcomes?

5. What types of instructional strategies are essential for ensuring academic success for all students? How can these be incorporated in daily lesson planning?

6. What are some effective active learning models for differentiating instruction?

7. How can labeling, tracking, and/or sorting of students be prevented?

8. What are some things teachers can do to enable students to learn more aggressively, extensively, deeply, and intrinsically?

9. How does one establish benchmarks for determining the degree of schooling success taking place?

10. What types of curricular reform are essential for ensuring academic excellence?

10 PLUS 5

Frequently Identified Goals of Public Education as Determined by Gallup Polls of Parents and Taxpayers

1. Students who are able to form and maintain positive relationships with others

2. Students who can function as part of a community

3. Students who are good problem solvers and creative/critical thinkers

4. Students who are literate

5. Students who are able to use technology constructively in the classroom

6. Students who are motivated to learn

7. Students who are competent in a specific skill or curriculum area

8. Students who are lifelong learners

9. Students who are confident enough to take risks

10. Students who are independent and can be self-advocates

11. Students who are accountable for their actions and decisions

12. Students who are able to make wise choices in work, recreation, leisure, and continued learning

13. Students who are contributing members of society

14. Students who are responsible citizens

15. Students who are global stewards

10 Traits Of Young Adolescents To Keep In Mind When Planning Lessons And Activities

As you plan activities, develop lessons, and deliver instruction, keep this information in mind:

1. Young adolescents have unique interests and varied abilities. They need opportunities to express their creativity.

2. Young adolescents identify with their peers and want to belong to the group. They must have opportunities to form positive peer relationships.

3. Young adolescents reflect a willingness to learn new things they consider to be useful; therefore, they require occasions to use skills to solve real-life problems.

4. Young adolescents are curious about their world. They need varied situations for exploration and extension of knowledge.

5. Young adolescents experience rapid and sporadic physical development. They require varied activities and time to be themselves.

6. Young adolescents are self-conscious and susceptible to feelings of low self-esteem. They need opportunities for success and recognition.

7. Young adolescents are at a time in their lives when they need adults but don't want to admit it. They need caring adult role models and advisors who like and respect them.

8. Young adolescents want to make their own decisions. They need consistency and direction.

9. Young adolescents prefer active over passive learning activities. They need hands-on and cooperative learning experiences.

10. Young adolescents are idealistic and possess a strong sense of fairness; therefore, they require situations appropriate for sharing thoughts, feelings, and attitudes.

10 Characteristics Each of Five Varied Learning Styles

1. TEN CHARACTERISTICS OF AUDITORY LEARNERS

1. Auditory learners like to be read to.
2. Auditory learners sit where they can hear.
3. Auditory learners are most likely to read aloud or sub-vocalize when they read.
4. Auditory learners enjoy music.
5. Auditory learners acquire information primarily through sound.
6. Auditory learners are easily distracted by noises.
7. Auditory learners may not coordinate colors or clothes, but can explain what they are wearing and why.
8. Auditory learners enjoy listening activities.
9. Auditory learners enjoy talking.
10. Auditory learners hum or talk to themselves or others when bored.

2. TEN CHARACTERISTICS OF VISUAL LEARNERS

1. Visual learners like to read.
2. Visual learners take copious notes.
3. Visual learners often close their eyes to visualize or remember.
4. Visual learners are usually good spellers.
5. Visual learners like to see what they are reading.
6. Visual learners tend to value planning and organization.
7. Visual learners are meticulous, neat in appearance.
8. Visual learners notice details.
9. Visual learners find something to watch when bored.
10. Visual learners find quiet, passive surroundings ideal.

3. TEN CHARACTERISTICS OF KINESTHETIC LEARNERS

1. Kinesthetic learners enjoy using manipulatives.
2. Kinesthetic learners speak with their hands and with gestures.
3. Kinesthetic learners remember what was done but have difficulty recalling what was said or seen.
4. Kinesthetic learners will try new things.
5. Kinesthetic learners rely on what they can directly experience, do, or perform.
6. Kinesthetic learners are outgoing and expressive by nature.
7. Kinesthetic learners tend to be messy in habits and dress.
8. Kinesthetic learners are uncomfortable in classrooms where they lack hands-on experience.
9. Kinesthetic learners like physical rewards.
10. Kinesthetic learners need to be active and in motion.

4. TEN CHARACTERISTICS OF RIGHT-BRAIN LEARNERS

1. Right-brain learners think intuitively and respond well to open-ended activities.
2. Right-brain learners have a common-sense approach to problems.
3. Right-brain learners remember faces.
4. Right-brain learners make subjective statements.
5. Right-brain learners are spontaneous, impulsive, flexible, and creative.
6. Right-brain learners solve problems through synthesis.
7. Right-brain learners are free with feelings.
8. Right-brain learners prefer essay tests.
9. Right-brain learners lack a strong sense of time and structure.
10. Right-brain learners "see the forest."

5. TEN CHARACTERISTICS OF LEFT-BRAIN LEARNERS

1. Left-brain learners are rational, logical, and verbal.
2. Left-brain learners like facts and knowledge.
3. Left-brain learners remember names.
4. Left-brain learners make objective judgments.
5. Left-brain learners respond to structure, order, and rules.
6. Left-brain learners solve problems through analysis.
7. Left-brain learners control feelings, emotions.
8. Left-brain learners prefer multiple-choice tests.
9. Left-brain learners like schedules and lists and have a well-developed sense of time.
10. Left-brain learners "see the trees."

10 PLUS 2

Characteristics of A Differentiated Curriculum and Alternatives for Instruction

1. Provide students with legitimate choices and decision-making options that are meaningful and manageable within a course of unit.

2. Offer alternative learning activities and tasks that cater to predetermined individual learning styles or preferences.

3. Arrange for students to have many encounters with varied learning materials and resources.

4. Enable students to pace their own learning with input and assistance from the teacher.

5. Select and develop both common and individual objectives or student performance standards based on both assessment and diagnostic data about students.

6. Provide some flexibility in scheduling "time on task" so that students have some choice in the way their time is spent on any given day or assignment.

7. Vary group size and individual study upon instructional purposes to be served.

8. Consider alternative assessment and evaluation measures for students and involve them in the process according to their abilities to participate.

9. Increasingly involve students in curriculum and instruction planning according to their abilities to participate.

10. Incorporate commercial, teacher-made, and student-generated materials as part of the delivery system to teaching content.

11. Base instruction on a combination of elements including interest, ability, achievement, and performance levels.

12. Finally, consider the following criteria when proposing and selecting learning alternatives for students:

. . . Are the alternatives designed for individual students with varying interests, learning styles, and levels of ability?

. . . Are the alternatives likely to help students accomplish the group and individual objectives for which they were designed?

. . . Are the alternatives explained fully and concretely so that students can use them and so that teachers can assess the results?

. . . Are there alternatives available for small group activity, individual activity, collaborative activity, and competitive activity?

. . . Are the alternatives appropriate for teaching the required curricular content and skills for the subject area?

. . . Are the alternatives written in such a way so as to include all essential information for the student including what he/she is to do; where he/she is to find information/resources; and what student products/evidence are expected from the alternative?

10 Ways to Differentiate Instruction and Five Examples of Each

Differentiate . . .

1. . . . assessment data.

    a. interest surveys
    b. learning style inventories
    c. left/right brain indicators
    d. skill competency checklists
    e. pre- and post-test results

2. . . . the content level of the material.

    a. different levels of textbooks
    b. different levels of resource materials
    c. textbook(s) on audiotape
    d. manipulatives
    e. audio/visual presentations

3. . . . the complexity of learning tasks.

    a. Bloom's Cognitive Taxonomy
    b. Williams' Creative Taxonomy
    c. Krathwohl's Affective Taxonomy
    d. Kohlberg's Stages of Moral Development
    e. Maslow's Hierarchy of Needs

4. . . . the kinds of resources.

    a. peer and volunteer resources
    b. library books and reference materials
    c. audio-visuals
    d. computers
    e. DVD and CD-ROM technologies

Differentiate . . .

5. . . . the instructional delivery systems.

    a. games and simulations
    b. learning/interest centers
    c. cooperative learning activities
    d. individual inquiry and study packages
    e. investigation cards

6. . . . the duration of learning activities.

    a. division of task into two or more sessions
    b. allowing students time to infuse personal interests
    c. reteaching as needed
    d. allowing for student choice
    e. providing enrichment

7. . . . the degree of student involvement in planning.

    a. development of organizational skills
    b. development of time management strategies
    c. establishment of goal-setting methods
    d. creation of feeling of ownership
    e. maintaining motivation

8. . . . the expected outcomes.

    a. gearing standards to individual abilities
    b. gearing standards to individual interests
    c. gearing standards to group norms
    d. setting criteria for quality of work
    e. setting criteria for quantity of work

9. . . . the evaluation process.

    a. self-evaluation
    b. portfolio evaluation
    c. product evaluation
    d. performance evaluation
    e. paper/pencil evaluation

10. . . . the types of recognition used in the classroom.

    a. a quiet pat on the shoulder
    b. papers displayed
    c. a rousing cheer and round of applause
    d. a happy-gram
    e. a personal note/stamp on the paper

Suggestions for Flexible In-Class Grouping

1. Use whole group instruction for introducing new content, concepts, and skills to students.

2. Use whole group instruction for showing movies, videotapes, slides, or other audio-visual images.

3. Use whole group instruction for conducting demonstrations or experiments.

4. Form smaller, short-term groups to follow up these whole group instruction tasks and to reinforce learning through practice and application tasks.

5. Provide in-class instruction for low-achieving and/or at-risk students whenever possible to do so in lieu of pullout classes and programs. Reduce in-class instructional tasks for those students who miss class for pullout options.

6. When grouping students of lower ability or achievement levels, make certain to deliver the same high-quality level of instruction as you do for those in higher performing groups to include varied learning materials and methods as well as infusion of higher order thinking skills. Keep in mind that all students can perform at all levels of Bloom's Taxonomy because one varies the sophistication of the content and not the level of the taxonomy.

7. Review and adjust groups as often as possible, moving students as interest, ability, and performance levels change from week-to-week and subject-to-subject.

8. Use cooperative learning groups for approximately one third of instructional time so as to balance it with both individualized learning and competitive learning. Keep in mind that high achieving students love competition whereas low achieving students prefer collaborative learning situations.

9. When grouping students for instruction, include tasks that require both group rewards and individual accountability.

10. Use small groups for peer tutoring and peer evaluation purposes to provide student feedback and support on their work. Keep in mind that kids often learn better from their peers than from their teachers.

11. When organizing small group work, allow students to select the students they want to work with from time to time as long as they can stay "on task." Do not hesitate to form a small group, with the teacher as facilitator, for those students who cannot or will not perform in peer group settings.

Concepts Essential to an Understanding of Standards-Based Education

1. **STANDARD**:
   A model that is used as a basis of judgment.

2. **PROGRAM or CONTENT STANDARDS:**
   The knowledge and skills expected of students at certain stages in their education which describe what students should know and be able to do.

3. **BENCHMARKS:**
   Specific skills/abilities and expectations of student performance by the end of predetermined organizational levels such as fourth, eighth, and twelfth grades.

4. **PERFORMANCE INDICATORS:**
   Student behaviors assessed by teachers to validate the achieved standards.

5. **COURSE STANDARDS:**
   Content and skill levels relative to a specific grade level or discipline area.

6. **UNIT STANDARDS:**
   Subject, topics, or themes contained in a specific course.

7. **LESSON STANDARDS:**
   Specific student behaviors for meeting unit standards.

8. **CONTENT/SKILLS:**
   What students need to know or be able to do that will enable them to achieve a standard for the grade, subject, or level.

9. **SCORING GUIDE:**
   A document used to determine whether the work is exemplary, proficient, progressing toward the standard, or not yet meeting the standard.

10. **RUBRIC:**
    The specific rules or criteria stated within the scoring guide.

10 Elements of Successful Lesson Planning for Middle Level Students

1. Are my objectives relevant and realistic in terms of intent and number?

2. Have I planned a varied delivery system to accommodate different learning modalities?

3. Have I organized my lesson into the quartile system (one-fourth of the class period each for direct instruction, class discussion, cooperative group work, and independent time)?

4. Are my directions clear and to the point?

5. Have I selected questions and activities representative of different levels of the cognitive and creative taxonomies?

6. What method of assessment best suites this lesson?

7. How and what will I need to differentiate (content level, learning tasks, resources, delivery systems) to meet my student's needs?

8. Have I provided alternatives to the textbook (posters, learning centers, audiovisuals, technology, etc.)?

9. Does the pacing fit into the planned time frame?

10. What materials, supplies, manipulatives, and resources do I need?

10 Questions For Teachers To Ask When Planning A Lesson

1. Are my objectives relevant and realistic in terms of intent and number?

2. Have I planned a varied delivery system to accommodate different learning modalities?

3. Have I organized my lesson into the quartile system (one fourth of the class period each for direct instruction, class discussion, cooperative group work, and independent time)?

4. Are my directions clear and to the point?

5. Have I selected questions and activities representative of different levels of the cognitive and creative taxonomies?

6. What method of assessment best suits this lesson?

7. How and what will I need to differentiate (content level, learning tasks, resources, delivery systems) to meet my students' needs?

8. Have I provided alternatives to the textbook (posters, learning centers, audio visuals, technology, etc.)?

9. Does the pacing fit into the planned time frame?

10. What materials, supplies, manipulatives, and resources do I need?

10 PLUS 5

Ways to Give Effective Feedback

1. Determine the technical reason. Why is it important to give this feedback?

2. Focus on what is to come, not what has passed. How could things be different in the future as a result of this feedback?

3. Use client data as the basis for feedback. What specific examples can you cite to document the feedback?

4. Put events in the right context. Is this a major problem or a small issue?

5. Be specific in your comments. Can you give concrete "for instances" of the behavior you want changed as a result of the feedback?

6. Make it timely. Can the person remember the event or circumstance of the feedback?

7. Determine whether the feedback should be given in public or in private. Is the feedback positive and therefore more beneficial if given in public, or is it negative and therefore more suitable to be shared in private?

8. Keep it simple and slow. Is there enough time for the person to digest the nature of the feedback?

9. Focus on behavior, not the individual. Can you limit the feedback to the behavior and not the personality of the individual?

10. Explain the impact. Can you use the feedback to explain the impact the behavior is having on one's peers, client, or team?

11. Speak only for yourself. Have you made certain that the feedback reflects only your feelings, and not a collective viewpoint?

12. Be honest and spontaneous. Is the feedback from the heart and immediate rather than superficial and long-term?

13. Be descriptive, not evaluative. Does the feedback avoid using language that tends to evaluate or judge the other person, putting him or her on the defensive?

14. Use "I" statements, not "you" statements. Can you express the feedback so that it is not accusatory but rather tells the person how the behavior makes you feel?

15. Consider the other person as well as yourself. Does the feedback serve the interests of the other person as much as it serves your interests?

10 Ways to Respond to Incorrect Student Answers

1. If the answer is incomplete, provide a hint or clue.

2. Rephrase the question in case it was not understood.

3. Supply the correct answer and discuss it with the student.

4. Give examples of possible answers in a positive way.

5. Tell the student where the answer may be found.

6. Ask the student to determine the question that he or she actually answered.

7. Ask a classmate to determine the question that the student actually answered.

8. Next time, after questioning, be sure to allow "wait time" for all students to think.

9. State reasons that the answer seemed logical.

10. Ask the student to explain his or her reasoning.

Potential Strengths of the Textbook

1. They are written by professional writers and not teachers.

2. They are kept up-to-date with revisions every three years.

3. They come with supplemental materials (workbooks, transparencies, black line masters, tests, etc.).

4. They come with comprehensive Teachers' Manuals that include classroom discussion questions and other suggestions for activities.

5. They contain alternative suggestions for meeting needs of special students such as gifted students, handicapped students, and ESOL students.

6. They are appropriate for designated grade level since readability formulas are used.

7. They are written for national distribution and therefore are designed to please all different geographical and cultural locations.

8. They include some information on just about every topic a teacher might want to teach in a given content area.

9. They make extensive use of colorful and attractive graphics, illustrations, maps, charts/graphs, and tables to increase student motivation and comprehension.

10. Race, sex, and other biases have been greatly reduced or limited.

11. Content is appropriate for designated grade level.

Potential Weaknesses of the Textbook

10 PLUS 1

1. Textbook programs are rarely field-tested or validated before publication.

2. Revisions are not based on feedback from teachers and revisions are minimal involving less than 10% change.

3. Supplemental materials are drill and practice types of tools with little emphasis on higher order thinking or problem-solving skills.

4. All students are required to read the same book for school year regardless of ability or background.

5. Readability standards have often resulted in shortened sentences and reduced vocabulary that often obscures meaning.

6. Mass-distributed books lack flexibility to meet the unique and specific needs of each state, district, or classroom.

7. Not enough information is presented on any one topic for meaningful instruction.

8. Sometimes the wealth of graphics can overwhelm the text and distract students from content.

9. Definitions of concepts are common, dictionary definitions rather than statements of defining attributes.

10. Many textbook revisions or changes are cosmetic and superficial rather than academic.

11. There is little improvement on standardized test scores as the result of textbook instruction.

10 Ways Teachers Can Integrate Thinking Skills Into the Curriculum

Teachers can integrate thinking skills into the curriculum by:

1. Stressing the importance of thinking daily through role modeling, poster/bulletin board displays, and class discussions on the subject.

2. Encouraging student interaction through such directives as . . .

   a. Asking a student to elaborate on a statement made by another student.

   b. Encouraging students to "agree" or "disagree" with an idea expressed by another student in the class.

   c. Using questions such as "Who will challenge the response just given by Student X or Student Y?"

   d. Encouraging students to paraphrase, summarize, or critique another student's ideas before adding to the discussion.

3. Asking open-ended and extension questions rather than closed and single-response questions.

4. Refraining from offering personal opinions, value judgments, or comments on the topic.

5. Giving a grade, reward, or extra credit mark for student participation and/or quality of student responses.

6. Developing wait time with students through such strategies as . . .

   a. Counting to twenty before calling on a student.

   b. Giving students a short writing assignment to answer a series of questions before calling on them.

   c. Distracting yourself by writing on the blackboard or on an overhead transparency.

   d. Waiting until at least half the class members have their hands up to respond before calling on anyone.

7. Keeping a tally of student responses to encourage widespread participation.

8. Organizing students into cooperative learning "think tanks" when doing complex-level thinking activities.

9. Using Bloom's Taxonomy when structuring discussion questions, worksheets, tests, or assignments so that students are working at all levels of the taxonomy.

10. Complimenting all students at the end of a group discussion for the quality of their thinking and their contributions.

IN SUMMARY: Thinking skills beneficial to students in career and life can be developed during the teaching of all disciplines through encouragement and rewards, effectively structured questions, the employment of higher-level thinking taxonomies, and the use of simple teaching strategies.

ACTIVE LEARNING STRATEGY:
Taxonomies That Teach

DESCRIPTION: What is it?

Taxonomies are models for smuggling thinking skills into the curriculum. The purpose of these taxonomies is to provide both teachers and students with a set of guidelines for developing learning activities that are flexible, creative, and developmental. Taxonomy is basically a hierarchy of levels of creative or critical thinking skills that correspond to a predetermined set of student behaviors or action verbs. Two effective taxonomies are Bloom's Taxonomy of Cognitive Development (Critical Thinking Skills) and Williams' Taxonomy of Creative Thought (Creative Thinking Skills). Charts for each of these taxonomies can be found on the following pages for easy use by both students and teachers in designing worksheets, discussion questions, classroom quizzes/tests, interdisciplinary units, homework tasks, and independent study guides.

DIRECTIONS: How do I get started?

1. Choose a topic of special interest to you or that needs to be taught in the classroom. Use Bloom's Taxonomy or Williams' Taxonomy to create an attractive, colorful, and interesting worksheet that includes one key activity for each level of Bloom's Taxonomy. Add graphics, borders, or bold print fonts to make your worksheet look special.

2. Prepare a set of questions for a discussion or for a quiz/test from a section or chapter of a textbook in one of the core subject areas. Design a question for each level of either Bloom's Taxonomy or Williams' Taxonomy. Notice how differently these taxonomies treat a given topic.

3. Develop an interdisciplinary unit that incorporates both Bloom's Taxonomy and Williams' Taxonomy in its organization. Choose a theme and try to include activities that relate to math, science, social studies, English, art, music, drama, physical education, and/or technology.

4. Create a series of ideal homework assignments in a subject area under study that focuses on either Bloom's Taxonomy or Williams' Taxonomy in its completion. Use these taxonomies to think up a wide variety of "points to ponder" or "projects to pursue" in this set of homework tasks.

5. Design an independent study project for extra credit that requires the student to apply all levels of both Bloom's Taxonomy and Williams' Taxonomy. Make the activities varied, research-based, and with a heavy emphasis on application of reading and writing skills.

10 PLUS 2

Active Learning Models and Methods for Differentiating Instruction in Any Subject Area

1.   Model One: Bloom's Taxonomy of Cognitive Development

2.   Model Two: Williams' Taxonomy of Creative Thought

3.   Model Three: Gardner's Multiple Intelligences

4.   Model Four: Cooperative Learning

5.   Model Five: Learning Logs and Dialogue Diaries

6.   Model Six: Games and Simulations

7.   Model Seven: Interactive Lectures

8.   Model Eight: Interdisciplinary Units and Thematic Instruction

9.   Model Nine: Virtual Field Trips

10.   Model Ten: Learning Stations

11.   Model Eleven: Student Contracts

12.   Model Twelve: Questioning and Discussion Sessions

1. MODEL ONE:
BLOOM'S TAXONOMY OF COGNITIVE DEVELOPMENT

Bloom's Taxonomy is a structure for classifying educational objectives so that teachers and students have a common framework for determining the types of desired changes in student behavior as learning takes place. Bloom suggests that there are at least six distinct levels of behavioral outcomes related to thinking and that each level is arranged in a hierarchy from the simplest to the most complex. These levels, defined in simple operational terms, are:

Knowledge Level:

Students learn information through remembering content, either by recall or recognition.

Comprehension Level:

Students understand information through translation, interpretation, or extrapolation (doing something extra with the material or event being comprehended).

Application Level:

Students use information in a context different from the one in which it was taught.

Analysis Level:

Students examine (break down) specific parts of the information in order to accomplish such tasks as reading between the lines, finding subtle implications, or completing a logical dissection of a communication.

Synthesis Level:

Students do something new and different with information in a process that is directly opposite to that of analysis. Synthesis requires integrating ideas in new and different ways.

Evaluation Level:

Students judge information by considering alternatives in making a judgment, establishing criteria for judging those alternatives, and by defending that final judgment among the established alternatives.

It is suggested that teachers use the Bloom Reference Chart with its collection of "verbs" or "behaviors" when designing their lesson plans, their tests, their classroom discussion questions, and their units of study so that students continue "to stretch their minds and tease their imaginations" in the teaching and learning process.

Bloom's Taxonomy (continued)

Bloom Action Verbs For Classroom Action

KNOWLEDGE: *Learn the Information.* Knowledge is defined as the remembering of previously learned material. This may involve the recall of a wide range of material, from specific facts to complete theories, but all that is required is the bringing to mind of the appropriate information. Knowledge represents the lowest level of learning outcomes in the cognitive domain.

RELATED ACTION VERBS

acquire	group	name	record
choose	identify	outline	repeat
count	indicate	pick	reproduce
define	know	point	select
distinguish	label	quote	state
draw	list	read	tabulate
fill in	locate	recall	trace
find	match	recite	underline
follow directions	memorize	recognize	write

COMPREHENSION: *Understand the Information.* Comprehension is defined as the ability to grasp the meaning of material. This may be shown by translating material from one form to another (e.g., words to numbers), by interpreting material (e.g., explaining or summarizing), and by estimating future trends (e.g., predicting consequences or effects). These learning outcomes are one step beyond the simple remembering of material and represent the lowest level of understanding.

RELATED ACTION VERBS

account for	draw	infer	reorganize
associate	estimate	illustrate	represent
change	expand	interpolate	restate
classify	explain	interpret	retell
conclude	express in	measure	reword
compare	other terms	outline	rewrite
contrast	extend	paraphrase	show
convert	extrapolate	predict	simplify
demonstrate	fill in	prepare	suggest
describe	find	put in order	summarize
determine	generalize	read	trace (on a map
define	give in own words	rearrange	or chart)
differentiate	give examples	recognize	transform
distinguish	group	reorder	translate

Bloom's Taxonomy (continued)

APPLICATION: *Use the Information.* Application refers to the ability to use learned material in new and concrete situations. This may include the application of such things as rules, methods, concepts, principles, laws, and theories. Learning outcomes in this area require a higher level of understanding than those under comprehension.

RELATED ACTION VERBS

apply	distinguish	keep records	prove (in math)
calculate	between	locate	put into action
choose	employ	(information)	put to use
classify	estimate	make	put together
collect information	examine	manipulate	record
complete	expand	model	relate
compute	experiment	modify	restructure
construct	express in a	operate	select
construct using	discussion	organize	show
convert (in math)	find (implies	participate	solve
demonstrate	investigation)	perform	track (in history,
derive	generalize	plan	development,
determine	graph	practice	process)
develop	illustrate	predict	transfer
differentiate	interpret	prepare	use
discover	interview	present	utilize
discuss	investigate	produce	

ANALYSIS: *Break the information down into its component parts.* Analysis refers to the ability to break down material into its component parts so that its organizational structure may be understood. This may mean the recognition of relationships between parts or the recognition of the organizational principles involved. Learning outcomes here represent a higher intellectual level than comprehension and application because they require an understanding of both the content and the structural form of the material.

RELATED ACTION VERBS

analyze	diagram	formulate	search
break down	differentiate	group	select
categorize	discover	identify	separate
classify	discriminate	illustrate	simplify
compare	distinguish	infer	sort
contrast	divide	inspect	subdivide
criticize	draw conclusions	order	survey
debate	draw inferences	outline	take apart
deduce	examine	point out	transform
detect	form	recognize	uncover
determine	generalizations	relate	

Bloom's Taxonomy (continued)

SYNTHESIS: *Put information together in new and different ways.* Synthesis refers to the ability to put together parts to form a new whole. This may involve the production of a unique communication (theme or speech), a plan of operations (research proposal), or a set of abstract relations (scheme for classifying information). Learning outcomes in this area stress creative behavior, with the major emphasis being on the formulation of new patterns or structures.

RELATED ACTION VERBS

arrange	devise	originate	rearrange
blend	develop	organize	reconstruct
build	document	perform	relate
categorize	explain	(in public)	reorganize
combine	form	plan	revise
compile	formulate	predict	rewrite
compose	generalize	prepare	specify
constitute	generate	prescribe	suppose
construct	imagine	present	summarize
create	integrate	(an original	synthesize
deduce	invent	report)	tell
derive	make up	produce	transmit
design	modify	propose	write

EVALUATION: *Judge the information.* Evaluation is concerned with the ability to judge the value of material (a statement, novel, poem, or research report) for a given purpose. The judgments are to be based on definite criteria. These may be internal criteria (organization) or external criteria (relevance to the purpose), and the student may determine the criteria given them. Learning outcomes in this area are highest in the cognitive hierarchy because they contain elements of all of the other categories, as well as conscious value judgments based on clearly defined criteria.

RELATED ACTION VERBS

appraise	critique	judge	standardize
argue	decide	justify	summarize
assess	defend	interpret	support
award	describe	measure	test
choose	determine	rank	validate
compare	discriminate	rate	verify
conclude	distinguish	recommend	
consider	evaluate	relate	
contrast	grade	select	

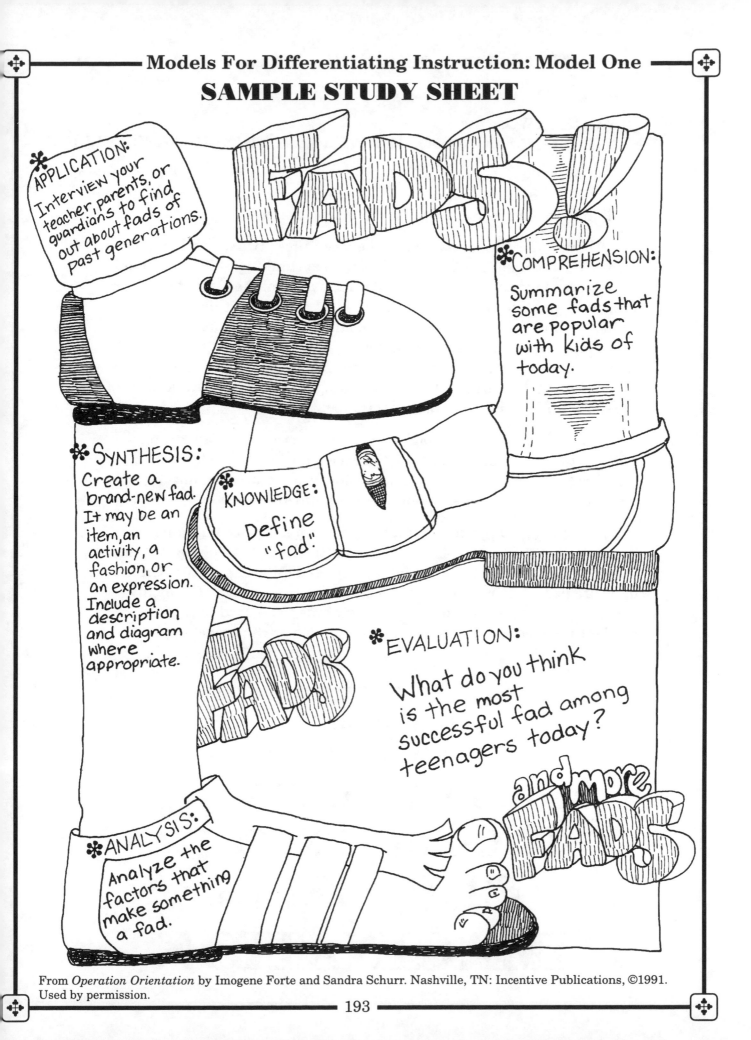

APPLICATION: Interview your teacher, parents, or guardians to find out about fads of past generations.

COMPREHENSION: Summarize some fads that are popular with kids of today.

SYNTHESIS: Create a brand-new fad. It may be an item, an activity, a fashion, or an expression. Include a description and diagram where appropriate.

KNOWLEDGE: Define "fad".

EVALUATION: What do you think is the most successful fad among teenagers today?

ANALYSIS: Analyze the factors that make something a fad.

FADS!

Fads

and more FADS

From *Operation Orientation* by Imogene Forte and Sandra Schurr. Nashville, TN: Incentive Publications, ©1991. Used by permission.

2. MODEL TWO:
WILLIAMS' TAXONOMY OF DIVERGENT THINKING AND FEELING

Williams' Taxonomy is an important model to use when teaching thinking skills. While Bloom's Taxonomy is used for teaching *critical* thinking skills, Williams' Taxonomy is used for teaching *creative* thinking skills.

Although there is a relationship between these two models, and even some overlap, it should be noted that critical thinking tends to be more reactive and vertical in nature while creative thinking tends to be more proactive and lateral in nature. Another way of saying this is that critical thinking tends to involve tasks that are logical, rational, sequential, analytical, and convergent. Creative thinking, on the other hand, tends to involve tasks that are spatial, flexible, spontaneous, analogical, and divergent. Critical thinking is "left brain" thinking while creative thinking is "right brain" thinking.

Williams' Taxonomy has eight levels, also arranged in a hierarchy, with certain types of student behavior associated with each level. The first four levels of the Williams' model are cognitive in nature, while the last four levels are affective in nature.

It is strongly suggested that a teacher keep a copy of Williams' Taxonomy in the lesson plan book so that the levels and behaviors can be an integral part of most lesson plans and student assignments. On the opposite page is a brief overview of the levels in Williams' Taxonomy. Each level is accompanied by a few cue words to be used to trigger student responses to a given creative stimulus or challenge.

FLUENCY

FLEXIBILITY

ORIGINALITY

ELABORATION

RISK TAKING

COMPLEXITY

CURIOSITY

IMAGINATION

Williams' Taxonomy of Creative Thought

FLUENCY

Enables the learner to generate a great many ideas, related answers, or choices in a given situation.
Sample Cue Words: Generating oodles, lots, many ideas.

FLEXIBILITY

Lets the learner change everyday objects to generate a variety of categories by taking detours and varying sizes, shapes, quantities, time limits, requirements, objectives, or dimensions in a given situation.
Sample Cue Words: Generating varied, different, alternative ideas.

ORIGINALITY

Causes the learner to seek new ideas by suggesting unusual twists to change content or by coming up with clever responses to a given situation.
Sample Cue Words: Generating unusual, unique, new ideas.

ELABORATION

Helps the learner stretch by expanding, enlarging, enriching, or embellishing possibilities that build on previous thoughts or ideas.
Sample Cue Words: Generating enriched, embellished, expanded ideas.

RISK TAKING

Enables the learner to deal with the unknown by taking chances, experimenting with new ideas, or trying new challenges.
Sample Cue Words: Experimenting with and exploring ideas.

COMPLEXITY

Permits the learner to create structure in an unstructured setting or to build a logical order in a given situation.
Sample Cue Words: Improving and explaining ideas.

CURIOSITY

Encourages the learner to follow a hunch, question alternatives, ponder outcomes, and wonder about options in a given situation.
Sample Cue Words: Pondering and questioning ideas.

IMAGINATION

Allows the learner to visualize possibilities, build images in his or her mind, picture new objects, or reach beyond the limits of the practical.
Sample Cue Words: Visualizing and fantasizing ideas.

Adapted from *Integrating Instruction in Language Arts: Strategies, Activities, Projects, Tools, and Techniques* by Imogene Forte and Sandra Schurr ©1996. Used by permission.

The Tropical Rain Forest
Via Williams' Taxonomy

FLUENCY:

List as many creatures as you can think of that inhabit the rain forest.

_____

FLEXIBILITY:

Classify the creatures on your list according to their specific rain forest habitat.

_____

ORIGINALITY:

Create a new rain forest creature and give it a scientific name.

_____

ELABORATION:

Describe ten important things or facts about your newly discovered creature.

_____

RISK TAKING:

State some fears that you would have about visiting the rain forest and encountering some of those wildlife creatures.

_____

COMPLEXITY:

Think of some explanations for why human beings continue to destroy or exploit the rain forest and its creatures even when they know of the dangers this will ultimately bring upon them.

_____

CURIOSITY:

There are many tribes native to the rain forest. If you could interview a tribe member about the wildlife creatures in their environment, what would you want to know?

_____

IMAGINATION:

Picture yourself living in the middle of a rain forest. Draw a picture of one of the unusual creatures you might cultivate as a pet.

_____

3. MODEL THREE:
GARDNER'S MULTIPLE INTELLIGENCES

Dr. Howard Gardner's Theory of Multiple Intelligences is an interesting way to teach a concept or skill in any subject area. Dr. Gardner has identified eight multiple intelligences. He defines these intelligences as eight different ways of knowing, perceiving, and understanding the world around us. Gardner also makes it clear that one or two intelligences are often stronger and more developed in a person, although everyone has the capacity for nurturing all eight. It is important that teachers design lesson plans with these multiple intelligences in mind and that students practice using all of these intelligences in their work.

INTELLIGENCE	DESCRIPTION	STRATEGIES	CAREERS
VERBAL/ LINGUISTIC	Involves ease in producing language, and sensitivity to the nuances, order, and rhythm of words	Journal writing, making speeches, storytelling, reading	Trial lawyers, poets, teachers, statesmen
LOGICAL/ MATHEMATICAL	Related to the ability to reasons deductively or inductively, and to recognize and manipulate abstract relationships	Developing outlines, creating codes, calculating, problem solving	Engineers, scientists, military strategists, computer programmers
VISUAL/ SPATIAL	Includes the ability to create visual-spatial representations of the world and to transfer them mentally or concretely	Drawing, using guided imagery, making mind maps, making charts	Architects, astronomers, artists, map makers

Gardner's Multiple Intelligences (continued)

INTELLIGENCE	DESCRIPTION	STRATEGIES	CAREERS
BODY/ KINESTHETIC	Involves using one's physical body to solve problems, make things, and convey ideas and emotions	Role playing, dancing, playing games, using manipulatives	Athletes, computer keyboarders, actresses, mechanics
MUSICAL/ RHYTHMIC	Encompasses sensitivity to the pitch, timbre, and rhythm of sounds as well as responsiveness to the emotional implication of these elements of music	Singing, performing, writing compositions, playing instruments, performing choral readings	Musicians, bandleaders, composers, singers
INTERPERSONAL	Refers to the ability to work effectively with other people and to understand them and recognize their goals, motivations, and intentions	Working with mentors and tutors, participating in interactive projects, using cooperative learning	Social workers, coaches, religious leaders, sales managers
INTRAPERSONAL	Entails the ability to understand one's own emotions, goals, and intentions	Using learning centers, participating in self-reflection tasks, using higher-order reasoning, taking personal inventories	Counselors, authors, philosophers, entrepreneurs
NATURALISTIC	Emphasizes the capacity to recognize flora and fauna, to make distinctions in the natural world, and to use the ability productively in activities such as farming and biological sciences	Observing, digging, planting, displaying, sorting, uncovering, and relating	Conservationists, forest rangers, farmers, biologists

A Sample Interdisciplinary Unit Using the Multiple Intelligences as its Organizing Structure

Note: Teachers can use the multiple intelligences for several purposes in the classroom. They can be used as a structure for identifying learning styles; they can be used as a structure for creating interdisciplinary or thematic units; and they can be used as a structure for setting up permanent learning stations.

"HISTORICAL HEROES"

VERBAL/LINGUISTIC TASK:

Choose a historical figure from the past that you consider a hero, and write a description of his or her major accomplishments, including the one that you would be most proud of if you were that individual.

LOGICAL/MATHEMATICAL TASK:

Create a timeline of the important events that made up the life of your historical hero.

VISUAL/SPATIAL TASK:

Draw a picture of something that you think this hero might accomplish today if he or she were alive at this time.

BODILY/KINESTHETIC TASK:

Act out or role-play a significant event from your historical figure's childhood. Get some friends to help you if needed.

MUSICAL/RHYTHMIC TASK:

Suggest three different types of music, composers, or instruments that you think best typify the personality of this historical hero, and give reasons for your choices.

INTERPERSONAL TASK:

Determine what leadership qualities this historical figure demonstrated that enabled him or her to get along with people. Give specific examples to support your viewpoint.

INTRAPERSONAL TASK:

Describe how your historical hero might have completed this starter statement:
> *"If I have one regret about my life, it is that . . ."*

NATURALIST TASK:

If this historical figure could live in one geographical part of the world today, where do you think he or she would decide to move, and why?

4. MODEL FOUR: COOPERATIVE LEARNING

Cooperative learning refers to small work groups for students. Five elements identified by experts Johnson and Johnson must be present in order for authentic learning to occur; these elements are:

(1) positive interdependence, which demands that students collaborate through group goals, shared resources, joint rewards, and interactive role assignments;

(2) face-to-face interaction, which encourages togetherness through mutual body language, eye contact, and collaborative problem solving;

(3) individual accountability, which advocates group goal achievement through individual efforts and tasks;

(4) interpersonal skills, which emphasize consistent application of basic social and communication skills among group members; and

(5) group processing, which provides the individual members with meaningful feedback and effective input on how they functioned as a group while completing the assigned task.

RANDOM WAYS TO GROUP STUDENTS

1. Drawing names out of a hat.

2. Using a deck of cards with all fours in a group or all kinds in a group.

3. Using academic procedures with all cities of same state, all math problems with same solution, all characters within same story, or all synonyms with same meaning in a group.

RULES TO GUIDE STUDENT BEHAVIOR IN GROUP

1. You are responsible for your own behavior.

2. You are accountable for contributing to the assigned task.

3. You are expected to help any group member who wants it, needs it, or asks for it.

4. You are able to ask the teacher for help only when everyone in the group has the same need.

5. You may not criticize another person in any way.

POSSIBLE SOCIAL SKILLS TO STRESS IN GROUP

1. Using quiet voices
2. Taking turns
3. Accepting and offering constructive criticism
4. Clarifying ideas
5. Expressing feelings
6. Using time wisely
7. Listening closely to others
8. Asking for help
9. Expressing honest appreciation/feedback
10. Staying on task

POSSIBLE ROLES FOR GROUP MEMBERS

1. Recorder
2. Checker
3. Artist
4. Reader
5. Timekeeper
6. Coordinator/Manager
7. Gopher
8. Encourager/Cheerleader

ALTERNATIVE WAYS TO GRADE GROUP WORK

1. Average members' individual scores; each member receives group average as grade.

2. Total members' individual scores so all members receive total score.

3. Issue group score on single product.

4. Randomly grade one member's paper/product; all group members receive that score.

5. Assign individual scores for each group member based on individual performance/ contribution.

STUDENT MEASURES OF SUCCESS

1. Setting achievable goals
2. Organizing to work together
3. Defining group roles
4. Accepting individual responsibility
5. Listening with respect
6. Taking turns to speak
7. Maintaining group order
8. Completing group task
9. Evaluating group progress
10. Applying social skills

Cooperative Learning Jigsaw Activity

DIRECTIONS

During the Jigsaw activity you will work in a group of six in order to learn something new about e-mail, and then teach this information to members of your home group. Follow these directions.

1. Assign a number from one through six to each member of your home group. Each student will list the members of his or her home group on his or her recording sheet.

2. With the help of your teacher, give each member of your group his or her corresponding paragraph describing some important aspect of e-mail. Do not let anyone see any paragraph except his or her own paragraph.

3. When the teacher gives you the signal, locate the other people in small home groups in your classroom who have a number the same as yours. Meet with them, and together learn the information discussed in your paragraph so that each of you becomes an "expert" on its content. You may take notes on the Recording Sheet. The group should then decide on a strategy for teaching what you have learned to the other members of your home group.

4. Return to your home team and teach the information in your paragraph to all of the other team members. Learn the information presented by them in their assigned paragraphs as well.

From *A to Z Media and Technology*. Nashville, TN: Incentive Publications, ©1997.

E is for E-mail Recording Sheet

Date: _____

HOME GROUP MEMBERS

STUDENT ONE _____

STUDENT TWO _____

STUDENT THREE _____

STUDENT FOUR _____

STUDENT FIVE _____

STUDENT SIX _____

DIRECTIONS TO STUDENT

Cut apart the paragraphs about e-mail. Give each section to the appropriate person in your group. Meet with the other students in the class who have the same number as you do and together learn the information discussed in the paragraph. Work with these same students to complete the follow-up task for your paragraph, and share the results with your home group as well.

From *A to Z Media and Technology*. Nashville, TN: Incentive Publications, ©1997.

E is for E-mail (continued)

STUDENT ONE

E-mail is the fastest, most efficient, and least expensive model of electronic communication in the world. The advantages of e-mail are:

1) it is as immediate as a phone call, but the other person does not have to be there to receive the message;

2) you can send e-mail wherever you want and the recipient can respond whenever he or she wants;

3) you can also attach files and communicate with hundreds of people with a single message.

TASK: As if for your local newspaper, design a simple classified advertisement that promotes the use of e-mail for the average home or business.

STUDENT TWO

With e-mail, you can send notes to friends or coworkers and send queries or requests to special addresses to receive information. You can even conduct classroom projects by gathering information, "talking" to an expert on a specific topic, or writing and receiving e-mail from keypads. You can even participate in group discussions on a specific topic because e-mail makes it possible to communicate with many people at the same time.

TASK: Generate a list of "experts" that you and your group might want to access through e-mail in order to learn something about a specific topic appropriate for a project in a special course or subject area.

STUDENT THREE

Anyone can use e-mail if they establish an account with an Internet service provider or a commercial on-line service. A special e-mail account and corresponding address makes it possible for people to send you e-mail messages. However, in order to send and receive e-mail you need to have an e-mail software program.

TASK: Write down a list of criteria that you might use when selecting an e-mail software program for student use in your classroom.

From *A to Z Media and Technology*. Nashville, TN: Incentive Publications, ©1997.

E is for E-mail (continued)

STUDENT FOUR

Every e-mail address has similar elements that are necessary in order for e-mail to be correctly routed to the recipient. The president's e-mail address, for example, is *president@whitehouse.gov*. The part of the address after the "@" is called the *domain name*, which is the name of the host or computer that is connected to the Internet from which the recipient receives his or her e-mail. The domain also gives the zone designation, telling what kind of host it is or where it is. Each part of the domain name is connected by "dots." In the president's e-mail address, the domain name is "whitehouse.gov" with "whitehouse" being the host and "gov" being the zone designation.

TASK: Work with a small group of peers to compose an e-mail message to send to the president of the United States. Send it if you can!

STUDENT FIVE

In the president's e-mail address *(president@whitehouse.gov)*, the combination of letters in front of the "@" is called the *user ID* or *username*. Most e-mail users choose their own username, which is often limited to eleven characters (letters and/or numbers). The username is like a mailbox in a large post office. The domain name would be the post office. If a mistake is made in an e-mail address, it will be returned to the sender.

TASK: Compile a list of "mock" e-mail addresses for the members of your class. What usernames and domain names will you use?

STUDENT SIX

Every e-mail message has the same elements, regardless of the computer system from which it was sent. Each message has an area for entertaining the recipient's address, another for "cc" addresses (which are names of other people who will receive this same message), another for the subject of the message, and another for the body of the message.

TASK: Design a series of standardized e-mail forms or formats that could be used for various types of messages to and from students and faculty members in your school.

From *A to Z Media and Technology*. Nashville, TN: Incentive Publications, ©1997.

5. MODEL FIVE: LEARNING LOGS AND DIALOGUE DIARIES

Another meaningful method of smuggling thinking skills into daily classroom events is through the continued and programmed use of learning logs and dialogue diaries maintained by students as an integral part of any study unit. This strategy is excellent for merging several of the thinking models into one integrated program.

The key to making log and diary entries successful with middle grades students is to make certain that the logs or diaries are evaluated and counted as part of the overall grade for the unit of study, receiving equal weight with other program components such as textbook readings and questions, tests, homework assignments, and classroom tasks. Daily log/diary questions, starter sentences, reaction statements, or short writing exercises that are structured according to any of the thinking skills models should be provided as well. Some sample student questions and directives based on the various models follow.

1. Use logs and diaries for self-assessment by writing entries to evaluate one's individual progress in a given subject area.

2. Use logs and diaries to explore personal reactions and responses to lectures, readings, viewings, recordings, and simulations.

3. Use logs and diaries to reflect on one's contributions to a class project, assignment, discussion, or field trip.

4. Use logs and diaries to record questions, observations, and insights in preparation for a student-teacher conference.

5. Use logs and diaries to keep track of one's independent research, reading, and study activities.

6. Use logs and diaries to maintain personal dialogues between oneself and the teacher or peers.

7. Use logs and diaries as source books for writing ideas for reports, research projects, writing assignments, and self-study topics.

8. Use logs and diaries as places for integrating subject matter and commenting on ideas or concepts learned.

9. Use logs and diaries for describing specific incidents and impressions arising from special events, challenges, opportunities, and excursions.

10. Use logs and diaries as sounding boards or trial runs for writing for a variety of purposes and a wider audience.

6. MODEL SIX: GAMES AND SIMULATIONS

Educational games play an important role in the middle-level classroom because kids have an inherent passion for games. When playing games, students can constructively interact with one another, apply their communication and decision-making skills in a non-threatening environment, and participate regardless of their ability level. They are evaluated by the outcome of the game and not by grades or body language of the teacher.

One interesting way to get students to apply thinking skills from any of the models is to assign them the task of constructing a game as the culmination of a unit of study. It is important to provide students with an outline of what should be included in this gaming project; some suggestions for this are given below. Make certain that students know that they must use one of the thinking skill models as the basis for designing all game questions, events, tasks, or challenges. Encourage them to include an outline of the thinking skill model as part of the game's directions.

REQUIREMENTS FOR YOUR GAME PROJECT

DIRECTIONS: You are to construct a game on a topic of your choice that is related to our recent unit on _____. Your game must require its players to use their best creative and critical thinking skills throughout the playing time. Before you actually begin creating your gaming masterpiece, you must decide on a thinking skill model as the foundation for your game design.

Your game should include:

1. An unusual title
2. Number of players
3. Learning outcomes and/or purposes of the game
4. Specific topic, theme, or subject
   from your recent study of _____.
5. Dice, spinner, or other method for specifying turns
6. Playing pieces for players
7. Question, task, statement, or activity cards
8. Chance or special direction cards
9. Answer key or booklet
10. Rules and directions for play
11. Playing board, deck of cards, or equivalent
12. Special container or package for game contents

10 PLUS 1

Guidelines for Developing Simulation Games to Encourage the Use of Thinking Skills

1. Determine the overall purpose of the simulation game for the students.

2. Determine the specific content (concepts) and skill (competency) objectives to be addressed as part of the gaming process.

3. Determine the major players, roles, groups, or organizations whose collective decisions will have an impact on the game's actions.

4. Determine the outcomes (influence, knowledge, etc.) desired most by the major players, roles, groups, or organizations.

5. Determine the resources that the major players, roles, groups, or organizations will have at their disposal throughout the game.

6. Determine the sequence of events and the information outlets that will occur among the major players, roles, groups, or organizations.

7. Determine the key guidelines, rules, and decision opportunities that will have an impact on the major players, roles, groups, or organizations.

8. Determine the external barriers or roadblocks that will limit the actions of the major players, roles, groups, or organizations.

9. Determine the rules and criteria by which winners will be selected from the major players, roles, groups, or organizations, making certain to accommodate the application of skills and content mentioned in Guideline Two above.

10. Determine the format and props for implementation of the game.

11. Determine the type of follow-up debriefing session you will have with the major players, roles, groups, or organizations.

7. MODEL SEVEN: INTERACTIVE LECTURES

Interactive lectures often referred to as informal or mini-lectures, break down the delivery of important information into manageable chunks for the students to remember. These lecture activities require some student participation in the form of questions, comments, or feedback as opposed to formal lectures, which are predetermined talks where student involvement is limited or nonexistent.

Following are seven different formats for the informal lecture:

1. THE FEEDBACK LECTURE:

Students are given a pre-reading assignment and an outline of the lecture notes prior to the lecture. The teacher lectures for ten minutes and then divides the students into small study groups for twenty minutes. Each study group is given a question to answer, a point to ponder, or a problem to solve related to the content of the lecture itself. The teacher then reconvenes the students for another ten-minute lecture segment and addresses the assigned question/point/problem in the lecture.

2. THE GUIDED LECTURE:

Students are given a list of three to five objectives for the lecture. They are then told to put their pencils down and listen to the lecture for twenty minutes without taking notes. At the end of this time segment, students are given five minutes to write down all the information they can recall individually. Students then work with a partner and together they combine their notes to reconstruct the lecture content. The teacher then fills in any gaps through a whole group recall and sharing session.

3. THE RESPONSIVE LECTURE:

Once a week, structure the lecture period so that its content reflects only questions the students have generated on a given topic. To prepare for this lecture method, give each student (or small group of students) a 3 x 5 file card and ask them to write an important question they have on a current topic or unit of study. Ask the class to order the questions in terms of general interest. The teacher then proceeds to answer as many questions as the time allows.

4. THE DEMONSTRATION LECTURE:
In this lecture format, the teacher prepares a twenty-minute lecturette that involves an active demonstration, experiment, or hands-on application related to the topic. Students respond by writing a conclusion, summary, or brief explanation of what happened and what they observed.

5. THE PAUSE PROCEDURE LECTURE:
Deliver a twenty-minute lecturette and have students take notes on the content. After five minute segments, the teacher pauses and gives the student two minutes to share his or her notes with a peer. It is sometimes helpful to give the students an outline that has a series of starter statements on the content which they must complete as the lecture is given.

6. THE THINK/WRITE/DISCUSS LECTURE:
The teacher prepares three questions to ask students throughout the lecture.

- The first question is a motivational question that is given before the lecture begins.

- The second question is given during the middle of the lecture, and requires the student to write a short response to clarify a point or concept presented in the lecture.

- The third question is given at the end of the lecture and is a feedback type question about something learned, something that needs further clarification, or something misunderstood.

7. THE BINGO LECTURE:
Prepare a bingo grid and in each cell put a key concept to be discussed during the lecture. As students hear the concept discussed during the lecture, they cover the appropriate space with a marker. The first person to get the cells completed across, down, or on a diagonal shouts "bingo" and wins that round.

ACTIVE LEARNING STRATEGY: INTERACTIVE LECTURES

TOPIC OF LECTURE: _____

DATE: _____

B	I	N	G	O

10 Guidelines for Making the "Lecturette" A Thinking Time and Learning Tool for Students

1. Limit the goal of the mini-lecture to one of the following: introducing or summarizing a unit of study, presenting or describing a problem, providing information otherwise inaccessible to students, sharing personal experiences of the teacher, clarifying important concepts associated with a unit of study, or reviewing ideas necessary for student retention.

2. Develop a set of specific content and process objectives for the mini-lecture.

3. Prepare and use an outline or set of notes for the mini-lecture.

4. Rehearse the delivery of the mini-lecture.

5. Enhance content of mini-lecture with audio-visuals and multi-sensory stimulation.

6. Lecture for ten minutes and then pause between two and five minutes, allowing time for students to reflect on their notes or discuss their notes with partners.

7. Use vocabulary and examples in the mini-lecture that are familiar to the students and appropriate for their age and ability levels.

8. Provide students with a written outline or study guide of the mini-lecture to serve as advanced organizers of the content to be covered.

9. Make modifications in the mini-lecture for students with special needs.

10. Maintain positive eye contact, body language, and voice pitch during the mini-lecture.

8. MODEL EIGHT: INTERDISCIPLINARY UNITS

Interdisciplinary units contain two or more different disciplines as their focus with a curriculum theme that should, according to James A. Beane, "emerge from the natural overlaps between the personal concerns of early adolescents and the larger issues that face our world." Thematic units are effective for these reasons:

(1) The real world is integrated.

(2) Students do best when learning is connected.

(3) Integrated programs are useful in tracking other areas of concern.

(4) It is difficult to teach subjects and skills in isolation during an instructional day even with the flexible block schedule in place.

10 Steps for Beginning to Integrate the Disciplines

1. **Step One:** Each teacher on a team should develop a workable definition of interdisciplinary instruction as he or she understands it. All team members compare and discuss individual interpretations of interdisciplinary instruction. Finally, the team synthesizes the best ideas from all team members and comes up with a workable definition for the group.

2. **Step Two:** Each team member brainstorms a wide variety of possible topics for interdisciplinary instruction that would most easily incorporate their core subject areas. Team members meet to share their respective lists, to eliminate duplicates or overlaps, and to compile a master list that appeals to all team members.

3. **Step Three:** Each team schedules a formal meeting to select any one of the designated themes for future implementation. Team members brainstorm related topics for each of the core subject areas. Next, teams locate resource materials on the topic and look for activities that lend themselves to science, social studies, math, or language arts.

Integrating The Disciplines

4. **Step Four:** The fourth step involves a series of team meetings that requires team members to complete an outline for teaching the interdisciplinary topic agreed upon in Step Three. Each teacher determines the key skills or concepts that are important parts of the interdisciplinary process.

5. **Step Five:** Team members exchange classes for at least one period, teaching one another's subject areas according to prepared lesson plans. For example, the science and math team members teach each other's classes for a session while the social studies and language arts team members do the same.

6. **Step Six:** Next, team members set aside the textbook in their subject area for a minimum of three consecutive days. Emphasis is placed on the use of other resources and delivery systems for teaching required basic skills and concepts. This requires team members either to practice using other types of reproducible materials for instruction with students or to develop individual activities of their own using varied tools and techniques to differentiate instruction.

7. **Step Seven:** Team members spend at least three days practicing the art of "creative questioning" within their disciplines. This approach encourages students to tease their minds and stretch their imaginations. Using the same types of higher-order questions in different subject areas can help the young adolescent to see the connectedness of both content and thinking skills.

8. **Step Eight:** Team members decide upon an individual skill such as drawing conclusions or the concept of measurement and develop a short lesson in science, math, social studies, and language arts to present to their students for one week. This activity will provide each team with a chance to approach a skill or concept from several interdisciplinary points of view.

9. **Step Nine:** The team composes a letter to parents or guardians outlining plans for the interdisciplinary unit and the involvement of the family. The content of the letter includes specific information about theme, purpose, length, objectives, varied activities, and projected outcomes. In addition, the letter invites parents to become involved in a variety of ways. The team members should also prepare their homeroom or group of assigned students for this interdisciplinary adventure, making certain that all stakeholders understand its purposes.

10. **Step Ten:** Finally, the interdisciplinary unit is field tested by team members with their students. The team designs a simple student evaluation form for assessing the unit's effectiveness. The evaluation form includes questions about all aspects of the interdisciplinary unit including appropriateness of the subject matter, activities, time span, team teaching, and learning resources.

Building An Interdisciplinary Planning Matrix

DIRECTIONS: With your team, sit down and list all the major concepts, units, skills, or topics each of you will be covering during the school year. Try to record by subject area and by month. Look for overlaps or changes which could be easily worked into interdisciplinary units.

Models For Differentiating Instruction: Model Eight

	SEPT	OCT	NOV	DEC	JAN	FEB	MAR	APR	MAY
SCIENCE									
MATH									
SOCIAL STUDIES									
LANGUAGE ARTS									
EXPLOR.									
P. E.									

10 Essential Elements of an Interdisciplinary Unit

1. THEME: Make it broad enough to:
  a. Include objectives from several subject areas
  b. Motivate and interest students and teachers
  c. Include several creative activities
  d. Accommodate small and large group instructional strategies
  e. Last from 3 to 5 days

2. TITLE: Make it creative and fun!

3. OBJECTIVES: List at least two objectives for each subject area: Language Arts, Social Studies, Math, Science, Industrial Arts, Art, Music, and Physical Education.

4. BACKGROUND INFORMATION ON TOPIC FOR STUDENT:
Write a one-page overview of the subject areas that provide students with the appropriate background or springboard information to effectively launch the unit.

5. GLOSSARY: Prepare a glossary of key terms, vocabulary, or concepts that are important to the mastery of the material.

6. STUDENT RECORD SHEETS: Maintain record sheets to keep track of student progress, or have students keep track of their own progress.

7. ACTIVITIES IN EACH DISCIPLINE: Use the same format in preparing your activities, including:
  a. Title
  b. Objective
  c. Materials Needed
  d. Procedure
  e. Evaluation

8. HOMEWORK AND/OR ENRICHMENT IDEAS:
Create a list of tasks that could be assigned as homework or enrichment for students.

9. POST-TEST/PROJECT PRESENTATION: Include a post-test and/or directions for a final project to serve as the evaluation for the unit in addition to those used as part of the activities.

10. BIBLIOGRAPHY: List resources/references for follow-up or for use during the unit.

9. MODEL NINE: VIRTUAL FIELD TRIPS

A virtual field trip is a simulated field trip using the latest Internet technology. Instead of an actual visit to a museum that consists of bricks, mortar, and real people, one visits the museum using hard drives, software, and digital information via computers and websites. There are several advantages to taking a virtual field trip to a place in cyberspace: these excursions are available at little or no cost, are conveniently located close to home, take only a few minutes to locate and tour, allow for revisits at a later date, and are self-directed rather than conducted by a tour guide.

SOME WEBSITES TO VISIT

a. Metropolitan Museum of Art: http://www.metmuseum.org

b. Museum of Science and Industry: http://www.mosi.org

c. Rock and Roll Hall of Fame: http://www.rockhall.com

d. NASA Kennedy Space Center: http://www.ksc.nasa.gov

e. National Museum of Natural History: http://www.mnh.si.edu

f. Sea World: http://www.seaworld.com

g. The Smithsonian Institute: http://www.smithsonianinstitute.com

h. National Baseball Hall of Fame: http://www.baseballhalloffame.org

i. The Electronic Zoo: http://www.netvet.wustl.edu/e-zoo.htm

j. George Washington's Mount Vernon: http://www.mountvernon.org

Note: Internet sites have been carefully chosen; however, the Internet changes daily.
Teachers and parents should review all sites before directing students to the sites.

10. MODEL TEN: LEARNING STATIONS

A learning station is a space in the classroom where students can go to participate in a wide variety of activities to learn or practice a new skill and/or to extend their knowledge on a given topic or concept.

Learning stations offer students choices and provide them with experiences for interaction and cooperation. Learning stations empower students to assume responsibility for their own learning, and they motivate students because the stations are rich in diverse materials and resources.

Learning stations come in many different sizes and shapes. They can be located on walls, easels, bulletin boards, tables, clotheslines, display boards, or counter tops, just to name a few possibilities. The entire classroom can be set up for learning stations, which would contain clusters of tables or desks. On the other hand, a single area of the classroom could house a single learning station or two for enrichment or reinforcement tasks.

Learning station tasks can be organized around Bloom's Taxonomy, Williams' Taxonomy, Multiple Intelligences, or any combination of these models to ensure higher order thinking skill tasks and to integrate a variety of learning styles.

CHECKLIST FOR CREATING AND USING LEARNING STATIONS

1. **TYPE OF LEARNING STATION**

. . . What major purpose or umbrella theme will the station serve?

. . . Will the station be an enrichment station, a skill station, or an interest station?

2. **OBJECTIVES OF LEARNING STATION**

. . . What student performance standards can best be met at this station?

. . . How do the performance standards relate to the abilities and interests of the students?

3. **DESIGN OF LEARNING STATION SPACE**

. . . How much and what type of space can be allocated to this station?

. . . What kinds of furniture and equipment are needed for this station?

. . . How will the location of the station affect other classroom activities?

4. **MATERIAL REQUIREMENTS FOR LEARNING STATION**

. . . What instructional materials are needed for the station?

. . . How will the materials be housed, stored, displayed at the station?

5. **ALTERNATIVE ACTIVITIES FOR LEARNING STATION**

. . . Are there varied activities and strategies available at the station?

. . . Are the activities and strategies compatible with the purpose or objectives of the station?

. . . Are the activities and strategies able to accommodate varying abilities, learning styles, and interests of students?

. . . Are the activities and strategies explained in such a way that the student knows what to do and how to do it?

. . . Do the activities and strategies require higher order thinking skills and active rather than passive tasks in their implementation?

6. GUIDELINES FOR STUDENT USE AT LEARNING STATION

. . . How many students can use the station at the same time, and how are they scheduled?

. . . What can students do at the station?

. . . What assessment, evaluation, or accountability measures are in place for assessing student work at station?

. . . What do students do with incomplete and with finished work?

7. MANAGEMENT OF LEARNING STATION PROCESS

. . . Is there a management system in place for the station?

. . . Is the management system appropriate for age and ability levels of students?

. . . Does the management system maximize student self-management and record-keeping?

. . . What arrangements are necessary for consultation between teacher and student on student progress and evaluation?

8. ORIENTATION OF STUDENT TO STATION

. . . Do students understand the purposes, procedures, and management of the station?

. . . Do students understand the relation of the station to other instructional activities in the classroom?

. . . Do students understand what behavior and academic standards are expected of them at the station?

Humor Learning Station à la Multiple Intelligences

VERBAL/LINGUISTIC INTELLIGENCE:

1. Write a descriptive paragraph based on one of these starter statements:
   . . . A funny thing that happened to me was . . .
   . . . People are funny who . . .
   . . . I had to laugh at myself when . . .

2. Write a classroom newsletter strictly on the lighter side.

3. Find, practice, and read something humorous to the class.

LOGICAL/MATHEMATICAL INTELLIGENCE:

1. Research to find information about the history and science of humor.

2. Analyze humorous literature or modern/classical art for types of humor.

3. Construct a chart to show your funniest choices when it comes to movies, television shows, classmates/friends, books, songs/recordings, jokes, riddles, and cartoons/comic strips.

4. Design a display that shows examples of Figural Humor, Verbal Humor, Visual Humor, and Auditory Humor.

VISUAL/SPATIAL INTELLIGENCE:

1. Do a humor collage of words, smiles, and faces.

2. Plan a silly hat day, funny T-shirt day, or a clever badge/button day for your class.

3. Use a Polaroid camera to take candid and spontaneous photos of a school event.

BODILY/KINESTHETIC INTELLIGENCE:

1. Learn signing of humor words as used by hearing impaired (words like smile, laugh, giggle).

2. Study the "art and science of clowns" and plan/perform a simple clown act for classmates.

3. Stock a toy box for the classroom full of fun games and props that anyone can use whenever things get tense or they have some free time.

MUSICAL/RHYTHMIC INTELLIGENCE:

1. Listen to humorous records or watch humorous videotapes. Write reviews of each record or tape.

2. Start a people chain with a joke and have others whisper or sing it to one another around the room. Summarize the funny things that happen.

3. Collect lyrics to humorous songs and post them for others to read and enjoy.

INTERPERSONAL INTELLIGENCE:

1. Establish a Humor/Joy/Fun committee for the class and rotate membership and responsibilities.

2. Organize a joke festival or marathon. Have a joke drop-box that students can read from when other work is complete. Have students rate submitted or performed jokes to determine their funniest rating. Does the rating scale have benchmarks for a grin, smile, grimace, loud laugh, or guffaw?

3. Start a humorous quotations collection to which students can add. Keep in file box or on a bulletin board.

INTRAPERSONAL INTELLIGENCE:

1. Maintain a "Laughter Log" that records your "humorous moments" during a given day, week, or month. Keep track of when and why you laugh.

2. Develop a personal plan for you and your family to celebrate Humor Week or National Humor Day April 15th.

3. Complete the inventory on the next page entitled: "DETERMINE YOUR HUMOR QUOTIENT."

11. MODEL ELEVEN: STUDENT CONTRACTS

An independent learning contract is a predetermined agreement between the student and the teacher in which the student commits to completing a series of learning activities within a specified period of time, and most often for some type of letter grade.

Contracts empower the student because they can be completed independently with a minimum of teacher direction and because they emphasize shared decision making between the teacher and student when setting up the terms of the contract itself. In short, a contract describes precisely what a student is to do and offers specific criteria against which the student is to be judged.

When first implementing student contracts on the classroom, *do* start with short-term contracts and *do* thoroughly explain the role and function of contracts to both students and parents. *Do not* expect all students to be able to use contracts effectively and *do not* assume that all instruction can take place through activities in the contracts without some supplementary teaching and monitoring sessions with the teacher.

Sample Contract for Study of Balloons

TOPIC: BALLOONS

OBJECTIVE CARD

1. The student will explain how a hot-air balloon can fly. (**Comprehension**)

2. The student will conduct two simple experiments using rubber balloons. (**Application**)

3. The student will create an original piece of writing related to balloons. (**Synthesis**)

4. The student will infer why Charles Goodyear is considered the father of the toy balloon.

5. The student will construct a balloon-related object and game.

INFORMATION CARD

Did you know that balloons rise because the gases inside them are lighter than the gases (air) outside them? Hot-air balloons are filled with air. The air in the balloon must be heated to make it lighter than the air around it. According to the law of convection, hot air rises.

Convection is a scientific process that happens when a gas is heated. With balloons, the gas is air. As the gas heats up, its molecules move faster and faster. As the molecules move faster, they move farther out. The gas expands (it takes up more space). This expanded gas is less dense, or lighter, than the gas around it. The heated gas rises. Cooler gas—air—moves in to take its place.

A burner, which runs on gas from a bottle, heats the air inside the hot-air balloon. Air heated by the burner begins to inflate the balloon. After the balloon is filled, the passengers jump into the basket.

Turning the burner's flame up or down controls the balloon. Increasing the flame heats the air inside the balloon, and the balloon rises faster. Turning down the flame lets the air cool, and the balloon drifts down.

A balloonist can control only the movement of the balloon up or down. Air currents control the movement of the balloon from one side to another.

Sample Contract for Study of Balloons (continued)

VOCABULARY CARD

Atoms Atoms are tiny building blocks of matter that are too small to be seen even with a microscope.

Burner A burner is an object that runs on gas that comes from a bottle.

Chemical changes Chemical changes occur when a substance is changed into something else because the molecules are altered.

Convection Hot air is not as dense as cool air, so cooler air pushes hot air upward. Heat can move from an energy source in a circular pattern, called convection current.

Elements All atoms are made up of protons, neutrons, and electrons (except the hydrogen atom). But not all atoms have the same numbers of these particles. So far, scientists have discovered 109 atoms with different combinations of protons, neutrons, and electrons and different properties. These 109 substances are called elements.

Helium Helium is a gas lighter than air. It is used to fill party balloons.

Inflate Inflate means to fill with air.

Molecules Atoms often group together with other atoms to form molecules. Some molecules are made up of the same element. Others are made up of combinations of elements. Molecules can contain from two to thousands of atoms.

INVENTORY CARD

• Assorted reference materials on hot-air balloons
• A set of colored photographs of hot-air balloons
• A collection of assorted balloons of all sizes and shapes
• A piece of wool
• A small bottle of vinegar
• A small package of baking soda
• Directions for making an origami balloon
• A cloth measuring tape
• A copy of Shel Silverstein's poem, "Eight Balloons," from *A Light in the Attic*

Sample Contract for Study of Balloons (continued)

STUDENT RECORD CARD BOX

NAME _____

DATE BEGAN LEARNING/STUDY KIT _____

DATE COMPLETED LEARNING/STUDY KIT _____

DIRECTIONS: As you complete each of the five required activities and the homework activity in this Learning/Study Kit, check it off. Keep all your work in a folder and turn it in to your teacher when everything is finished. Record your grade as well.

_____ 1. *Homework Activity*

_____ 2. *Who is Charles Goodyear?*

_____ 3. *Experimenting with Balloons*

_____ 4. *"Eight Balloons" by Shel Silverstein*

_____ 5. *Balloons are Made for Writing*

_____ 6. *Balloon Games*

HOMEWORK CARD

Choose one of these balloon projects to complete as a homework assignment:

1. Use a balloon as the basic form for making a papier-maché animal.

2. Use a series of balloons to make an origami paper balloon.

3. Use several balloons to twist and turn into animal shapes.

4. Make an ornament by dipping a piece of yarn, lace, string, or ribbon into liquid starch and wrapping it around an inflated balloon. When it is dry, pop the balloon.

Sample Contract for Study of Balloons (continued)

REQUIRED ACTIVITY CARD

Activity One: *Who is Charles Goodyear?*

Research to discover ten facts about Charles Goodyear, and why many consider him to be the "father of the toy balloon." Put each fact on a separate file card and write a short paragraph of elaboration about each fact.

REQUIRED ACTIVITY CARD

Activity Two: *Experimenting with Balloons*

1. Rub a balloon using the woolen cloth in this kit. Then place the balloon near your head. Explain what happens and why you think it happens.

2. Pour 1/2 cup of vinegar into a soda bottle and put 1 tablespoon of baking soda into a balloon. Place the end of the balloon over the top of the bottle. What causes the chemical reaction that you see?

3. Inflate a balloon, pinch it closed, and then let it go. What happens and why? Can you learn to control the flight of the balloon?

4. Measure the circumference of an inflated balloon. Put it in the freezer for at least 30 minutes. What happens when you measure it again? Why do you think this is so?

REQUIRED ACTIVITY CARD

Activity Three: *"Eight Balloons" by Shel Silverstein*

Read Shel Silverstein's poem entitled "Eight Balloons." Draw a picture to go with it!

Sample Contract for Study of Balloons (continued)

REQUIRED ACTIVITY CARD

Activity Four: *Balloons are Made for Writing*

Complete one of the following writing tasks:

1. Write an autobiography of a balloon at a special party or celebration.

2. Create a tall tale about a balloon that was as big as a house and still growing.

3. Compose a free verse poem about a balloon.

4. Complete a series of journal entries about your first hot-air balloon ride.

5. Invent a comic strip character and use "balloons" in each frame to tell a story.

REQUIRED ACTIVITY CARD

Activity Five: *Balloon Games*

Think of five different games that could be played with a balloon at an outdoor event.

Sample Contract for Study of Balloons (continued)

HOW MUCH DID YOU LEARN? CARD

1. Who was Charles Goodyear?

_____

_____

_____

_____

2. Write out a good question for each of these balloon-related answers:

Question: _____

_____

Answer: convection

Question: _____

_____

Answer: molecule

Question: _____

_____

Answer: chemical change

Question: _____

_____

Answer: helium

3. Briefly explain the principle behind the hot-air balloon.

4. List three facts or conclusions you learned from completing the science experiments with balloons.

5. Draw a simple diagram of a hot-air balloon and label its parts.

12. MODEL TWELVE: QUESTIONING AND DISCUSSION SESSIONS

Both large and small group discussions should be a common instructional practice in every classroom setting and should focus on the use of higher order questioning skills in their dialogues and interactions. Group discussions are important for these reasons:

a. They provide the teacher with feedback about student learning.

b. They lend themselves to higher order thinking skills.

c. They help students develop interests and values and attitudes.

d. They allow students to become more active participants in their learning.

e. They enable students to hear and offer alternative points of view and to explore complex issues.

On the other hand, there are some disadvantages to discussion sessions that need to be kept in mind:

a. Difficulty in getting student participation as they may be threatening to students because of peer pressure to excel.

b. They are time consuming to conduct properly.

c. They are not always well suited to covering significant amounts of content.

d. They require more forethought and planning on the part of the teacher than lecture.

e. They provide the teacher with less control than other means of instruction.

10 PLUS 4

Tips for More Effective Discussions

1. **ASK FOR FEELINGS AND OPINIONS**
Example: What is your reaction to . . . ?
or
How do you feel about . . .?

2. **PARAPHRASE**
Example: Are you saying that . . . ?
or
What I think I am hearing is . . .

3. **ENCOURAGE PARTICIPATION**
Example: Susan, how would you answer that question . . . ?
or
Before we move on, let's hear from John . . .

4. **ASK FOR SUMMARY**
Example: Will someone please summarize what has been said?
or
Summarize your major objections . . .

5. **ASK FOR CLARIFICATION**
Example: Explain your last comment further . . .
or
Can you expand on that idea . . . ?

6. **ASK FOR EXAMPLES**
Example: Will you give us some examples of what you mean?
or
Expand on what you said . . .

7. **TEST FOR CONSENSUS**
Example: Does everyone accept the idea that . . . ?

or

Before we go on, can we agree that . . . ?

8. **INITIATE ACTION**
Example: How do you think we should . . . ?

or

How would you suggest we proceed on this . . . ?

9. **EXPLORE AN IDEA IN MORE DETAIL**
Example: What are some more things we could consider . . . ?

or

What would you add to what has been said . . . ?

10. **CONDUCT A QUICK SURVEY**
Example: How many agree with this idea . . .

or

How does everyone feel about this . . . ?

11. **SUGGEST A PROCEDURE**
Example: Would it help if we put the items in order of importance . . . ?

or

Let's go around the room to see how others would feel . . .

12. **COMPLIMENT A GOOD POINT**
Example: That's a good point . . .

or

I wish I had thought of that . . .

13. **MEDIATE DIFFERENCES OF OPINION**
Example: I think you aren't really disagreeing with each other, but expressing yourselves differently . . .

or

Let's see how your views are alike. . .

14. **CHANGE THE GROUP PROCESS**
Example: Let's break into smaller groups and . . .

or

Let's stop the discussion for a moment and . . .

10 PLUS 1

Points To Ponder When Setting Up A Classroom Discussion To Promote Thinking Skills

1. Why is a classroom discussion important to the teaching of this topic or subject?

2. What specific content and process objectives do I have for this discussion?

3. How do I want to physically arrange the room and student seating for this discussion?

4. What ground rules should I establish for student participants before starting this discussion?

5. What plans do I have for dealing with students who dominate the discussion or who will not participate in the discussion?

6. What preparations should the students make before the discussion?

7. What roles will I play throughout the discussion?

8. How can I actively involve all students in the discussion?

9. What classroom activities would be appropriate as a follow-up to this discussion?

10. How long should the discussion last and should students be graded for their participation in class discussion? If so, how?

11. What are the key questions that I should prepare for leading the discussion?

10 Findings from the Published Literature about Curriculum and Instruction

1. FINDING:
Allan A. Glatthorn summarizes:

Authentic learning is more likely to occur if the required curriculum is characterized by these qualities:

(1) It is based on and derived from quality standards.

(2) It emphasizes depth of learning, not coverage.

(3) It values generative knowledge—knowledge that is used in solving problems.

(4) It makes specific provisions for flexible implementation, so that the teacher can enrich it, make it meaningful to the students, and respond to the special needs of students.

If the curriculum emphasizes the coverage of too much content, values only the comprehension of facts and formulas, and tries to control teaching completely, then authentic learning is very unlikely to occur.

In judging curriculum quality, you cannot always rely on the correspondence of the district guide with state standards. In a review of state curriculum standards, three experts gave them an overall grade of D+ (Finn, Petrilli, & Vanourek, 1998). Because you are required to implement the district curriculum, your best response, when working with a required curriculum that seems deficient, is to teach the main concepts and skills while adding elements that will strengthen the district guide.

SOURCE: Glatthorn, A. A. (1999) Performance standards and authentic learning. Larchmont, NY: Eye on Education. 28-29.

2. FINDING:
Brian J. Caldwell predicts:

Ten strategic intentions that contribute to a gestalt, or vision, of the new school in action include:

1. Subject boundaries will be broken, and learning will be integrated across the curriculum as the new learning technologies become universal, challenging rigidity in curriculum and standards frameworks.

2. School buildings designed for the Industrial Age will be redesigned to suit the needs of the knowledge society.

3. Schools will establish a richer range of professionals to work with and support teachers. Some will be on site and some will be located in other places.

4. Teachers will have access to the best resources to support their work, with many of these resources accessed from CD-ROMS and the Internet.

5. Students, teachers, and other professionals will increasingly work in teams, reflecting a pattern that is widely evident in workplace arrangements in other fields.

6. Schools will expand their policies and practices for the pastoral care of students to include cyber-policy on care in virtual schools.

7. Pastoral care for teachers will be important given the shift to the new professionalism and major changes in roles, responsibilities, and accountabilities, with professional development, individually and in teams, being one element in the strategy.

8. Issues of access and equity will be addressed in school cyber-policy, with a range of strategies including the sharing of resources among schools, partnerships with the private sector for donations and subsidies, and the creation of community-based learning centers.

9. Virtual schooling will be a reality at every stage of schooling, but there will be a place called school, with approaches to virtual schooling including the neighborhood educational houses.

10. New cultures for learning will take hold in schools for the knowledge society. There will be "lifelong learning" and "just-in-time-learning" that allows state-of-the-art approaches to learning and teaching to be designed and delivered on short notice in any setting for all learners.

SOURCE: Caldwell, B. J. (1999). Education for the public good: Strategic intentions for the 21st century. Marsh, D. D. (Ed.). ASCD Yearbook, 1999. Alexandria, VA: Association for Supervision and Curriculum Development. 56-57.

3. FINDING:

Fenwick W. English emphasizes:

To be effective in schools, a curriculum must have at least three essential characteristics.

    (1) As a work plan, a curriculum must provide for consistency (or coordination).

    (2) It must provide for continuity (or articulation).

    (3) A curriculum must also provide for flexibility in adaptation as teachers interact with students.

Flexibility means that the curriculum must be open to some interpretations in terms of how and under what classroom circumstances the content is most optimally taught. This means that the curriculum must be capable of being changed by alerting the sequencing and pacing of its delivery without fundamentally altering its design fidelity. Effective school curriculum never attempts to standardize students but must, as a work plan, provide for focus and connectivity (coordination and articulation) without leading to slavish conformity where every teacher has exactly the same lesson on the same day from the same page in the same textbook. Such a situation would be profoundly unproductive and ineffective.

SOURCE: English, F. W. (1992). Deciding what to teach and test. Newbury Park, CA: Corwin Press, Inc. 16

4. FINDING:

Carol Ann Tomlinson says:

In differentiated classrooms, teachers begin where students are, not the front of a curriculum guide. They accept and build upon the premise that learners differ in important ways. Thus, they also accept and act on the premise that teachers must be ready to engage students in instruction through different learning modalities, by appealing to differing interests, and by using varied rates and types of instruction along with varied degrees of complexity. In differentiated classrooms, teachers ensure that a student competes against himself as he grows and develops more than he competes against other students. In short, teachers in differentiated classrooms begin with a clear and solid sense of what constitutes powerful curriculum and engaging instruction. Then they ask what it will take to modify that instruction so that each learner comes away with understandings and skills that offer guidance to the next phase of learning.

SOURCE: Tomlinson, C. A. (1999). The differentiated classroom: Responding to the needs of all learners. Alexandria, VA: Association for Supervision and Curriculum Development. 2.

5. FINDING:
Robin Fogarty and James Bellanca stress:

A steady current of experts favor explicit skill instruction for the thinking curriculum. In some areas, consensus among the many thinking skills advocates embodies these beliefs:

... Thinking is most often taught indirectly, but a direct approach is needed.

... Learning how to think is not an automatic by-product of studying certain subjects.

... Students will not learn to think better simply by being asked to think about a subject or topic.

... Youngsters do not learn how to engage in critical thinking by themselves.

... There is little reason to believe that competency in critical thinking can be an incidental outcome of instruction directed, or apparently directed, at other ends.

... Instructions for the skills must be direct and systematic prior to, during, and following students' introduction to the skills and use of them in the classroom.

SOURCE: *Fogarty, R. & Bellanca, J. (1995). Cognition in practice: Best practices for the learning-centered classroom. Palatine, IL: IRI/Skylight Publishing, Inc. 73.*

6. FINDING:
Dale Parnell concludes:

The application of these principles to instructional development can facilitate learning in the classroom and help students transfer that learning to real-life settings outside the classroom.

A. THE PURPOSE PRINCIPLE: Teachers help students understand the purpose of any study unit; not only what they should learn, but why they should learn it.

B. THE BUILDING PRINCIPLE: New knowledge and new units of study are deliberately and specifically connected with students' prior knowledge or past learning so that the new learning builds on prior experience.

C. THE APPLICATION PRINCIPLE: New knowledge is specifically related to its practical, real-life application—especially how it relates to students' future roles as citizens, workers, consumers, family members, lifelong learners, healthy individuals, and participants in cultural and leisure activities.

D. THE PROBLEM-SOLVING PRINCIPLE: Students are encouraged to become active (rather than passive) learners by using new knowledge and skills to solve problems.

E. THE TEAMWORK PRINCIPLE: Students learn teamwork and cooperation by working together to solve problems.

F. THE DISCOVERY PRINCIPLE: The classroom slogan is "Try it!" Students are guided toward discovering new knowledge rather than having the answer (or multiple answers, as is often the case) handed to them. Teachers help students explore, test, and seek their own answers, often with the help of learning partners.

G. THE CONNECTION PRINCIPLE: Teachers help students see the connections between context and content, knowledge and application, one discipline and another. Divisions between traditional disciplines are minimized.

SOURCE: Parnell, D. (1995). Why do I have to learn this? Waco, TX: Center for Occupational Research and Development, Inc. 8-9.

7. FINDING:

Terry J. Foriska stresses:

Curricula clarity of focus begins with identifying the content standards all students are expected to achieve by the time they complete the specific program, whether the math program, science, social studies, or others. These subject area standards tell us why a particular subject is important and what skills and knowledge students will need for the future. For many years, these learning standards were not identified. Subjects were taught because everybody knew we needed this curriculum or because the state required it. In preparing content area standards, developers and teachers should ask such questions as the following:

. . . What should students know or be able to do as a result of studying this subject for X number of years in our grades/schools?

. . . What do experts in the field believe?

. . . What does the current research tell us?

. . . Have national standards been defined?

. . . What are the local, state, and national trends?

. . . What do we believe from our own craft experience and knowledge?

SOURCE: Foriska, T. J. (1998). Restructuring around standards: A practitioner's guide to design and implementation. Thousand Oaks, CA: Corwin Press, Inc. 35.

8. FINDING:
Donald C. and Sally N. Clark say:

The core curriculum of a middle level school is composed of the content and skills considered to be basic for all students. This content, a core of common learning, is for the most part determined by the state and by the school district, which also determine the procedures for assessing mastery. In most cases, the core of common learning required by middle level schools consists of courses in reading/language arts, social studies, mathematics, and science. Students are usually enrolled in these classes the entire time they are in the middle level school. It is the core curriculum where most of the current emphasis on performance standards is being placed.

An essential part of the middle level curriculum, the exploratory and elective curriculum provides for essential, less structured, learning experiences (exploratory courses) and student-selected enrichment, participatory experiences (elective courses and activities). The exploratory/elective curriculum, however, is more than just a sequence of courses. It is a process that provides opportunities for students to "explore their aptitudes, interests, and special talents and to develop an accurate and positive self-concept across the entire range of the middle-level school curriculum. Included in the required sequence are courses such as foreign language, art and music, physical education, technology, and the more traditional home economics and industrial arts."

There is also a social curriculum that should be emphasized. First, there are many planned activities that take place at school that facilitate socialization both in and out of the classroom. The centerpiece of the social curriculum is the teacher advisory program where the focus is on helping students develop effective socialization skills. The social curriculum, however, goes far beyond the experiences typically found in advisories. Some of these experiences include cooperative learning and task groups, student activities, participation in school governance, peer mediation, sports, and youth service. Second, in many respects the social curriculum is much like the hidden curriculum. Values and attitudes are being projected by teachers, administrators, and other adults in ways that may positively or negatively affect young adolescents.

SOURCE: Clark, D. C. & S. N. (2000, April). Developmentally responsive curriculum and standards-based reform: Implications for middle level principals. Bulletin, National Association of Secondary School Principals. 5-7.

9. FINDING:
Robert C. Spear points out:

Techniques for individualization within regular classroom activities can help students. Allowing an oral presentation to be given in front of a teacher, counselor, and/or peer instead of the entire class can be an appropriate modification. When teachers utilize a lecture-direct instruction format, some techniques for individualization are allowing students to diagram rather than write or outline ideas and information; shortening the time requirement of a lesson into smaller segments or allowing some segments to be presented by tape; allowing for note cards; and providing an outline of points to be covered or learned.

Techniques to individualize reading assignments would include

   (1) providing lower-level texts for students,

   (2) allowing students to highlight the regular textbook;

   (3) preparing taped presentations of text material,

   (4) assigning reading of specific points and providing vocabulary assistance, and

   (5) using visual clues to assist comprehension.

Other approaches could include:

   (1) permitting substitution of written assignments with projects, oral reports, and computer assignments;

   (2) allowing extra time;

   (3) emphasizing quality, not quantity; and

   (4) permitting students to tape lengthy assignments rather than write them.

SOURCE: Spear, R. C. (1992). *Appropriate grouping practices for middle level students.* Irvin, J. L. (Ed.). *Transforming middle level education.* Needham Heights, MA: Allyn and Bacon. 267.

10. FINDING:
James A Beane states:

Surely middle school educators must sense in their work a persistent tension between the school and early adolescents that sensitivity and organizational changes have failed to resolve. While this tension may well reside in complicated issues involving the society and schools in general, it is also likely that it is at least partially located in that curriculum question.

Progress toward creating a genuine "middle school" curriculum must begin with serious conversations about the curriculum questions as well as classroom adventures to bring those conversations to life. This is not, however, work in which "anything goes." While there is no specific map, there is a compass to guide us.

This compass amounts to guidelines that suggest a middle school curriculum ought to have certain qualities:

> a focus on general education;
>
> the exploration of self and social meanings;
>
> respect for the dignity of young people;
>
> grounding in democracy;
>
> prizing of diversity;
>
> personal and social significance;
>
> lifelike and lively content and activities; and
>
> rich opportunities for enhancing knowledge and skill.

How the actual curriculum looks may be as diverse as there are middle schools and classrooms. Wherever we go and whatever we may see in the name of "curriculum," though, we ought to see those guidelines brought to life in the school experiences of early adolescents.

SOURCE: Beane, J. A. (1993). A middle school curriculum: From rhetoric to reality. Columbus, OH: National Middle School Association. 24.

Curriculum and Instruction Teacher's Wrap-Up, à la Bloom

KNOWLEDGE
Define formal curriculum, core curriculum, and hidden curriculum.

COMPREHENSION
Give examples of things teachers can do to ensure that the curriculum is planned to result in authentic learning.

APPLICATION
Outline a presentation for faculty in-service on "Differentiating Instruction" to meet the needs of widely varying student learning styles and abilities.

ANALYSIS
Compare and contrast three major taxonomies and/or models for teaching or strengthening thinking skills and promoting academic success for all students.

SYNTHESIS
Create a lesson plan, classroom activity, or assignment designed to differentiate instruction.

EVALUATION
Summarize in three sentences or less your interpretation of the phrase "smuggling authentic learning into cognitive instruction."

Advisory

and

Affective

Education

Affective Education and Advisory Overview

AN AFFECTIVE EDUCATION PROGRAM MAY BE DEFINED AS:

• An important component of the educational program is designed to focus on the social, emotional, physical, intellectual, psychological, and ethical development of students.

• A program affording structured time during which special activities are designed and implemented to help adolescents find ways to fulfill their unique needs.

• Including an advisory program which provides consistent, caring, and continuous adult guidance through the organization of a supportive and stable peer group that meets regularly under a teacher serving as advisor.

• Helps to promote the fourth "R" as a recognized component of the curriculum. Traditionally, the schooling process has emphasized the three R's—reading, writing, and arithmetic—as the key curricular areas for middle level programs. In the complex and technological world of the Information Age, however, a fourth R, referred to as "relationships," has taken on new meaning and new responsibility.

• Plays a major role in helping our young people through the turbulence and hurdles of early adolescence.

• A special program to help students bridge the gap between elementary school and the independent world of high school. It offers middle school students the best of both worlds because it provides every student with an advisor who has a special concern for the student as an individual and encourages independence and personal growth needed for high school success.

• Affective education helps students build self-awareness and personal esteem.

• An advisory program can serve as a prescriptive antidote for the unmotivated learner or the at-risk student who can be coerced into negative behaviors. It may at the same time be structured to meet the special needs of academically or otherwise talented students. Recognizing that all students have needs to be met in ways unique to their own situations, activities, and projects will be included to accommodate a variety of learning styles and interests.

• Finally, an advisory program is needed to help students feel good about themselves and the contributions they can make to their school, community, and society.

• In the years ahead, society will be dependent on the middle level students of today. An effective advisory program will help young adolescents become happy, fully-functioning citizens of our world.

10 PLUS 17

Important Questions to Find Answers for Related to Affective Education, Character Education and Advisory

1. How do we define "affect?"

2. What is the relationship of affective growth to cognitive growth in an educational setting?

3. Why is affective education critical in today's complex and technological world?

4. How do you define a morally responsible person?

5. Is it possible for attitudes to be taught?

6. How would you defend or negate this statement: The moral fiber of this country (or world) is in rapid decline and is reflected in the behavior of today's adults and children?

7. What problems are created by the notion of "the hurried child" in this new millennium and how may such a phenomenon be controlled in an ever-changing and accelerated world?

8. What contradictions exist in today's early adolescent that are brought about by their unique needs and characteristics?

9. Are all adolescents at risk, and if so, what unique needs and characteristics of this age group seem to contribute most to this problem?

10. How would you define a teacher advisory (TA) program?

11. How can advisory ease the transition between elementary and middle school, and between middle and high school?

2. What are some things advisors can do to become better prepared to meet individual needs in a group setting?

3. How can an advisory program that has gotten off to a bad start be redirected and revitalized to become a positive influence in students' lives?

4. What steps can administrators take to positively influence a school wide advisory program?

5. How can parents be effectively involved in advisory activities?

6. What went wrong with advisory programs in middle schools of the last 80s and 90s that caused them to fall short of their original and noble purposes?

7. How can after-school and community enrichment activities be incorporated into an advisory program?

8. What are some pitfalls new advisors should be alert for and how can experienced advisors help them avoid these pitfalls?

9. What factors have most influenced the arguments for dealing more aggressively with the affective needs of kids in our schools today?

20. What are some activities that should be the "heart and soul" of effective advisory programs?

21. How can teachers make a difference in the moral lives of the students they teach.

22. Why is a well-defined character education program an important component of an effective middle school curriculum?

23. How would you define values?

24. How do values fit into a character education program?

25. How does one accumulate a set of values over time and what does it take to change or modify values as part of the growth or maturation process?

26. Why is it important for students, teachers, and administrators to have a common understanding and acceptance of the advisory program?

27. How is self-esteem of students connected directly or indirectly to school achievement?

10 PLUS 12 Decisions that Must Be Made When Planning A Teacher Advisory Program

1. What is the overall mission or purpose of the advisory program?

2. Who does what in an advisory program? Consider administrators, counselors, teachers, and other support staff.

3. Who can and should be advisers?

4. What kind of planning is required to establish a quality advisory program and should it involve a Steering Committee organization structure?

5. How does one schedule an advisory program, and are there optional time formats to consider?

6. How should advisory groups be formed, and is there an ideal advisor/advisee teacher/pupil ratio?

7. How does one prepare to be an advisor? What type of training is required?

8. How do advisory classes differ from the academic classes and how do they support the academic program?

9. How does one involve the parents in the advisory program?

10. What qualities are desired or essential to the role of advisor and should all teachers in a building be required to have an advisory group?

11. How do teachers separate their roles as advisors from their roles as instructors in a specific discipline?

12. How do teachers and counselors separate their roles and responsibilities?

13. How are students assigned to advisors and designated advisory groups?

14. Should advisers keep their advisees for more than one year?

15. Should students be involved in the planning and implementation of an advisory program?

16. How does one prepare students for an advisory program?

17. What kinds of activities work best in an advisory program?

18. What are some sources for advisory activities and experiences?

19. How does one evaluate the advisory program and assess its effectiveness in meeting the needs and characteristics of early adolescents?

20. What problem areas or pitfalls is one aware of when setting up an advisory program?

21. How does one keep an advisory program going and viable over time?

22. What student and teacher outcomes are most evident in a successful advisory program?

10 PLUS 2

Definitions Essential to Advisory and Character Education

1. Advisory or Advisor/Advisee Program: The unique organizational structure that contains one small group of students facilitated by an educator whose role it is to nurture, advocate for, and guide through the schooling process the individuals within that group.

2. Affective Domain: The area of education that focuses on the attitudinal/emotional development of students, which includes a host of "whole person" areas such as self-esteem, emotional and social adjustment, and personal beliefs.

3. Character Education: The movement in values and moral education that has the goal of teaching certain traditional values and virtues.

4. Cognitive Domain: The area of education that focuses on memory, reasoning, thinking, imagining, and the conscious intellectual activities associated with academics.

5. Growth Spurts: The brain growth of children that happens in chunks rather than in a continuous and uninterrupted process; this calls for various instructional strategies throughout adolescence.

6. Maturation: The process of growth and development that occurs over time as the result of the interaction of one's experience and one's genetically programmed potential.

7. Metacognition: The theory which states that learners benefit by thoughtfully and reflectively considering the things they are learning and the ways in which they are learning them.

8. Moral Development: The theory or set of theories that postulates that individuals pass through various and predetermined stages of moral reasoning such as the theory developed by Lawrence Kohlberg.

9. Self-Esteem: The estimation individuals place on their own perceived attributes, capacities, intentions, and behaviors.

10. Values and Moral Education: The conscious attempt to help others acquire the knowledge, skills, attitudes, and values that contribute to more personally satisfying and socially constructive lives.

11. Socialization: The process whereby individuals are inducted into norms, values, rules, etc. of a group.

12. Values Clarification: The process by which an individual is helped to make free value choices after studying a spectrum of options, to prize the choices made, and to behave in a manner that reflects his/her commitment to the value(s) chosen.

Krathwohl's Affective Taxonomy

Much like other taxonomies, the Affective Taxonomy provides a useful way to describe and classify educational objectives. When used as a model for creating advisory tasks, it becomes possible to design instruction that focuses on the non-intellectual aspects of individual growth. Such practices as the improvement of self-concept, enhancing interpersonal relationships, and dealing with moral or value issues no longer needs to be left to accident or chance.

LEVEL I — RECEIVING-ATTENDING

This level establishes an essential condition for learning to occur. The teacher prompts, gains, and guides the attention of the learner. Students are attending when they are being aware, being conscious of what is happening; being willing to receive, open to instruction; and controlling attention, focusing on the given task.

LEVEL II — RESPONDING

This level expresses a "willingness" on the part of the student. The student wants to understand, is willing to participate, and responds to instruction. The student participates, cooperates, contributes, and gains satisfaction in doing so. Students are responding by complying with given directions, participating willingly, and gaining in satisfaction or pleasure.

LEVEL III — VALUING

This level involves the determination of values, the worth of something established. The individual becomes associated with an attitude or belief. Students are valuing by determining the worth of something, expressing preferences, and making a commitment to beliefs.

LEVEL IV — ORGANIZATION

This level provides for the examination of evidence, the making of comparisons, and the prediction of outcomes. Attitudes and beliefs are weighted, ranked, and organized into a value system. Students are building a value system by comparing beliefs that are held; bringing values into an ordered relationship; and establishing a pattern of sentiment, beliefs, and values.

LEVEL V — CHARACTERIZATION

This level takes into account the behavior of the individual as guided by the attitudes, beliefs, and values that are held; values are internalized, acted upon, and reflected as one's philosophy of life. Students are acting on values by responding according to their beliefs, being consistent in their responses, and affirming their attitudes and beliefs.

Steps to Using Krathwohl's Taxonomy

To use Krathwohl's Taxonomy as a model for infusing affective values, beliefs, attitudes, and feelings into the advisory program, use the following steps:

STEP 1: Familiarize yourself with these five levels of the taxonomy, which are in hierarchical order.

STEP 2: Analyze several different advisory or character education activities to determine which levels of Krathwohl's Taxonomy are being emphasized. Determine what distinguishes one level from the next during this review process.

STEP 3: Create some "teachable moment" advisory or character education tasks from current events, news broadcasts, or community events. Try to include as many levels of Krathwohl's Taxonomy as you can for each lesson plan. Use the cue words in the chart on the next page to help with this activity.

STEP 4: Compare the cue words of Krathwohl's Taxonomy with those of Bloom and Williams. Reflect on why some behaviors occur in more than one level and/or in more than one taxonomy remembering that it is the context for the behavior or cue word (verb) that makes the distinction.

Note: A bulletin board, mural, poster, or set of transparencies may be prepared to assist students with the understanding and application of Krathwohl's Taxonomy as a model for internalizing behaviors associated with attitudes, values, beliefs, and feelings.

AFFECTIVE GOALS
Operational Definitions

AFFECTIVE GOAL	OPERATIONAL DEFINITION	CUE WORDS
RECEIVING Pays attention, is aware, takes information into account	The pupil displays attentiveness; listens, notices, and observes	listen, notice, see, observe, attend to, hear, follow, heed, regard, recognize, be alert to, consider, look for, examine, scan, review, inspect, scrutinize, smell, sense, touch, experience, absorb, be mindful of, be conscious of
RESPONDING Willingness to respond, motivated, gains satisfaction if responding	The pupil wants to discuss or explain	show, tell, explain, express, answer, respond, follow, proceed, volunteer, practice, interact, contribute, attempt, perform, display, offer, complete, share, discuss, find, seek, consult, try, reject, inspire
VALUING Accepting, preferring, and making a commitment to a value	The pupil chooses a concept or behavior that he/she believes is worthy	choose, select, rank, reject, adopt, decide, support, recommend, rate, defend, approve, pick, favor, challenge, specify, compare, estimate, state preference, judge, assess, appraise, subscribe to, turn down, state belief, oppose
ORGANIZATION Recognizes pervasive values, determines inter-relationships of values, organizes value system	The pupil reviews, questions, and arranges his/her values into an ordered system or plan	review, determine, organize, compare, arrange, classify, sort out, systemize, rank order, figure out, consider, examine, advocate, design, group, propose, structure, prescribe, set in order, index, methodize, assign, prepare, dispose of, form
CHARACTERIZATION Internalization of a value / Value system is consistent with behavior	The pupil voices his/her beliefs and affirms his/her values	act out, resolve, practice, behave, treat, avoid, rely on, respond, honor, affirm, declare, resist, confide, adopt, recommend, reflect, accept, disclose, stand for, state, profess, announce, assert, acknowledge

Checklist for Developmental Needs of Students that may be Addressed through Advisory and/or Character Education Program

___ **1.** Need for movement and physical activity.

___ **2.** Need for peer relationships and interactions.

___ **3.** Need for active over passive learning experiences.

___ **4.** Need for confronting moral and ethical questions head on.

___ **5.** Need for diversity.

___ **6.** Need for adult approval and affirmation of love.

___ **7.** Need for opportunities for self-exploration and self-definition.

___ **8.** Need for clear limits and structures that are fair and reasonable.

___ **9.** Need for meaningful participation in school community.

___ **10.** Need for confirmation of body changes and growth spurts as normal.

___ **11.** Need for introspection and reflection in personal thoughts and feelings.

___ **12.** Need for recognizing relevance of what is learned in school to real world situations.

___ **13.** Need for idealism and ambiguity when it comes to the meaning of life.

___ **14.** Need for optimism and hope when it comes to the future.

___ **15.** Need for competence and achievement in accomplishing tasks.

___ **16.** Need for exploring options, making choices, and investigating alternatives as part of the schooling process.

10 PLUS 10

Calendar Activities for a Core Value in a Character Education Program

Responsibility: Taking Care of Your Duties and Your Actions

Day One:
Discuss the meaning of the word responsibility.

Day Two:
Give examples of how boys and girls in your school demonstrate responsibility for their own health and well-being.

Day Three:
Whose responsibility is it to see that 1) your homework is done 2) your supplies are organized for the day 3) the school building is clean 4) the playground is safe?

Day Four:
Make a poster to encourage people your age to accept responsibility for conserving earth's natural resources.

Day Five:
Send a "thank you" message to someone in your community who carries out a responsibility that makes the community a nicer place to live.

Day Six:
Name and describe the ways members of the military forces assume special responsibility for citizens of the country they serve.

Day Seven:
Prepare a journal entry about family members' responsibilities to each other.

Day Eight:
Suggest to your teacher improvements that could be made in the way irresponsible student behavior is dealt with in your school.

Day Nine:
Rate yourself _ good _fair _ poor on responsibility for 1) your own rights and possessions 2) the rights and possessions of others 3) your own health and safety 4) the health and safety of others. Ponder your answers!

Day Ten:
Find a news story about a leader who behaved in an irresponsible manner that resulted in pain for the people he or she is responsible for.

Day Eleven:
Tell how yesterday's story would have been different had the leader behaved in a responsible manner.

Day Twelve:
Select a hero from the past or present whose behavior exemplifies a special sense of responsibility for other people. Retell the story to someone else.

Day Thirteen:
Read *Horton Hatches the Egg* by Dr. Seuss (see page 47 for list of books).

Day Fourteen:
Design an award for a member of your class that you have observed demonstrating responsibility for the good of the entire class.

Day Fifteen:
Think of a time when you were held responsible for someone else's behavior. Write or tell about the outcome and how you felt.

Day Sixteen:
Write a creative story based on one of the following 1) The life guard whose heroic actions saved a drowning person 2) The lady who rescued a bird with a broken wing 3) A passing teenager who snatched a toddler from the path of a speeding car.

Day Seventeen:
Ask three people you respect to define responsibility in their own words. Compare the meanings they give you with your own definition. What are the main differences?

Day Eighteen:
Create a poster or banner to promote awareness of the importance of school spirit and individual responsibility for team efforts.

Day Nineteen:
Compose a set of guidelines for developing student and teacher responsibility for a creative and challenging classroom climate.

Day Twenty:
Reflect on what embracing responsibility as a lifelong value means to you personally.

From *Character Education Year 1; Grades K-6* by John Heidel and Marion Lyman-Mersereau. Nashville, TN: Incentive Publications, ©1999.

Decisions to Make in Planning an Advisory Program

1. WHO IS INVOLVED?

. . . All students in the school are assigned to an advisory group that is facilitated by a teacher or an administrator. Advisory groups should have no more than 20–22 students in a group. The students may be assigned by grade level or across grade levels. The principal and guidance counselor of the school are not advisors because it is the job of these two people to coordinate and monitor the entire advisory process. The Advisory Steering Committee assists them in this role. Sometimes other staff members of the school may also serve as advisors if they are trained properly. These may include the secretary, the school nurse, the custodian, or a teacher's aide.

. . . The Advisory Steering Committee is responsible for researching, planning, implementing, and evaluating the advisory program. Members of the Advisory Steering Committee must include administrative, teacher, guidance, parent, and student representatives. They meet regularly to monitor the progress of the advisory concept.

. . . Any educator who would not benefit from the advisory program should be given alternative responsibilities during the school day, which could range from supervisory tasks to clerical tasks. No individual should be forced to serve as an advisor.

2. WHAT IS THEIR PURPOSE?

. . . Advisory groups use the unique needs and characteristics of the early adolescent as the foundation for their organizational structure.

. . . These groups are designed to focus on the affective domain in which one small group of students identifies with and belongs to one advisor who nurtures, advocates, and guides through school the individuals assigned to this group. It is the goal of the advisory program to provide every student with an opportunity to know one adult in the school better than any other so that a special trust and bond is established in this relationship.

. . . Advisory groups also make it possible for students to belong and affiliate with a small group on a regular basis so that the advisor can express concern in a personal and more intimate setting, focusing on student feelings and attitudes as well as more academic needs.

3. WHY ARE THEY IMPORTANT?

. . . Society has changed dramatically and schools have had to take on the role of surrogate parent in many instances. A restructured economy has seen a dramatic increase in the number of two working adult households or the single parent struggling with two different job settings.

. . . Family mobility has broken down extended family support systems and we no longer have a situation in which children are raised in a friendly neighborhood or community environment where everybody knows and nurtures everybody else.

. . . Child care centers, facilities, and after school programs have segregated children from older generations so that intergenerational activities and events are almost non-existent. "Words of wisdom" and "personal stories" of older people no longer contribute to the personal growth and experiences of children.

. . . There is continual decline of households with school-age children, which in turn impacts on the budgets and politics of allocating resources to the schools. The welfare of kids all too often is taking a back seat to the welfare of senior citizens.

. . . Today's adolescents are all grown up with no place to go. In previous generations, kids were considered an asset in a family as they helped with family chores, jobs, and services, while today they are considered more of a liability because there is little that a young person can do to make a difference in the quality of family or community life.

4. WHEN ARE THEY SCHEDULED?

. . . Ideally, advisory groups should meet on a daily basis for 20 to 30 minutes a week. If this is not possible, advisory groups should meet at least a minimum of three times a week.

. . . Ideally, advisory groups should meet first thing in the morning to get the school day off to a good start and to establish the climate for the day's activities.

. . . Three traditional ways to schedule advisory time are: (1) The school day is extended for 30 minutes to provide additional minutes for advisory sessions and interactions. (2) Student begins each day with advisor. They spend 10 minutes on housekeeping tasks. On two designated days each week, 5 to 10 minutes are deducted from each class period so that an additional or longer advisory period is created and inserted between two other periods. It is during this time that the organized curriculum is implemented. (3) A school can also institute a "drop period" schedule to accommodate the advisory program. For this option, a period is eliminated from the daily schedule on a rotating basis (either two, three, four, or ideally five days a week), and the advisory class is put in its place.

. . . Two alternative ways to schedule advisory time are:

(1) Organizing teams in a type of block-time and modified self-contained program, where the teacher has the same students for

two or three periods per day and teaches them two or more subjects, often referred to as an "extended time advisory program," which promotes trust and facilitates teacher guidance.

(2) Planning full day advisory experiences that include three to six full-day experiences throughout the year. These activities usually begin with a kick-off breakfast and can feature everything from community service projects and field experiences to artists-in-residence programs or city bus tours.

5. WHERE DO THEY FIT IN THE CURRICULUM?

. . . The curriculum should include both preplanned topics or themes and varied instructional strategies that are interdisciplinary and that complement the academic disciplines.

. . . The curriculum should infuse critical and creative thinking skills at all levels of the taxonomy and should be applied in both the affective and cognitive domains of knowledge.

. . . The curriculum should incorporate multiple learning styles and intelligences that cater to the diversity that exists among and between students.

. . . The curriculum should allow for "teachable moments" as they surface through local, regional, national, and global news events and human-interest stories.

. . . The curriculum should use as its foundation a research-based commercial program such as the A to Z Advisory Program or the ADVISORY program published by Incentive Publications, then supplement this resource with additional materials on a need basis. The commercial program offers the following advantages over a locally developed program:

(1) universal themes appropriate for the early adolescent;

(2) scope and sequence of both content and skills to be taught;

(3) activities that have been field tested with target populations;

(4) infusion of quality educational models for addressing varied learning styles and thinking skills; such as Bloom's Taxonomy, Williams' Taxonomy, Krathwohl's Taxonomy, and Gardner's Multiple Intelligences; and

(5) focus on a wide range of active learning tools and techniques.

10 PLUS 10

Potential Goals for an Effective Advisory Program

The following checklist may be used to critique an advisory curriculum consisting of a variety of tools and techniques to meet established program goals.

1. Teaching conflict resolution skills among peers

2. Building a positive relationship between students and teachers

3. Assisting students to set and achieve personal goals

4. Creating a school climate of culture that is caring and encourages pride

5. Promoting attitudes of acceptance and collaboration among diverse groups

6. Enhancing abilities to make decisions and solve problems through the use of educational thinking skill models such as Bloom's Taxonomy for Cognitive Development, Taxonomy for Creative Thinking, and Krathwohl's Taxonomy for the Affective Domain

7. Providing opportunities for self-exploration and the discovery of special interests, aptitudes, hobbies, and capabilities

8. Introducing and reinforcing healthy study habits and skills

9. Experimenting with technology and the Internet as important resources, but also recognizing their limitations and problem areas

10. Aiding in the building of personal friendships

11. Charting present and past academic and behavioral performances

12. Introducing and applying a variety of instructional delivery systems and thinking skill models

13. Becoming test-wise and practicing test-taking strategies

14. Investigating the world of work and career choices for the future

15. Planning and implementing service learning projects

16. Integrating art, music, and fitness into the schooling process

17. Understanding the elements of good communication skills, including reading, writing, speaking, and listening

18. Examining the media and the current events reported in the newspapers

19. Evaluating one's personal relationships, values, morals, and beliefs

20. Self-assessment through experiences with learning style inventories and multiple intelligences

10 PLUS 8

Key Elements of a Successful Advisory Program

1. Each advisor plays the role of a child advocate representing that student at team meetings, screening meetings, parent conferences, and other student/staff sessions as needed.

2. Each advisor initiates intervention procedures and referrals both within the advisory setting and if necessary, in collaboration with counseling services.

3. Each advisor maintains a line of communication with the advisee's academic teachers and with the advisee's parents or guardians.

4. Each advisor engages in individual conferences with advisees on a predetermined and consistent basis.

5. Each advisor maintains accurate records on advisees, including such tools as an advisee information folder, advisee academic plan card, advisee attendance/behavior record, advisee report card and progress report, and advisee test scores, to name a few.

6. Each advisor supports the advisory concept and works to improve his/her performance in the advisory role and setting.

7. Each advisor is well informed on the unique needs and characteristics of the early adolescent and of the advisees assigned in his/her advisory class.

8. Each advisor becomes the single most important adult in the school for his/her advisees.

9. Each advisory class has a reasonable teacher-pupil ratio.

10. Each advisory class has a specific time and place to meet that is regularly scheduled.

11. Each advisory class meets a minimum of three times a week for an average of 20 to 30 minutes a day, or meets on an alternative predetermined plan.

12. Each advisory class provides advisees with activities that are varied, active, and student-centered.

13. Each advisory class has a common core curriculum with flexibility in its implementation.

14. Each advisory class represents a place where both advisors and advisees look forward to advisory time and tasks.

15. Each advisory class places a high emphasis on individual learning styles.

16. Each advisory class maintains a balance of individual, small group, and large group activities.

17. Each advisory class infuses higher order creative and critical thinking skills whenever able to do so.

18. Each advisory class emphasizes an advisee's academic, social, emotional, physical, psychological, or self-concept in its program.

10 PLUS 30

Assets Crucial to a Child's Healthy Development for Life

as Identified by the Search Institute

The Minneapolis-based Search Institute, founded in 1958 to advance the well-being of children, has conducted research involving nearly 600,000 young people nationwide to formulate the Healthy communities/Healthy Youth initiative. The goal is to provide the training and technical assistance needed to motivate and equip communities to nurture competent, caring, and responsible children. The average young person has fewer than half of the 40 developmental assets the institute has identified as necessary for healthy development.

This list of 40 assets may be used as a guide or check point for planning or evaluating an advisory program's goals and objectives. The list also may be found helpful in determining how well a specific school and parent community currently meet these developmental needs young people have, keeping in mind that the more they are met, the less likely the young people are to use drugs and alcohol, or to engage in sexual activity or violence. Activities and programs may be planned to promote these 40 assets and to help fill the gaps in character education and thereby assume more responsibility for our nation's youth.

1. Family support
2. Positive family communication
3. Other adult relationships
4. Caring neighborhood
5. Caring school climate
6. Parent involvement in schooling
7. A community that values youth
8. A useful role in the community
9. An hour or more of community service per week
10. Feeling of safety at home, school, and in neighborhood

11. Clear rules and consequences at home

12. Clear rules and consequences at school

13. Neighbors take responsibility for monitoring behavior

14. Positive adult role models

15. Positive peer influence

16. High expectations from parents and teachers

17. Three or more hours a week in music, theater, or other arts

18. Three or more hours a week in sports, clubs, or organizations

19. One or more hours a week in religious activities

20. Time at home at least five nights a week

21. Motivation to do well in school

22. Actively engaged in learning

23. At least one hour of homework every school day

24. Cares about his/her school

25. Reads for pleasure at least three hours a week

26. Values helping others

27. Values equality and reducing hunger and poverty

28. Stands up for beliefs

29. Tells the truth even when it isn't easy

30. Accepts personal responsibility

31. Shows restraint from sexual activity, drugs, and alcohol

32. Can plan ahead and make choices

33. Has empathy, sensitivity, and friendship skills

34. Is comfortable with people of different backgrounds

35. Can resist negative peer pressure

36. Seeks to resolve conflict nonviolently

37. Sense of control over things

38. High self-esteem

39. Sense of purpose

40. Optimistic about the future

Major Roles of Individual Responsible for an Advisory Program

1. ROLE OF ADMINISTRATION

A. To generate a total school philosophy and mission statement that supports advisory as an essential element in the school's program

B. To promote and market the advisory program within the school and throughout the community

C. To establish an organized structure that facilitates the implementation of an advisement program, such as an Advisory Steering Committee

D. To assign competent personnel — students, and community representatives to the Advisory Steering Committee to coordinate the program

E. To provide time and space within the school for both planning and implementing advisory activities

F. To identify and provide quality in-service training for all individuals involved with the program

G. To participate actively in all in-service activities as a means of lending both support and expertise as needed

H. To monitor the progress of the program and visiting advisement groups

I. To find ways to include the performance of staff, in their roles as advisors, as part of the annual performance evaluation process.

2. ROLE OF ADVISORY STEERING COMMITTEE

A. To facilitate the program, which involves scheduling, calendars, materials, in-service training, parent conferences, etc.

B. To establish goals and objectives for the program

C. To provide input and to serve as a liaison between the administration and faculty as well as between the faculty and the parent community

D. To monitor advisement procedures and activities

E. To provide support and enthusiasm for advisors

F. To design ongoing in-service necessary for continued growth

G. To assist in the assessment and evaluation of the advisory program

3. ROLE OF GUIDANCE COUNSELOR

A. To assist in the development of advisory philosophy, themes, and activities

B. To coordinate the advisory program through leadership of the Advisory Steering Committee

C. To coordinate and conduct in-service training

D. To review and respond to referrals about advisees from advisors

E. To communicate with advisors about their advisees as needed

F. To meet periodically with advisors in conferences for the purposes of encouragement and for solving problems

G. To assist with monitoring and evaluating the program

4. ROLE OF ADVISOR

A. To provide a caring and nurturing relationship with advisees

B. To work with guidance counselor to insure proper guidance services for all students

C. To attend all in-service training sessions

D. To plan and implement advisory activities

E. To provide a time and place for advisees to meet and share concerns

F. To respond to individual needs of advisees

G. To refer advisees for counseling and/or social services on a need basis

H. To communicate with parents and guardians of advisees

I. To provide increased academic and career advisement

J. To monitor academic progress and maintain accurate records on advisees

K. To encourage advisees' academic, personal, and social development

10 Possible Barriers to Successful Advisory Programs

1. Insufficient planning time before implementing the program

2. Inadequate support of advisory concept by administrators, teachers, and/or parents

3. Incomplete curriculum of advisory topics, activities, and active learning strategies

4. Lack of budget for advisory training and materials

5. Poor scheduling of advisory time and space

6. Teachers uncomfortable with the role of advisor because of reluctance to share personal experiences and affective self

7. Teachers reluctant to take time from academic disciplines to teach affective content and skills

8. Teachers taking on too much of the counseling role and/or unprepared to take advantage of referral options and services

9. Advisory program lacking adequate evaluation and assessment processes to determine its effectiveness with students

10. Students seeming to undervalue the advisory time

10
PLUS 14

Do's and Don'ts of Advisory Programs

DO'S

1. Do research the advisory concept through review of the literature, visitations to other school advisory programs, and dialogue with other teachers who serve as advisors, using the Internet as a resource.

2. Do allow plenty of time to plan for the implementation of the advisory concept.

3. Do a need assessment to determine what programs and procedures are already in place at the school for meeting the affective needs and characteristics of students. The advisory program can either enhance these elements and/or fill in the gaps.

4. Do organize an active Advisory Steering Committee to oversee the development, implementation, and evaluation of the advisory program.

5. Do create a quality-marketing plan to promote the advisory concept with all stakeholder groups including administrators, teachers, support staff, students, and parents.

6. Do develop a realistic timeline with checkpoints for planning and implementing the advisory program from the very beginning of its inception.

7. Do arrange for open forum meetings and get-togethers with constituent groups to present tentative plans and to encourage input/feedback.

8. Do spend quality time and dollars arranging for comprehensive in-service and training programs designed to meet the needs of advisors and steering committee members.

9. Do seek out a comprehensive curriculum for the advisory program that combines the materials of an established publishing house with supplementary materials for those "teachable moments" that occur during any given school year.

10. Do plan an ongoing evaluation program to monitor the progress of the advisory program that includes a variety of assessment tools, including interview forms, observation checklists, and individual surveys or questionnaires.

11. Do interface the advisory program with other successful program options in the school so that they complement one another rather than compete with one another.

12. Do be flexible and consider changes and modifications to the program as it progresses.

DON'TS

1. Don't expect the planning, implementation, and evaluation process for advisory to progress without problems to be solved, plans to be altered, and timelines to be adjusted.

2. Don't try to censor suggestions for improvement, feedback for change, or criticisms of existing policies. Keep the lines of communication open and encourage two-way exchanges at all times.

3. Don't get discouraged or frustrated when setbacks and disappointments occur. Think of these as creative tensions to be resolved.

4. Don't duplicate another school's program and expect it to work without considerable modification.

5. Don't skimp on the training for advisors and don't fail to offer ongoing assistance and in-service throughout the advisory program's implementation and evaluation phases.

6. Don't attempt to implement an advisory program without a predetermined curriculum, complete with themes, topics, activities, strategies, and supplementary or optional materials.

7. Don't overlook alternative methods for scheduling and/or using advisory time. Try out different ways of delivering the program until a satisfactory formula has been achieved.

8. Don't focus on the quantitative dimensions of the advisory program but consider the quality of the advisory experiences and activities.

9. Don't expect all advisors to handle their advisory responsibilities in like manner, but allow for differences in personalities and learning or teaching styles.

10. Don't doom the program to failure by complaining about it, especially during the developmental and early implementation phases. Make the criticism constructive about potential for improvements in the program.

11. Don't expect each advisee to respond to the program in like manner as students, like teachers, have different needs and perceptions of what advisory is supposed to accomplish.

12. Don't forget to have fun with the kids and learn from your mistakes as well as your successes.

10 PLUS 15

Alternative Ways to Use Advisory Time

Procedural Suggestion: Examine each of the activities listed here as potential uses for a quality advisory period. Try to think of a particular task that you have done successfully in the classroom for each of the given categories. Be ready to share the task with others who might want to field test it with their own group of advisees.

1. Small and whole group discussion

2. Impromptu and mini-speeches or talks

3. Games or simulations

4. Book, movie, and television reviews

5. Role plays and case studies

6. Study and test review sessions

7. Community field trips and experiences

8. Speaker's bureau of adults from the community at large

9. Virtual field trips to special web sites using the Internet

10. Learning log or journal entries

11. Learning stations or portable desk top centers

12. Spelling bees, contests, and other academic competitions

13. Skits and plays

14. Silent sustained reading sessions with follow-up book dialogues

15. Demonstrations or exhibits

16. Experiments or investigations

17. Interviews, surveys, or questionnaires

18. Conflict resolution exercises

19. Panels, debates, and round table conversations

20. Current events

21. Films, movies, or videotapes

22. Holiday celebrations

23. Special club or activity days

24. Career and workplace explorations

25. Individual counseling and conference sessions

10 PLUS 10

Springboards For Discussion Starters And Journal Writing In Advisory

1. A reaction to a particular point with which you strongly agree or disagree

2. A question about a concept that confuses you

3. A description about a situation that frustrates you

4. A paraphrase of a difficult or complex idea that interests you

5. A summary of a special time or feeling

6. A comment on what you think about a given person, place, or thing

7. A reaction to an idea that confirms or questions a particular belief you hold

8. A discussion of the pros and cons of an issue important to your well-being

9. A comparison and contrast of two opposing ideas that intrigue you

10. A history of a significant emotional event you experienced

11. Which is the stronger sex—male or female?

12. Is it easier in today's world to be a kid or an adult?

13. Would you rather have good looks or good grades?

14. If you could see into your future, would you want to?

15. Which is better for you— cooperation or competition?

16. How would you define maturity?

17. What makes an ideal hero?

18. How would you recognize a perfect day?

19. Do people learn more from their mistakes or from their successes?

20. What would be the best thing that could happen to you?

10

PLUS 2

Quotations From Well-Known Figures To Use As Discussion Sparkers

1. Golda Meir: *You cannot shake hands with a clenched fist.*

2. Winston Churchill: *The price of greatness is responsibility.*

3. Albert Einstein: *The most beautiful thing we can experience is the mysterious. It is the source of all true art and science.*

4. Dwight D. Eisenhower: *Leadership is the art of getting someone else to do something you want done because he wants it done.*

5. Henry Ford: *Failure is only the opportunity to begin again more intelligently.*

6. Mahatma Gandhi: *No culture can live if it attempts to be exclusive.*

7. Henry Van Dyke: *For the woods would be very silent.*

8. Martin Luther King: *Injustice anywhere is a threat to justice everywhere.*

9. Vince Lombardi: *It's not whether you get knocked down, it's whether you get up.*

10. Margaret Thatcher: *Being powerful is like being a lady. If you have to tell people you are, you aren't.*

11. John Mosley: *All things are difficult before they are easy.*

12. Alexander Pope: *A man should never be ashamed to say he has been wrong, which is but saying in other words that he is wiser today than he was yesterday.*

SOME DISCUSSION QUESTIONS TO CONSIDER:

1. Do you generally agree or disagree with this quotation? Explain.
2. Give an example from history or personal experience to illustrate the idea behind this quotation.
3. Why do you think the author of this quotation chose to say what he or she said?
4. How might you restate the quotation in your own words?

(sample) Student Interest Inventory

Write a spontaneous personal reaction to complete each sentence below.

1. The thing I do that I am proudest of is _____

    _____

    because _____ .

2. My favorite leisure time activity is _____ .

3. I would like to make improvement in _____

    _____

    because _____ .

4. My favorite book is _____ .

5. One thing I enjoy doing with my family is _____

    _____

    because _____ .

6. I think my family's rules are _____

    _____

    because _____ .

7. One thing I enjoy doing with my friends is _____ .

8. One thing I would change about my home is _____

    _____

    because _____ .

9. I would like for my friends to think I am _____

    _____

    because _____ .

10. When I am an adult I would like to _____

    _____

    because _____ .

11. One thing I would change about my community is _____

_____

    because _____ .

12. When I think of school, I feel _____

_____

    because _____ .

13. The thing I like best about school is _____

_____

    because _____ .

14. The thing I like least about school is _____

_____

    because _____ .

15. The trait I admire most in a teacher is _____

_____

    because _____ .

16. I think homework is _____

_____

    because _____ .

17. I think our school rules are _____

_____

    because _____ .

18. My favorite school subject is _____

19. One thing I would change about my school is _____

_____

    because _____ .

20. I hope ADVISORY will help me to _____

_____

Adapted from *Advisory Middle Grades Advisee/Advisor Program* by Imogene Forte and Sandra Schurr. Nashville, TN: Incentive Publications, ©1991. Used by permission.

Advisory Program Scheduling

OPTION ONE:

Student begins each day with advisory teacher for a designated 20–30 minute period of time.

Advantages:
1. Student starts the day on a positive note with small advisory group and teacher advocate.
2. Academic school day is not broken up by affective advisory program.
3. Schedule is consistent and easy to follow.

Disadvantages:
1. Advisory time can too easily be used up for housekeeping and administrative tasks with little time left for advisory activities.
2. Student has no time to report or reflect on how school day is going.
3. Advisory preparation time adds to burden of school-day preparation.

OPTION TWO:

Student begins each day with advisor. They spend 10 minutes on housekeeping or administrative tasks. On two designated days each week, 5–10 minutes are deducted from each class period so that an additional or longer advisory period is created and inserted between two other periods. It is during this time that the organized curriculum is implemented.

Advantages:
1. Two advisory periods are available on selected days, one for advisory tasks and one for administrative tasks.
2. Student begins each day on a positive note with advisory group and teacher advocate.
3. Administrative or housekeeping tasks are not taken away from academic time.
4. Advisory is easy to schedule as advisory time can be scheduled between any two periods.

Disadvantages:

1. Advisory tasks possible only two days a week, so advisory becomes more administrative than affective in nature.

2. Advisory adds to school-day preparation time.

3. Teacher must teach an additional period two days per week.

OPTION THREE:

A school can institute a "drop period" schedule to accommodate the advisory program. For this option, a period is eliminated from the daily schedule on a rotating basis (either two, three, four, or, ideally, five days a week), and the advisory class is put in its place.

Advantages:

1. The planner has a fair amount of scheduling freedom. When advisory time is scheduled daily, two days can be devoted to formal advisory curriculum activities, one is set aside for administrative tasks, and the remaining two days may be used for alternative advisory activities. When fewer days are allotted for advisory classes, the scheduler will, of course, plan other combinations of advisory activities.

2. The burden of giving up academic time to make room for advisory time is shared among the teachers.

3. Scheduling is easy as a period is eliminated from the daily schedule on a rotating basis.

4. Advisory time is scheduled in place of something else and not in addition to everything else.

Disadvantages:

1. Some effort is required to plan a rotating schedule.

2. May be difficult to meet state guidelines for prescribed academic day.

Adapted from *Advisory Middle Grades Advisee/Advisor Program* by Imogene Forte and Sandra Schurr. Nashville, TN: Incentive Publications, ©1991. Used by permission.

10 MINUS 3

Evaluation Tools To Use In Measuring Effectiveness of Advisory Programs

TOOL NUMBER ONE: SEARCHING FOR FEELINGS

Directions: Circulate throughout the room and try to locate someone who experienced each of the designated feelings below in a work-related advisory session during the past week. Have them briefly tell you why they felt as they did. Record a comment or two as a memory aid for discussion purposes in a sharing session. If possible, try not to use any individual for more than one response.

Find Someone Who Had the Feeling of . . .	Person's Name	Comment
1. excitement		
2. pessimism		
3. disappointment		
4. optimism		
5. competence		
6. anger		
7. pride		
8. camaraderie		
9. anxiety		
10. security		

TOOL NUMBER TWO: SELF-ANALYSIS OF MY READINESS TO BE AN ADVISOR

Directions: Complete each of the items listed below to self-assess your current state of readiness for taking on the role of student advisor or for completing your role as student advisor for the current semester or academic school year. Be honest in your rankings and be ready to share your reasons for each choice.

1. I enjoy teaching and/or facilitating the learning of key concepts, skills, attitudes, and beliefs associated with the affective domain.

    Usually   Sometimes   Rarely

2. I am comfortable and willing to share my personal feelings and experiences with my advisees.

    Usually   Sometimes   Rarely

3. I show considerable interest in and enthusiasm for the advisory program.

    Usually   Sometimes   Rarely

4. I am willing to try new things and take reasonable risks with my advisory responsibilities.

    Usually   Sometimes   Rarely

5. I am prepared and organized when leading my advisory sessions.

    Usually   Sometimes   Rarely

6. I look forward to each advisory period.

        Usually   Sometimes   Rarely

7. I can spark students' interest in the challenges and purposes of the advisory concept.

        Usually   Sometimes   Rarely

8. I believe that all students can benefit from an advisory program.

        Usually   Sometimes   Rarely

9. I know how to help students apply problem-solving and decision-making skills to their daily lives.

        Usually   Sometimes   Rarely

10. I know how to help students identify and reach their academic potential.

        Usually   Sometimes   Rarely

11. I know how to help students build a strong and positive sense of self.

        Usually   Sometimes   Rarely

12. I am a positive role model as an advisor for my students.

        Usually   Sometimes   Rarely

TOOL NUMBER THREE: POLLING FOR ADVISORY ISSUES AND ADVISOR FEEDBACK

This form may be reproduced and made available to all advisors for their completion. A portion of a staff meeting, a department meeting, a team meeting, or an Advisory Steering Committee meeting should be scheduled for discussing the results.

Directions: Please take a few minutes to fill out this Advisor Polling Feedback Form and turn it in to a member of the Advisory Steering Committee. Note that the results of this poll will be made available at the next _____ (Type of Meeting) scheduled for _____ (Date/Time/ Place of Meeting). Part of this meeting's agenda will be devoted to a discussion of the results.

PART I. Check three of the advisory-related areas listed below that are of particular interest to you. The top priority issues of the school's advisors from this list will be discussed in more detail at the above meeting.

_____ 1. Support from administration and social service specialists for my role as an advisor

_____ 2. Scheduling advisory time

_____ 3. Using the advisory period effectively

_____ 4. Implementing the advisory curriculum adequately

_____ 5. Defining expectations of advisory program, role of advisor, and role of advisees

_____ 6. Meeting with parents of advisees

_____ 7. Meeting with academic teachers of advisees

_____ 8. Supplementing the predetermined advisory curriculum with alternative materials and "teachable moment" opportunities

_____ 9. Maintaining records on advisees

_____10. Integrating advisory with the core academic areas of the curriculum

PART II. Please indicate your preference for dealing with the poll results at the above meeting so that planning may be made accordingly.

_____ 1. I prefer a whole and large group discussion of results.

_____ 2. I prefer smaller cooperative learning groups for discussing the results.

_____ 3. I prefer hearing an expert's or consultant's input on the results.

_____ 4. I prefer a panel to discuss the implications of the results.

_____ 5. Other (please specify) _____

TOOL NUMBER FOUR: MAKING ADVISORY TASKS ACCOUNTABLE AND MEASURABLE

Designing advisory activities for students in such a way that they also meet standards-based curricular requirements is both a necessity and a challenge. Advisory must never be viewed as a "frills" time-out period for students, but rather as a support program for the various core discipline areas. One way to accomplish this goal is to gather samples of student work that result from assigned advisory tasks. These student work samples can then be used to help judge the worth or value of both the advisory assignments and the quality of student responses to these activities.

Directions: Organize a group of advisors by grade level, team level, or department level. Provide these advisors with a set of guidelines for aligning classroom work in advisory with standards from one or more of the other designated subject areas. Allow sufficient time for this process to take place. Repeat the steps outlined below on a variety of advisory tasks as needed to validate a variety of curricular outcomes.

Step One: First, instruct advisors to have students complete the designated advisory task according to the directions given.

Step Two: Advisors then collaboratively identify each of the curricular standards that apply to this particular task designating subject area(s) to which it applies.

Step Three: Next, advisors work together to develop a scoring guide derived from both the standards and the assigned task.

Step Four: Advisors collectively score the student work using this scoring guide.

Step Five: Finally, advisors discuss and determine whether or not the work meets the standards making any adjustments necessary to ensure that it does.

NOTES: Write down some thoughts about the above process as you field test selected advisory activities from the curriculum. Think about the sequence of steps and which ones are most difficult for the advisors to implement. Determine how this process can validate what you do during advisory time. How does this make the advisory program more accountable and measurable?

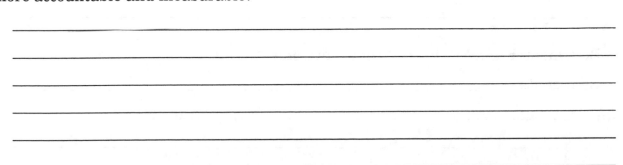

TOOL NUMBER FIVE: ALTERNATIVE STAFF DEVELOPMENT OPTIONS FOR ADVISORS

Directions: There are many alternatives to the traditional workshop or in-service training session designed for improving the attitudes and skills of teachers serving as advisors. In fact, learning styles of staff member in any school setting differ as widely as they do for the students they teach.

It is suggested here that advisors be given several options for improving their effectiveness in advisory classrooms by choosing one or more alternative methods of staff development. Consider each of the following methods for improving one's competencies in the advisory classroom and record an advantage (or disadvantage) and a benefit (or problem area) for each of the alternatives listed below from your perspective as an advisor.

1. Conduct an action research project with your group of advisees.

   Comments: _____

   _____

   _____

2. Observe an advisory classroom and analyze it as a teaching case.

   Comments: _____

   _____

   _____

3. Plan and critique an advisory lesson with an advisor colleague.

   Comments: _____

   _____

   _____

4. Be a mentor and coach a colleague advisor.

   Comments: _____

   _____

   _____

5. Conduct research or visit advisory websites on the Internet.

   Comments: _____

   _____

   _____

6. Give an advisory presentation or a model lesson before an audience of peer advisors at a conference.

   Comments: _____

   _____

   _____

7. Read journal articles or professional monographs on the advisory concept. Try writing an advisory-related article of your own.

   Comments: _____

   _____

   _____

8. Maintain an advisory reflection log or learning journal of your own.

   Comments: _____

   _____

   _____

9. Design a self-assessment tool around your advisory role and use it to analyze your own behavior and teaching in the advisory classroom.

   Comments: _____

   _____

   _____

10. Videotape your performance in an advisory session and ask a group of peers to view the tape and give you feedback.

    Comments: _____

    _____

    _____

TOOL NUMBER SIX:
JOIN A WHOLE-FACULTY STUDY GROUP

Directions: Study groups within individual schools have become excellent tools for determining the value of a program, the success of a concept, or the affective and academic growth of a student. It is strongly suggested that the Advisory Program become the basis for a series of study group projects as part of the evaluation process for judging the worth of advisory in the secondary school program.

According to study group experts Carlene U. Murphy and Dale W. Lick, a "study group of teachers is a small number of individuals joining together to increase their capacities through new learning for the benefit of students. There are whole-faculty study groups where all faculty members at a given school are members of professional study groups and there are independent or stand-alone study groups that do not depend on organizational support."

Murphy and Lick outline the following steps in forming study groups which could be organized to examine the strengths and weaknesses of the existing advisory curriculum or overall advisory program with a given school setting. *"Try it, You'll Like it!"*

1. Keep the size of the group to no more than six to keep the study group process manageable.

2. Do not worry about the composition of the study group, as the content most often dictates the membership.

3. Establish and keep a regular schedule on a weekly basis. Regular and shorter meetings are preferable to irregular and longer meetings.

4. Establish group norms at the first meeting of the study group so that every member understands and supports the rules and follows the acceptable standards for behavior.

5. Agree on an action plan for the study group and adjust the timeline and tasks at regular intervals on a need basis.

6. Complete a log after each study group meeting that is a written summary of what happened at the meeting and that gives the study group a history or track record.

7. Encourage members to keep individual logs for their personal reflections.

8. Establish a pattern of study group leadership that encourages each member to serve as the study group leader on a rotating basis.

9. Give all study group members equal status and equal responsibilities.

10. Have a curriculum and instructional focus because the function of study groups is to support the implementation of curricular and instructional innovations, to integrate and give coherence to a school's instructional practices and programs, to target a school wide instructional need, and to monitor the impact of instructional changes on students.

11. Plan ahead for transitions, as most study groups stay together for a school year.

12. Make a comprehensive list of learning resources, both material and human.

13. Consider a variety of data sources as part of the action plan, including such options as student work, student grades, attendance or discipline reports, parent participation in school events, student or staff surveys, promotion/detention/suspension records, student participation in school events/activities/projects, courses/teachers selected. Teacher observations, or state assessments.

14. Include training in the study group's agenda.

15. Evaluate the effectiveness of the study group.

For more information read: Murphy, C. & Lick, D. (1998) Whole-faculty study groups: A powerful way to change schools and enhance learning. Thousand Oaks, CA: Corwin Press, Inc.

TOOL NUMBER SEVEN: STUDENT FEEDBACK ACTIVITIES

Student feedback on implementation of the advisory program is very important and can easily be incorporated into the advisory curriculum itself. Try these two student activities to solicit their input on how "things are going."

Activity One: The Advisory Collage

Directions: Provide students with old magazines/newspapers, magic markers, and large pieces of poster board, drawing paper, or newsprint. Instruct students, as individuals or in small groups, to create a collage that represents what they have learned in the advisory sessions. Encourage them to cut out words from magazine/newspaper headlines or use the magic markers to insert key words and phrases where appropriate to do so. Ask students to use the blank space below to write in some ideas to be graphically portrayed as visual images in the collage.

Activity Two: The Television Commercial

Directions: Work with a small group of peers and follow these steps to complete the task outlined below:

1. Discuss your favorite television commercials and give reasons why they are special.

2. Describe ways that producers of television commercials use gimmicks to make their messages creative and appealing. Consider such elements as humor, sex appeal, animation, well-known personalities, slogans, music, comparisons, figurative language, and surprises.

3. Create a thirty-to-sixty second television commercial that advertises the advisory program, emphasizing its value to you as students.

4. Perform your television commercial for an audience of peers or parents/guardians.

5. Create a print version of your advisory television commercial and post it on the classroom bulletin boards or walls.

6. Draw a rough sketch of your television commercial idea below.

Findings from the Published Literature Related to Advisory Programs

1. FINDING:
Hoversten, Doda, and Lounsbury write: Advisory programs carry myriad objectives. For example: (1) Provide an environment and activities that will foster bounding with an advisory group so that students will feel accepted and valued by teachers and peers. (2) Help students cope with academic concerns and set goals that will facilitate positive school experiences. (3) Give students avenues to discover their uniqueness so that they might come to appreciate the many differences among people. (4) Help students develop positive relationships through experiences that utilize group dynamics. (5) Promote critical thinking skills through discussion and problem-solving activities so that students can learn to make responsible choices. (6) Develop listening skills and an understanding of the roadblocks that hinder effective communication. (7) Build self-esteem in students so that they might become confident, capable young people who accept responsibility for their own actions. (8) Heighten student awareness of good citizenship through providing opportunities for extensive involvement through shared decision-making. (10) Improve home/school communication and relationships.

The list is representative of the variety of objectives that may be incorporated in these advisory programs. In fact, almost any type of activity that one can think of or devise could be included because no universally accepted definition of these programs currently exists. Given this diversity, it is difficult to discuss advisory programs as a single conceptual entity and it is also misleading to do so as two advisories may differ greatly in terms of their objectives and/or activities.

Reference: Galassi, J., Gulledge, S. & Cox, N., (1998). Advisory definitions, descriptors, decisions, and directions. Columbus, OH: National Middle School Association.

2. FINDING:
An advisory system in any middle school helps overcome the impersonality and alienation that secondary students often feel. Using staff as advisors guarantees that each student has an advocate who knows the student well. Those who know this process can say with certainty that an advisory system makes school a more personal

place; gives all advisors a chance to share something powerful; provides students and parents a specific person in the school to whom they can turn with questions, concerns, or offers of help; and has a generally salutary effect on the overall culture of a school. The fact that every single student knows there is one person in a school building who is her advocate, one person a student can seek out to vent anger to or ask a question of, is comforting. As time goes by, an advisor becomes a combination mentor, advisor, and adult friend—but always a mature professional with a student's best interests in mind and an understanding of who that student is. An advisory system gives each student the support young people crave and helps defeat an alienation from school that too many students feel in an educational bureaucracy.

Reference: Goldberg, M. (1998). How to design an advisory system for a secondary school. Alexandria, VA: Association for Supervision and Curriculum Development.

3. FINDING:

Pearl G. Solomon concludes: Sample criteria for evaluating the content standards of a grade-level curriculum are as follows:

   . . . Meet mandated state, district, local standards, or non-mandated professional standards.
   . . . Articulate with the commencement and benchmark standards or outcomes.
   . . . Are realistic in terms of available resources of time.
   . . . Are realistic in terms of space.
   . . . Are realistic in terms of available resources of human energy.
   . . . Are realistic in terms of available resources of materials.
   . . . Are developmentally appropriate for the student.
   . . . Respond to evidence from recent research on how learning happens.
   . . . Challenge all students to reason with higher-order thinking skills.
   . . . Are comprehensive and comprehensible.
   . . . Pay attention to the potential for cross-disciplinary connections.
   . . . Prepare children for life in a world of cultural and political differences.
   . . . Are measurable by a matching performance standard.
   . . . Meet the child's needs to succeed in the present and future societal context.

SOURCE: Solomon, P.G. (1998). The curriculum bridge: From standards to actual classroom practice. Thousand Oaks, CA: Corwin Press, Inc. 78.

4. FINDING:

Irene McHenry states that schools are a fertile ground for moral development in today's culture. As the new century begins, it is imperative that schools give priority to the development of the skills necessary to survive by creating a society in which people value integrity in their relationships, in which active listening to the perspectives and feelings of others is an automatic first step in dialogue, in which effective and responsible communication is given a high priority, in which we believe in and value the richness of diversity and the conflict that differences may bring, in which emphasis on community values is at the forefront of all learning, and in which embrace tension and conflict as an opportunity for moral growth. We must create educational institutions that reflect the best of humanity,

SOURCE: McHenry, Irene. "Conflict in Conflict: Fertile Ground for Moral Growth," Phi Delta Kappan, Bloomington, IN. November 2000, Vol. 82, Number 3, p. 227.

5. FINDING:

A song from a Broadway show a few decades ago asked, "What's the matter with kids today? Why can't they be like we were, perfect in every way?" It was a playful satire on the tendency of adults of every generation to worry about the behavior of youth.

But it's not nostalgia or crankiness that provokes our concern these days; it's a frightening increase in violent behavior and a seeming lack of basic human values among some young people. Teachers contend with shocking levels of aggression and profanity. Police are witness to weekend parties where teenagers get drunk and use drugs. And every major city now has drive-by shootings and gun battles on school playgrounds.

I don't mean to condemn an entire generation; lots of young people lead productive, healthy lives. But many are not "like we were," and for good reason; the factors that shape their lives are very different. Because of social and economic changes, family patterns and work arrangements had irrevocably altered. Consequently, many children receive less guidance from their parents. Fewer adults in the community make it their responsibility to know and look out for children. Instead, children learn about values and how to behave largely from television and their peers.

SOURCE: Brandt, Ron. (1993, November). Overview: What can we really do? Educational Leadership (51) 3.

6. Finding:

J. Howard Johnston summarizes the reasons advisory programs in the late 80s and 90s went astray from their original, important, and noble purposes.

One: Many advisory programs were initially developed by guidance departments and took on a group guidance format that made teachers uncomfortable and resistant.

Two: Some advisory periods were scheduled simply to provide unstructured, free time for adults and children to interact with one another so that the bulk of the interaction was among the students themselves rather than between teacher and students. In other cases, teachers created "activities" designed primarily to engage students in some form of structured task. Because they were unconnected to discernible school goals, these were often seen as trivial or simply a waste of time.

Three: Other programs took on an "issues" or "hot topics" focus in which students had an opportunity to discuss matters of personal or school-wide concern. While this approach is the one that is probably most closely related to the original purposes for the advisory function, many of these topics such as drug and alcohol use, sexual behavior, peer relations, and values education, became controversial and invited a great deal of public and parent scrutiny. To quell community concerns about the treatment of these topics, many programs abandoned them altogether or couched them in vague, non-offensive topics and activities that were less controversial. These "sanitized" versions of major issues also came to be seen as trivial by many teachers and students.

Four: In addition, the advisory curriculum seldom coincided with problems as they appeared in the lives of the children. If we talk about "death and loss" in October, but my dog dies in May, the advance preparation may not help me deal with the loss at the time it occurs.

In short, the advisory period became a supervised time for study or socialization among students. Indeed, the most common advisory activities cited by teachers in order of frequency were: . . . Informal conversation among students

. . . Silent reading or study time

. . . Teacher discussion with group

. . . A group activity or game

. . . Teacher discussion with individual student

SOURCE: Johnston, J.H. (1997, March/April). What's Going On?: from Advisory Programs to Adult-Student Relationships: Restoring Purpose to the Guidance Program. Schools in the Middle: Theory into Practice. (6)4

7. FINDING: The Violent Generation. The E-Generation. The Scapegoat Generation. The Hollywood Generation. The Ambitious Generation. From sociologists and journalists to parents and educators, adults categorize today's teenagers with a slew of conflicting labels. But what do we really know about this group of 12-to-18 year olds, a population of more than 30 million people? Can we adequately generalize about today's youth culture in a way that makes sense not just to those who label teens, but also to teens themselves? Part of the difficulty involves the ambivalent images of today's youth. Some see that teenagers are outperforming their teachers and parents in technology. But others worry that they are "secretive," unsupervised—just a website or a video game away from becoming dangerous and violent. Some argue that the media exploit teens through advertising and television, whereas others feel that today's teens, the savvy children of baby boomers, actually control an increasingly teen-driven market. Generation X, that nebulous population characterized by shopping malls, cynicism, and 1970s television reruns, has finally given way to the next generation, raised more on the Internet and video games than on "The Brady Bunch" and "Schoolhouse Rock." Who are they? How are they represented? And what, if any, common experiences do they share and bring into the classroom?

SOURCE: Tell, Carol. "Generation What? Connecting with Today's Youth," Educational Leadership, Association for Supervision and Curriculum Development, Alexandria, VA. December 1999/January 2000, Volume 57, No. 4, p. 8.

8. **F**INDING:
So what should advisory look like today? It is not a good option to simply use advisory time for a study hall or revert to an administrative homeroom model. Students at this age need opportunities to talk about issues that they are concerned about, they need to feel a sense of belonging, and they need to connect with an adult who cares. If teachers view their students as emerging adults and acknowledge the needs and concerns of young adolescents, then it makes sense that the teacher's role must also include facilitating opportunities for student discussion and skill building in the social and emotional areas. All of these things happen in a well-developed and carefully facilitated advisory program.

SOURCE: Pitton, Debra A. "The School and the Child and the Child in the School." Middle School Journal, National Middle School Association, Columbus, OH. September 2001, Vol. 33, No. L, p. 17.

9. **F**INDING:
Anne Wheelock summarizes a school culture for standards-based reform allows every student to feel "safe to be smart." Such a culture puts the focus on student work and communicates explicit expectations for the work required from every single student. It draws strength from relationships of trust and beliefs about learning that allow students to risk working hard, making mistakes, and persisting. It is grounded in assignments that every student can find engaging, and its credibility rests on routines that build the support students need to succeed in the regular school day. It communicates that every student will learn by asking for help and by helping others do good work, so that it is not only "safe" but exciting to "be smart."

SOURCE: Wheelock, Anne. Safe To BE Smart: Building a Culture for Standards-Based Reform in Middle Grades. National Middle School Association, Columbus, OH. 1998, p. 184.

10. **F**INDING: Educational philosopher Jane Rowland Martin proposes a new way of thinking about what should be considered basic knowledge for all students. Noting some of the many ways society is different today than it used to be—e.g. both men and women are in the workplace, more single-parent families—she argues for changing our conception of school from that of a "school house" to one of a "school home." . . . The notion of a "school house" suggests the major purpose of school is preparing students to be future workers and public citizens, what Martin refers to as the "productive" aspects of society . . . The "school home" would teach the 3 R's along with what she calls the 3 C's: care, concern, and connection. The 3 C's would prepare students for what she calls the "reproductive" aspects of society, such as caring for others, raising children, and maintaining a home. Quality of life depends not only on student's future successes as workers and citizens in the public arena but also as caring, competent parents and good neighbors in private homes and personal relationships.

SOURCE: Dodd, Anne W. "Making Schools Safe for All Students: Why Schools Need to Teach More than the 3 R's, Bulletin, National Association of Secondary School Principals, Reston, VA., March 2000, Vol. 84, No. 614, pp. 26-27.

Affective Education and Advisory Teacher's Wrap-Up, à la Bloom

KNOWLEDGE
Define the concepts of "affective domain" and "cognitive" domain as they relate to the advisory program.

COMPREHENSION
Summarize the major findings in the literature related to the role of affective education in today's middle level schools.

APPLICATION
Outline the major elements of a successful advisory program.

ANALYSIS
Compare and contrast the "dos" and "don'ts" of effective advisory programs.

SYNTHESIS
Create an original advisory lesson plan that would work well in most middle school settings.

EVALUATION
Name and rank order seven evaluation tools suggested in this module to measure the effectiveness of advisory programs from the most interesting or least from your perspective and give reasons for your first and last choices.

STUDENT
ASSESSMENT
AND
EVALUATION

Student Assessment and Evaluation Overview

Assessment is:
- The testing or grading of students according to a given set of criteria.
- Referred to as authentic when methods of assessing achievement or performance are as close to real-life situations as possible.
- Valuable to both teachers and students as feedback on the effectiveness of classroom delivery systems and outcome expectancies.
- The use of a wide variety of methods and techniques, avoiding overuse of any one testing strategy.
- The need to assess individual student growth in both cognitive and affective areas.
- The use of tests, quizzes, products, portfolios, and performance assessments to stimulate student interest, enthusiasm, quest for knowledge, and improved self-esteem.
- Provisions for prompt, accurate, and concise feedback to students and parents.
- A non-threatening environment and avoidance of personally embarrassing situations.
- New and different approaches to provoke student interest and positive behavior.
- Measurement of innovative delivery systems such as cooperative learning, peer tutoring, exploratory and mini-courses, and thematic and research- and literature-based units as well as teacher-directed lessons and lectures.
- State and national standards

Effective assessment devices characteristically:
- Identify both strengths and weaknesses.
- Make provisions for student involvement in a personal sense in the overall assessment process.
- Take into account differences in student learning styles, attitudes, interests, and talents.
- Honor all student efforts and neither downgrade nor glorify varying exceptionalities at either end of the grading spectrum.
- Make provisions when feasible for collaborative efforts while taking into account individual differences within the group.
- Employ a multifaceted scoring procedure rather than one rigid grading system while avoiding "fuzzy and unclear" terminology or evaluative criteria that has little actual meaning for any stakeholder in the assessment process.
- Provide timely and specific feedback for teacher evaluation and future planning.
- Contribute to the student's sense of self-worth and academic achievement.

10 PLUS 10

Important Questions To Find Answers For Related to Assessment

1. Under what circumstances are teacher-made tests more effective than standardized tests? Explain your answer and give at least one example of an occasion when just the opposite would be true.

2. What are some advantages and some disadvantages of the use of true-false questions as a measure of major concepts and understandings gained and processed?

3. What are some guidelines for developing matching and/or sentence completion questions?

4. What are some common pitfalls to avoid when developing and using multiple-choice questions?

5. What can teachers do to make sure that assessment results are reported and interpreted in a manner that is actually meaningful and useful to parents and students?

6. What are some major guidelines for writing and scoring essay tests?

7. What are some commonalities of portfolio, performance, and product assessment? Explain the strengths and weaknesses of each and give one example of a situation in which each would be a valid means of assessment.

8. How would you define outcomes-based education? In your own words, explain an effective approach to outcomes-based assessment.

9. What are some ways middle level students can be prepared for taking essay tests?

10. What are some advantages of portfolio assessment over traditional testing? Give at least three advantages for the student.

11. Why are student products good assessment tools? How can they be used to encourage creativity?

12. What are some things to keep in mind when designing, scoring, and using performance tests and evaluating their results?

13. What are some major advantages of including student self-evaluation as an ongoing part of a structured assessment program?

14. What are the most valuable components of a student portfolio as viewed by the teacher?

15. What are the most valuable components of a student portfolio as viewed by the student?

16. How can teachers assigned to the same team work together to develop a plan to more effectively assess individual students within the group?

17. What steps can teachers take to become more proficient in selecting, administering, recording, and making use of assessment tools and results?

18. How can total group assessment devices be tailored to acknowledge and make positive application of differences in individual learning styles?

19. What are some informal methods of assessing student understanding of material covered during instruction?

20. How can assessment be used to help students develop a positive self-image and capitalize on individual strengths and weaknesses?

10
PLUS 10

Definitions Essential to Assessment Success

1. **Authentic Assessment** refers to methods of assessing student achievement or performance that are as close to real-life situations as the setting allows.

2. **Assessment** is the testing or grading of students according to a given set of criteria.

3. **Summative Evaluation** is the process used to determine the general value or worth of programs, curricula, or organizational settings. It describes what was accomplished, what the negative or positive consequences were, what the final intended or unintended results were, and, in some cases, whether the benefits justify the costs.

4. **Measurement** implies the assignment of a numerical quantity to a given assessment or evaluation procedure.

5. **Outcomes-Based Education** focuses curriculum, instruction, and measurement/assessment on the desired student outcomes—the knowledge, competencies, and qualities students should be able to demonstrate when they finish school.

6. **Outcomes-Based Assessment** is assessment in the context of outcomes-based education. It is those skills, competencies, experiences, talents, and attitudes which the student is intended to have after graduation for the purpose of employment or personal human development that are assessed.

7. **Validity** refers to the extent to which a test measures what it was intended to measure.

8. **Reliability** is the consistency of performance on the test from one taking of the test to another by the same individual.

9. **Portfolio Assessment**: A meaningful collection of student work that exhibits the student's overall efforts, progress, and achievements in one or more areas.

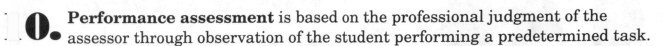

10. **Performance assessment** is based on the professional judgment of the assessor through observation of the student performing a predetermined task.

11. **Product assessment** is an assessment that requires a concrete end result such as a display, videotape, learning package, experiment, script, production, manual, or exhibit.

12. **Authentic Learning**: A type of learning that requires students to encounter and master situations that resemble real life.

13. **Benchmarks**: Specific skills/abilities developed by the end of predetermined organizational levels.

14. **Concept map**: A person's graphic, diagrammatic, or schematic representation of his/her understanding of a concept.

15. **Formative Evaluation**: Its purpose is to provide those responsible for the program with ongoing information about whether things are proceeding as planned and whether expected progress is being made. Formative evaluations address these issues:
(1) What conditions are necessary for success?
(2) Have those conditions for success been met? and
(3) Can the conditions be improved? Formative evaluation occurs during the operation of a program or activity.

16. **Journals**: Journals are written in narrative form, are subjective, and deal more with feelings, opinions, perceptions, or personal experiences. They tend to be descriptive, long, open-ended, and free flowing compared to learning logs.

17. **Learning Logs**: Logs consist of short, objective entries that contain descriptions or explanations of problem-solving processes, observations during experiments, questions about the information presented, lusts of outside readings, details of assignments, etc. They are usually brief, factual, and impersonal.

18. **Metacognition**: A theory which states that learners benefit by thoughtfully and reflectively considering the things they are learning and the ways in which they are learning them.

19. **Observation Checklists**: These are strategies to monitor specific skills, behaviors, or dispositions of individual students or all of the students in a class. They can also serve as a record-keeping device. Quality checklists include the student's name, space for four or five targeted areas, a code or rating to determine to what degree the student has or has not demonstrated the skill, and a space for comments or anecdotal notes.

20. **Rubrics**: Rubrics are a set of guidelines containing criteria based on stated performance standards and a descriptive rating scale for purposes of distinguishing between performances or products of different quality.

10 PLUS 10

Formative/ Summative Evaluation Formats for Teachers to Use in the Classroom

1. Teacher Observations and Daily Recordings on Note cards

2. Student Learning Logs or Journal Entries

3. Peer Observations

4. Student Performance Tasks

5. Student Products or Projects

6. Peer Assessments

7. Student or Teacher Interviews

8. Role-Playing or Case Studies

9. Anecdotal Comments or Records

10. Student Self-Assessment or Reflective Comments

11. Small or Large Group Projects

12. Teacher-Assigned Formal Tasks

13. Written Tests

14. Oral Quizzes

15. Open-Ended or Guided Responses

16. Demonstrations or Exhibits

17. Graphic Organizers or Visual Designs

18. Portfolios

19. Interactive Lectures

20. Discussion/ Panel Participation

Things to Keep in Mind About Portfolios

1. Portfolios are collections of a student's work assembled over time to document individual growth and academic progress.

2. Portfolio assessment measures require the student to assume primary responsibility for making decisions about what goes in the portfolio, how the portfolio is organized, and what type of self-reflection experiences are to be included.

3. Portfolios provide students with opportunities for goal setting, for tools of discussions with peers and adults, for demonstrations of student skills and acquisition of concepts studies, for evidence of student learning, for making connections between carried subject areas, and for invitations to reflect on work that has been done.

4. Portfolio contents can be housed in a number of different containers including file boxes, show boxes, shopping bags, cardboard magazine holders, photo albums, scrapbooks, and expandable file or pocket folders.

5. Portfolios should contain front and back covers and information about time span represented by artifacts. They should also contain a Table of Contents, an overview of the organizational structure employed by the portfolio, a collection of at least ten different artifact formats, reflections on all included artifacts, and a self-evaluation to analyze overall student strengths and weaknesses.

6. Portfolios can be graded in many ways. Individual pieces can be graded over a predetermined time period. A completed portfolio can be graded on such criteria as visual appeal, organization, creativity, reflections, form or mechanics, evidence of growth, knowledge of concepts/skills demonstrated, and completeness.

7. Some performance type activities to be considered for portfolios might be: debates, exhibitions, display, skits or plays, speeches, audio/video tapes, choral readings, dances, presentations, oral lab reports, newscasts, court trials, panel discussions, travelogues, surveys, role plays, case studies, or personal interviews.

8. Some product type activities to be considered for portfolios might be: poems, booklets, charts/graphs, diagrams/flow charts, reviews, newspaper/editorials, collages, posters, banners, glossaries, journal entries, letters, lists, murals, puzzles, games, book reports, transcripts, scrapbook, stories, experiments, magazines, games, or models.

9. Some test type activities to be considered for portfolios might be: teacher-made tests, student-generated quizzes, take-home tests, criterion-referenced tests, standardized tests, open book exams, oral tests, textbook tests, cooperative learning group tests, or district/state-mandated tests.

10 MINUS 4

Steps for Planning A Portfolio System

1. Determine the overall purpose and intended audience of the portfolio.
. . . How will the portfolio document student growth and learning?
. . . What is the timeline for this portfolio?
. . . Who will view the portfolio?

2. Specify the curricular areas to be included in the portfolio.
. . . Will this be a single course portfolio or a team portfolio?

3. Decide on the selection criteria for items placed in the portfolio.
. . . Who selects the pieces - student, teacher, parent, or some of each?
. . . How many pieces should be represented?
. . . What types of pieces should be represented?
. . . How often should pieces be included?

4. Plan a management system for the portfolio process.
. . . What type of container will house the portfolio?
. . . How will students organize and maintain their portfolio?
. . . How will students update their portfolio?

5. Establish a set of priority uses for the portfolio.
. . . How can I make certain that students see the value of the portfolio?
. . . How can I oversee the selection of the most appropriate pieces to accurately reflect student growth over time?
. . . How can I make optimal use of the portfolio with parents?
. . . How can I use the portfolio for celebration of work well done?
. . . How can I interface the portfolio process with grading of report cards?
. . . How can I use the portfolio to provide me feedback as a teacher? As a parent?

6. Focus on a manageable assessment process for measuring the success of portfolios.
. . . How will I know the portfolio assessment process is working?
. . . How do I grade the portfolios?
. . . How do I get students to apply self-evaluation and metacognitive techniques?
. . . What is done with the portfolios at the end of the marking period, semester, or school year?

10 PLUS 2

Questions to Ask During Portfolio Conference Sessions

1. How is your portfolio organized and how did you decide on this organizational pattern?

2. How did you go about selecting your portfolio pieces?

3. What pieces are you most proud of in this portfolio and why do you feel as you do?

4. What piece on the portfolio do you wish was not there and how could you improve it?

5. Of all the assignments represented by the pieces in the portfolio, which one was hardest for you to do and which one was easiest? What makes this so?

6. How do these pieces reflect your overall growth this marking period, semester, or year?

7. What makes you feel proud when you review the work in this portfolio?

8. How would you improve this portfolio process for next time?

9. What does this portfolio say about you, the student, and you, the person?

10. What do you hope happens to the contents of this portfolio?

11. What advice would you give to another student about to begin the portfolio process?

12. How does the work in this portfolio affect your grade in this class/course? How should it affect the grade in this class/course?

Steps for Designing A Performance Task

A performance assessment task focuses on real-life applications or real-life problems where possible to do so. Performance tasks are realistic, are complex, are comprehensive, are time-consuming, and are most often scored using rubrics. Performance tasks are characterized by high levels of student choice, elaboration or core knowledge/content, application of higher order thinking skills, explicit scoring systems, broad audiences, and structured plans that fit a specific set of instructional objectives or performance standards. Educators should follow these steps when designing a performance test:

1. Identify content area(s) to be assessed including factual/conceptual understandings.

2. Select the process or inquiry/thinking skills you wish to measure.

3. Write a detailed description of the performance task.

4. List the criteria to be used to evaluate the performance.

5. List the resources required to complete the task.

6. Write directions for the students that include appropriate language for clarity.

7. Decide on how to interpret results—comparison with other students or with self.

8. Develop scoring procedures that focus on performance, not content.

9. Determine who will rate or evaluate the performance—teacher, peers, or self.

10. Administer a trial test wherever possible to do so.

11. Modify or revise elements of the performance task according to trial test results.

Things to Keep in Mind About Performance Assessment

1. A performance assessment task involves using real-life applications to real-life problems or at least in simulated settings. Performance tasks are realistic, are complex, are comprehensive in nature requiring extended time to complete, and involve greater use of judgment in scoring.

2. Some important characteristics of performance tasks include: student choice, elaboration of core knowledge content, application of process and higher order thinking skills, an explicit scoring system, a broad audience, and a structured plan to fit a specific instructional objective or performance standard.

3. Performance tasks are often preferred over more traditional assessment tasks because: educators are dissatisfied with selected-response and paper/pencil tests; educators feel that process or procedural knowledge is as important as content knowledge and this can best be measured through performance tasks. Educators feel that conventional tasks are harmful because they encourage high stakes testing and a focus on low level instructional tasks.

4. Educators should follow these steps when designing a performance test:

Step One: Identify content area to be assessed including factual/conceptual understandings.

Step Two: Select the process or inquiry/thinking skills you wish to measure.

Step Three: Write a detailed description of the performance task.

Step Four: List the criteria to be used to evaluate the task.

Step Five: List the resources required to complete the task.

Step Six: Write directions for the students that include appropriate language for clarity.

Step Seven: Decide on how to interpret results—comparison with other students or with self.

Step Eight: Develop scoring procedures that focus on performance, not content.

Step Nine: Determine who will rate or evaluate performance—teacher, peers, or self.

Step Ten: Administer a trial test wherever possible to do so.

5. Some specific types of possible performance tasks are:

COMPARISON AND CONTRAST TASK:

DEMONSTRATION TASK:

INFERENCE TASK:

PREDICTION TASK:

APPLICATION TASK:

EXPERIMENTAL TASK:

GENERALIZATION TASK:

Descriptions of Performance Task Options for Students and Teachers to Consider

1. COMPARISON AND CONTRAST TASK: The student is asked to compare two or more people, places, or things by presenting both similarities and differences.

2. DEMONSTRATION TASK: The student is asked to show or perform a specific skill or act.

3. INFERENCE TASK: The student is asked to look for and identify subtitles and between-the-lines meanings when reviewing ideas and/or information.

4. PREDICTION TASK: The student is asked to make realistic guesses about what could have happened or will happen in the future.

5. APPLICATION TASK: The student is asked to use his or her knowledge or skill in a new context or situation different from the one in which it was learned.

6. EXPERIMENTAL TASK: The student is asked to set up an experiment to test a hypothesis.

7. GENERALIZATION TASK: The student is asked to draw conclusions from a given set of data.

8. INVESTIGATION TASK: The student is asked to follow a reasonable set of guidelines for conducting an inquisition or in forming generalizations about an assigned topic or problem.

9. ANALYSIS TASK: The student is asked to break down a whole into its component parts, looking for relationshipS between parts or the recognition of the organizational principles involved.

10. PERSPECTIVES TASK: The student is asked to consider two or more different perspectives, then to choose the perspective he or she supports.

11. INVENTION TASK: The student is asked to create, compose, design, develop, or produce something new and unique.

12. APPRAISAL TASK: The student is asked to determine the worth or value of a person, place, thing, event, or idea.

13. DECISION-MAKING TASK: The student is asked to identify the factors or variables that caused a certain decision to be made.

14. PROBLEM-SOLVING TASK: The student is asked to create a solution to a specific problem.

15. EVALUATION TASK: The student is asked to identify the pros and cons or advantages and disadvantages of a given situation.

10 Reasons Student Products Make Good Assessment Tools

1. They come in a variety of sizes, shapes, colors, and formats. They may involve learning logs, video or audiotapes, computer demonstrations, dramatic performances, informative bulletin board displays, debates or panels, formal speeches or presentations, student experiments and inventions, investigation reports, physical constructions, or role-playing and case study scenarios.

2. They are more likely to be initiated or generated by students rather than teachers that then reflect individual student learning styles and interests.

3. They can show dimensions of student creativity and originality not always evident in more traditional kinds of assessment such as quizzes and paper-pencil tests.

4. They can demonstrate student grasp or understanding of academic content or knowledge in new and different ways.

5. They can improve student attitudes towards learning because of their hands-on approach and emphasis on action.

6. They can make the classroom come alive as students interact collaboratively with one another sharing ideas, resources and know-how during activity periods.

7. They lend themselves to subject matter integration more easily than other forms of evaluation.

8. They require more flexible time frames for completion, which in turn allows for better differentiation of instruction between and among students.

9. They represent more concrete expressions of what has been learned in the eyes of the students who do not always see evidence of knowledge demonstrated in test-taking situations.

10. They encourage mutual goal setting and planning between both student and teacher.

Things to Know About Rubrics and Checklists

1. A checklist is used to identify the critical attributes of specific end products and most often have a simple "yes" or "no" box to check which follows each identified attribute. Most checklists focus on these main assessment categories:
  . . . Organization and preparation
  . . . Content
  . . . Mechanics

2. A rubric is a generic scoring tool used to evaluate a student's performance in a given outcome area. Rubrics consist of a fixed measurement scale and a list of criteria that describe the characteristics of products or performances for each score point. Criteria are the guidelines, rules, or principles by which student responses, products, or performances are evaluated.

3. Three tips for scoring rubrics are:
  . . . When reading a response or examining a product, refer to the rubric frequently to keep the criteria in mind.
  . . . Remember that a specific level such as a "2" includes work that is an exact "2" or a "plus 2" or a "minus 2", and a plus or minus could be helpful in this process.
  . . . Focus only on the criteria specified in the rubric, and not on other elements.

4. Some characteristics of effective rubrics are:
  . . . They reflect the most significant elements related to the assigned task.
  . . . They help to be more accurate and consistent when pinpointing competence levels.
  . . . They help teachers grade student work more accurately and fairly.
  . . . They encourage student self-evaluation as part of the process.
  . . . They provide more information than a checklist of skills or attributes.

5. Some preliminary guidelines to consider before constructing quality rubrics are:
  . . . Define quality performance in a given subject or content area.
  . . . Determine what distinguishes quality work from mediocre or unacceptable work.
  . . . Collect samples of rubrics from various disciplines to examine and critique.
  . . . Collect samples of student work that reflect varied degrees of competence.
  . . . Generate a master list of potential criteria (descriptors) for several degrees of proficiency in student work.

Steps for Creating and Using Rubrics with Students

1. Determine the overall objectives and proficiencies expected of students at completion of task.

2. Decide on specific criteria to be demonstrated by students.

3. Create a rubric with four to six degrees of proficiency of each criterion and express in language common to students.

4. Weight each criterion to determine percentage of number of points each criterion is worth.

5. Distribute and explain purpose and contents of rubric to students.

6. Require students to set goals for themselves and determine what level of proficiency they are most comfortable with at this point in time.

7. After assigned task is completed, ask students to self-evaluate using the rubric sheet.

8. After task is completed, teacher evaluates the student using the rubric sheet and discusses any discrepancies between the two set of results.

9. Instruct students to revise work that does not meet minimum standards.

10. Encourage students to collaboratively develop rubrics with criteria for their future projects as they gain experience in their use and purpose.

11. Experiment with three types of scales when constructing rubrics with the students. Consider these options:

. . . Numerical Scale—Example:	0	1	2	3	4
. . . Verbal Scale—Example:	Not Yet	Needs Improvement	Making Progress	Proficient	
. . . Numerical / Verbal Scale—Example:	0	1	2	3	4
	Whoops!	Not Good		O.K	Cool!

1. They are easy to use and explain.

2. They focus, streamline, and standardize curriculum planning.

3. They make scoring of complex work products more manageable.

4. They establish consistent criteria for student self-assessments.

5. They identify steps students must take to improve a performance.

6. They offer specific information to share with parents.

7. They provide criteria for writing report cards.

8. They make teacher expectations very clear.

9. They provide students with more informative feedback about their strengths and areas in need of improvement when compared with more traditional forms of assessment.

10. They support and do not inhibit learning from a student and parent perspective.

11. They support the combined development of skills, concepts, and good thinking.

12. They can determine how well students are meeting school and district performance standards.

13. They can inform and improve one's teaching.

14. They are both visual and graphic which appeals to multiple learning styles.

15. They provide quality alternatives to other assessment measures and make excellent artifacts for portfolios.

10 Benefits of Self-Evaluation For Students

Self-evaluation:

1. Places the assessment burden on the individual.

2. Answers students' two most basic questions: "How am I doing?" and "Where do I go from here?"

3. Provides the basis for agreement between student and teacher on academic priorities.

4. Improves effectiveness, as opposed to efficiency, in the schooling process.

5. Encourages objective analysis of one's own attitudes and aptitudes.

6. Relates progress to performance by answering such questions as "Are we doing the right things?" and "Are we doing the right things right?"

7. Assists in preparation for added growth and responsibility.

8. Promotes a feeling of personal accomplishment.

9. Encourages individual goal setting.

10. Acknowledges differences in learning styles.

Generic Rubric Assessment Form

Directions: Use this form to plan and construct a rubric for an assessment task.

DESCRIPTION OF TASK, PRODUCT, OR PERFORMANCE

_____

_____

_____

_____

_____

KEY ELEMENTS OF TASK, PRODUCT, OR PERFORMANCE

_____

_____

_____

_____

_____

CRITERIA FOR JUDGING SUCCESS OF IDENTIFIED KEY ELEMENTS

_____

_____

_____

_____

_____

_____

Next page for scoring

SCORING GUIDE FOR JUDGING CRITERIA EFFECTIVENESS

STRONG

_____

_____

_____

_____

SATISFACTORY

_____

_____

_____

_____

NEEDS SOME IMPROVEMENT

_____

_____

_____

_____

NEEDS CONSIDERABLE IMPROVEMENT

_____

_____

_____

_____

NOT ACCEPTABLE

_____

_____

_____

_____

Teacher/Student Conference Form

Use this form in duplicate to record the important points that were discussed at the conference. One copy is for the teacher and one copy is for the student.

STUDENT NAME: _____ **Date:** _____

Purpose of Conference

_____

_____

Items Discussed

_____

_____

_____

Student Reaction and Follow-up

_____

_____

_____

_____

_____

Teacher Reaction and Follow-up

_____

_____

_____

_____

_____

Date and Plans for Next Conference

_____

_____

Student Self-Assessment Checklist

DIRECTIONS: Use this form to record the individual tasks you do on a daily basis to complete an assignment.

STUDENT NAME: _____ **Date:** _____

Assigned Task *(Please describe)*

_____

_____

_____

Things I have Done	Yes	No
1. _____		
2. _____		
3. _____		
4. _____		
5. _____		
6. _____		
7. _____		
8. _____		
9. _____		
10. _____		

Observation Checklist Form

Use this form as a guide for observing individual or small groups of students in a specific learning situation or behavior setting.

LEARNING SITUATION/SETTING _____

DATE _____ **SUBJECT/CLASS** _____

Student Observed	Skill Observed	Times Observed	Comment
1.			
2.			
3.			
4.			
5.			
6.			
7.			
8.			
9.			
10.			

Peer Editing Review Form

Work with a peer partner to review your work. Ask your partner to use this form for critiquing your work.

TITLE OF WORK _____

TYPE OF WORK _____

1. The part of this piece I like best is . . .

   _____

   _____

   _____

2. A part of this piece that is not clear and that is confusing to me is . . .

   _____

   _____

   _____

3. A suggestion I have for improving this piece is . . .

   _____

   _____

   _____

4. Some other things you might want to change are . . .

   _____

   _____

   _____

5. To me, the strength of this piece is . . .

   _____

   _____

   _____

Created By _____ Reviewed By _____

Group Presentation Rating Scale

Use the rating scale to evaluate your contribution and that of your peers to the group presentation.

1 Not Acceptable   2 Somewhat Acceptable   3 Acceptable

4 Mostly Acceptable   5 Completely Acceptable

	Self Evaluation	Peer Evaluation
1. creativity of ideas		
2. Quality of content		
3. Organization of information		
4. Attention to detail		
5. Enthusiasm for topic		
6. Use of visuals and props		
7. Appropriate speech and body language		
8. Technical skill and expertise		
9. Value and interest of audience		
10. Overall performance		

10 PLUS 10

Reflective Questions To Use With Students

1. Tell me about this piece of work.

2. How did you begin this task?

3. How did you plan this project?

4. What did you want to happen as a result of this idea?

5. What evidence do you have to support the notion that this work is the best you can do?

6. What would you do differently next time?

7. How would you describe this project to another student?

8. What questions or concerns about your work do you want to discuss today?

9. Was the work on this task satisfying to you and why or why not?

10. What is something you can do now that you could not do as well before?

11. What can I learn about you from this piece of work?

12. What is something you want people to notice about this project?

13. Do you feel that this product reflects your abilities?

14. I wonder what else you might want to say about . . . ?

15. How pleased are you about . . . ?

16. I am not clear what you mean by . . . Could you give me an example?

17. Why do you think . . . ?

18. How would you go about improving . . . ?

19. What advice would you give somebody who wanted to replicate your work?

20. What did you most enjoy (or least enjoy) about this assignment?

10 Questions Students Need To Have Answered Before A Test

Questions:

1. Is this going to be a quiz, test, or exam?

2. What type of quiz/test/exam will it be?
(Take-home, oral, collaborative, individual, or open book?)

3. What kind of questions will it have?
(Multiple choice, essay, fill-in-the-blank, true/false, or short answer?)

4. How much time will I be given to complete the quiz/test/exam?

5. How long will it be? How many questions will it have?

6. What information will be covered?
(Notes, textbook, lecture, outside readings, discussions?)

7. Do the answers have to be written in complete sentences, and will spelling count?

8. Can I hand in the test as soon as I finish?

9. How can I best review for the quiz/test/exam?

10. How will the test be graded or scored?

10 Ways Students Can Use Test Time Wisely

1. Read through the entire test before you begin writing the answers.

2. Budget your time by setting time limits for each section of the test.

3. Complete all questions for which you know the answers first. Then go back and work on questions of which you are not as certain.

4. Underline or circle key words and phrases in each set of directions on the test.

5. Use intelligent guessing strategies for those questions you do not know. Try not to leave any questions unanswered unless there are penalties for making a "best guess."

6. Never go back and change an answer unless you are absolutely sure you made a mistake.

7. Allow a few minutes at the end of the test to go back and review all questions and answers.

8. Be sure your name is on each page of the test.

9. Do not worry about what other students are doing on the test or how they are pacing their time.

10. If you had to transpose answers from one place to another on the test or answer sheet, double check to make sure you were not careless in doing so.

10 PLUS 1

Ways to Prepare Middle Level Students for Taking Essay Tests

1. Define the concept of "essay test" for students and discuss how it differs from other types of test questions and formats.

2. Give examples of various question types including multiple choice, matching, short answer, true/false, and essay questions. Examine the strategies used by students when answering each type of question.

3. Point out the benefits and challenges of taking essay tests over other types of more traditional tests.

4. Review the process for taking an essay test with students emphasizing what constitutes good writing for essay questions.

5. Provide students with multiple examples of essay questions from past years along with student responses that were both satisfactory and unsatisfactory as models for what to do and what not to do.

6. Encourage students to develop their own essay type questions on a given topic and then write possible responses to their own student-generated efforts. Critique student responses and have them rewrite their question accordingly.

7. Show students how essay questions are related to the required student performance standards for the language arts or English curriculum in the school.

8. As a group, make a list of guidelines to "do's and don'ts" for writing quality responses to essay questions. Impress upon students how correct grammar principles, spelling, and readable handwriting can influence the grade given to essay question responses.

9. Consider giving extra points or extra credit to students who voluntarily elect to rewrite unacceptable or inadequate responses to essay questions on a given test or exam.

10. Begin the process of administering essay tests to students on either open book-tests or take-home tests when students have more time and some study aids to help with the writing of responses.

11. Provide students with copies of the Essay Direction Words charts on the following pages to use as helpful tools during essay tests situations.

 **Plus 21 Essay Direction Words**

IF YOU ARE ASKED TO:	YOU SHOULD DO THE FOLLOWING:	EXAMPLES:
Analyze	Break down or separate a problem or situation into separate factors and/or relationships. Draw a conclusion, make a judgment, or make clear the relationship you see based on your breakdown.	Analyze the main story line in Chapter 2 and tell how it sets the stage for Chapter 3.
Categorize	Place items under headings already labeled by your teacher.	Categorize the items on the left under the proper headings on the right.
Classify	Place items in related groups; then name or title each group.	Listed below are 20 items. Classify them in 4 main groups; then name each group.
Compare	Tell how things are alike; use concrete examples.	Compare the American government system with that of the German government.
Contrast	Tell how things are different; use supporting concrete examples.	Contrast the writing styles of Shakespeare and Bacon.
Criticize	Make a judgment of a work of art or literature and support your judgment.	What do you think about the end of Shakespeare's tragedy, *Romeo and Juliet*? Explain your answer.
Deduce	Trace the course; derive a conclusion by reasoning.	Deduce the following logic problem to arrive at one of the conclusions listed below . . .
Defend	Give enough details to prove the statement.	Defend the statement "innocent until proven guilty."
Define	Give the meaning.	Define the word *plankton*.
Describe	Give an account in words; trace the outline or present a picture.	Describe Grand Coulee Dam.

IF YOU ARE ASKED TO:	YOU SHOULD DO THE FOLLOWING:	EXAMPLES:
Diagram	Use pictures, graphs, charts, mind maps and flowcharts to show relationships of details to main ideas.	Diagram the offices of the federal government.
Discuss	Consider the various points of view by presenting all sides of the issue.	Discuss the use of chemotherapy in the treatment of cancer.
Distinguish	Tell how this is different from others similar to it.	Distinguish the three types of mold we have studied in class.
Enumerate	List all possible items.	Enumerate the presidents of the United States since Abraham Lincoln.
Evaluate	Make a judgment based on the evidence and support it; present the good and bad points.	Evaluate the use of pesticides.
Explain	Make clear and plain; give the reason or cause.	Explain how a natural disaster can help man.
Illustrate	Give examples, pictures, charts, diagrams or concrete examples to clarify your answer.	Illustrate the use of a drawbridge.
Interpret	Express your thinking by giving the meaning as you see it.	Interpret the line "Water, water everywhere and not a drop to drink."
Justify	Give some evidence by supporting your statement with facts.	Justify the decision to bomb Nagasaki, Japan.
List	Write in a numbered fashion.	List 5 reasons to support your statement.
Outline	Use a specific and shortened form to organize main ideas supporting details and examples.	Outline the leading cause of World War II.

IF YOU ARE ASKED TO:	YOU SHOULD DO THE FOLLOWING:	EXAMPLES:
Paraphrase	Put in your own words.	Paraphrase the first paragraph of the Gettysburg Address.
Predict	Present solutions that could happen if certain variables were present.	Predict the ending of the short story written below . . .
Prove	Provide factual evidence to back up the truth of a statement.	Prove that the whaling industry has caused the near-extinction of certain varieties of whales.
Relate	Show the relationship among concepts.	Relate man's survival instincts to those of animals.
Review	Examine the information critically. Analyze and comment on the important statements.	Review the effects of television advertisements on the public.
State	Establish by specifying. Write what you believe and back it with evidence.	State your beliefs in the democratic system of government.
Summarize	Condense the main points in the fewest words possible.	Summarize early man's methods of self-defense.
Synthesize	Combine parts or pieces of an idea, situation or event.	Synthesize the events leading to the Civil War.
Trace	Describe in steps the progression of something.	Trace the importance of the prairie schooner to the opening of the West.
Verify	Confirm or establish the truth of accuracy of point of view with supporting examples, evidence and facts.	Verify the reasons for the writing of the Declaration of Independence.

 **PLUS 2**

Informal Methods Of Assessing Student Understanding Of Material Covered During Instruction

1. IN BASKET

Ask each student to write at least one good question on a 3" x 5" file card about a key topic or set of concepts previously taught in class. Place each of these cards in a box or envelope and randomly select one card at a time to read aloud to the class. Students volunteer to respond to the questions presented and earn "points" for each correct answer. Students may gain additional points for embellishing or adding to someone else's response as well. Several of these student-generated questions could be used on a test to be given at a later date.

2. GROUP PROFILE

Distribute one file card to each student and have each record a number from 1 to 10 that best describes how well he or she understands ideas recently taught during a lecture, discussion, textbook reading assignment, videotape, homework task, etc. Provide students with at least three benchmarks on the rating scale to use in making their decisions. For example, one continuum might look like this:

| 1 | 2 | 3 | 4 | 5 | 6 | 7 | 8 | 9 | 10 |

1 = I don't understand much of anything I read or heard.

5 = I understand about half of the ideas presented.

10 = I understand the material well enough to take a test on it or to teach it to someone else.

Collect the file cards (no names on them, please) and record all responses on the board, a transparency, or a piece of chart paper. Use this to determine the percentage of the class that has knowledge of the material that was assigned or taught.

3. SMALL GROUP CONSENSUS REPORT

Divide students into small groups of three or four. Instruct them to reach consensus on the five most important facts they have learned and should remember from the day's lecture, discussion, or assigned reading. Have each group write responses on a large piece of newsprint and post around the room for all to see. Ask each group's recorder to share his or her small group's responses and justify its choice of five facts.

Look for similar responses from each group and reach a large-group consensus on the most important information recorded on the charts. Have students copy these in their notebooks to study for a test at a later date.

4. PICTURE CARDS

Provide each student or small group of students with a duplicate set of Picture/Symbol Cards that you have prepared in advance. Picture/Symbol Cards can be made by drawing, pasting, or printing a series of individual pictures or symbols on 3" x 5" cards or sections of card stock. Possible pictures or symbols for this activity might include: a heart, eagle, dollar sign, hourglass, flag, globe, light bulb, bell, star, firecracker, etc.

Have students select one or more picture/symbol cards from the group and use them as springboards or catalysts for use in expressing feelings or emotions in any given area. This works well in getting students to use analogies when making informal judgments about people, places, or things. For example, one might instruct the students to select a picture/symbol card from the group that represents their feelings about a recent court decision, about an editorial from the newspaper, about a historical event from the textbook, or about an incident from a novel.

5. STUDENT PANEL

Divide students into small groups and have them generate a list of tasks in school that they find difficult to do and a list of tasks they find easy to do. Have them graph the results of their brainstorming. Share graphs with the entire class. Next, choose a task with which many students have difficulty. Form a panel of students from the class who felt the task was easy for them and use this group to share concrete ideas about how they mastered this task. Allow time for the class to ask questions of this "panel of experts."

6. CONVINCE THE PANEL OF EXPERTS

Each student is instructed to prepare for class one well-written summary paragraph stating his or her position or collection of facts on a key concept, issue, idea, problem, or situation related to a given unit of study. Each person reads or shares the paragraph with a panel of "student experts" (three selected class members).

The panel "rates" the information on prepared flashcards (1–10, with 10 being high). The teacher tabulates each total and announces the "best performances" at the end of the time period.

This activity should be followed with a large-group discussion using such questions as:

a. How many students gained at least one new idea or perspective today?

b. Did this process spark any additional ideas in your minds?

c. What criteria were used by the "panel of experts" to judge the summary paragraphs?

d. How could we help each other on our presentations so that all would receive 10s?

7. CAKE WALK

Prior to this activity, write ten important questions about a topic being studied in the classroom. These questions are written on a blackboard, transparency, or large piece of chart paper so they are visible to everyone in the room.

Students then form two concentric circles in which each person of the outer circle faces another person of the inner circle to form pairs. Instruct the students in each group to move counter to one another while background music is being played. When the music stops, the students also stop moving, still facing one another. They then have two minutes to discuss the answer to the first question on the board, overhead, or chart paper.

When the music starts again, the students move again until the music stops and they are facing a new partner. This time they are to discuss the answer to the second question given. The process is repeated until all ten questions have been addressed. This makes an excellent review activity at the end of a unit of study.

8. EQUATION QUIZ

The teacher prepares a series of equations that represent a variety of important concepts being studied as part of an instructional unit. Students are given the equations and asked to use their notes, textbooks, or worksheets to figure them out. If time permits, students should also be given the opportunity to create their own equations representing information that they think is important. Examples of equations for several content areas are given below.

Math Examples

2000 = P. in a T.	(2000 = Pounds in a Ton)
90 = D in an R. T.	(90 = Degrees in a Right Triangle)
23 Y. – 3 Y. = 2 D.	(23 Years minus 3 Years = 2 Decades)
32 = D. F. at which W. F.	(32 = Degrees Fahrenheit at which Water Freezes)

Social Studies Examples

T. = L. S. State	(Texas = Lone Star State)
7 = W. of the A. W.	(7 = Wonders of the Ancient World)
M. + M. + N.H. + V. + C. + R.I. = N.E.	(Maine + Maryland + New Hampshire + Vermont + Connecticut + Rhode Island = New England)
S. + H. of R. = U.S. C.	(Senate + House of Representatives = United States Congress)

9. RESPONSE CARDS

Provide each student with a set of color-coded feedback cards. One set of cards should have the word *True* on one card and the word *False* on another. A second set of cards should have 'A' on one card, 'B' on a second card, 'C' on a third card, 'D' on a fourth card, and 'E' on a fifth card.

Inform the class that the cards will be used to provide the teacher with feedback in response to his or her questions. The teacher then proceeds to make a series of True/False statements, and the entire class should hold up the appropriate alphabet card signifying their best response to the choice offered.

Variations of this activity include using other card options, such as sets of blank cards on which students should write responses to short-answer questions, or alphabet cards for matching questions.

10. ALPHABET REPORTS

Students are given a piece of paper with the 26 letters of the alphabet printed vertically down one side. They are directed to select 26 related concepts, terms, events, or persons that show what they have learned about a given topic. Each item should begin with a different letter of the alphabet and students should be encouraged to think of more than one word for each letter as they record their ideas. Next, students should try creating meaningful phrases with each cluster of words recorded next to the appropriate letter of the alphabet so that the reading of the report flows like a free verse poem.

11. CONCEPT PUZZLES

Students are instructed to select the most important terms, concepts, or ideas associated with a textbook chapter or teaching unit. They are to develop brief definitions or identifying phrases for each, as well. Next, students are told to construct a crossword puzzle that incorporates each of the items and to fill in the appropriate numbers, crossword-puzzle style. These can be exchanged among peers to "test" one another on their understanding of information taught.

12. BINGO BONANZA

Students are directed to generate a set of 25 questions and answers that are important to their understanding of a completed textbook chapter, lecture, assigned reading, or instructional unit. The questions should be organized or sorted into five major categories, and students should create some identity for each category name using the letters B, I, N, G, and O. Next, BINGO cards should be designed according to one of these formats:

(A) Generic cards (like traditional BINGO cards) using a 5" x 5" matrix with numbers in the 24 designated cells and the FREE spot designated in the center. In this case, the teacher reads a question with an associated number, and if the student has the number and can correctly write in the answer, he or she fills in the appropriate cell.

(B) Specific cards with the cells previously filled in using 24 of the key concepts, ideas, terms, etc. If the student believes that one of the answers on the card fits the question being read, he or she writes the question number next to it. As in BINGO, the first student to complete the answers in a row horizontally, vertically, or diagonally calls out BINGO and wins the game!

10 PLUS 15

Assessment Tips, Tools, and Test Formats

1. Use oral and open-book tests. Have students demonstrate reference and research-location skills while taking an open-book test and then share their knowledge through an oral quiz. Oral exercises are more accurate and less threatening than paper and pencil tests.

2. Provide opportunities for students to test one another and grade the results. Kids are fair and teachers have fewer papers to grade.

3. Encourage students to write and submit test questions for an upcoming exam. This serves as an excellent review technique.

4. Show students how to solve problems through a wide variety of techniques which include:
   . . . Looking for patterns
   . . . Constructing a table
   . . . Making an organized list
   . . . Guessing and then checking
   . . . Drawing a picture or diagram
   . . . Using objects or acting the scenario out
   . . . Working backwards from end to beginning
   . . . Writing an equation in words, symbols, or numbers
   . . . Simplifying the problem by breaking it down into component parts
   . . . Changing one's point of view or perspective

5. Offer teacher-made percent tickets worth from 1% to 5%. A percent ticket is a document worth percentage points for tests, essays, or reports. Students earn tickets for good behavior or good work and then can turn them in to raise a grade on an assignment.

6. Create a legitimate "test-type" paper and pencil question sheet to serve as a review for an upcoming classroom quiz or test. After each question, write down the page number in the textbook where its answer can be found if the student does not know it.

7. Design an Alphabet Test that requires students to write down key words, concepts, definitions, names, or other relevant information for each letter of the alphabet. They may write down more than one item for each letter and receive points for each correct response.

8. Write a series of open-ended test items that require the student to apply critical thinking skills. For example, select a topic and instruct the students to do on of the following analytical tasks: Compare and contrast; Give pros and cons; State advantages and disadvantages; think of causes and effects.

9. Require students to maintain scrapbooks of all their work assignments for a given unit of study. Students glue their worksheets, homework, quizzes, reports, etc. in the scrapbook as they are assigned/graded and then use these items for review at the end of the unit.

10. When reviewing for a test, provide the students with a series of topics related to a unit of study. Students, one at a time, draw a topic out of a hat and give a one-minute speech on all they know about it. Pass out the topic slips of paper at the beginning of class so that students have some time to think and plan their impromptu speeches.

11. For fun and variety, prepare a set of cards (like a deck of playing cards) that equals the number of students in the class. On most of the cards write the words *REGULAR ASSIGNMENT*. On a few cards write the words *FREE ASSIGNMENT*, *MODIFIED ASSIGNMENT*, or *EXTRA ASSIGNMENT.* Students randomly draw a card from the deck and do their work accordingly. Kids either do the regular assignment, a reduced assignment, an extra assignment, or do not have to do the assignment at all.

12. On every test, allow students to argue for any two questions they missed/ answered incorrectly. In order to win the argument, the student must write a detailed explanation supporting his/her answer from his/her perspective. All or partial credit can be given to the question if the argument is logical and convincing to the teacher. This strategy is helpful because students perceive it as fair, as an opportunity to control or raise a grade, and as an invitation to go back and review the material.

13. Divide students into pairs and give each pair of students three chairs for their group, placed side by side. All sets of chairs are placed in a circle around the room. The first set of chairs (Group 1 chairs) is the only cluster that has someone sitting in all three chairs. The teacher prepares a set of test review questions and asks the first question to Group 1. The first student to blurt out the answer moves to empty chair in Group 2. The teacher then asks a question of Group 2 and the first person to blurt out the correct answer moves to the empty chair in Group 3. The process is continued and the first person to get back to their original group chair wins the game.

14. Instead of an honor roll for a classroom setting, why not instigate a PROGRESS ROLL that records names of students who are honor students and also those who are making progress in a given academic area.

15. Solicit lecture or hand-written discussion/textbook notes from good students in the class and, with their permission, copy and distribute these notes to others in the class who need or want them. Reward these special note-takers with rewards such as coupons for free time, extra library time, more computer time, or a pass on an upcoming test/assignment.

16. Once or twice a year, allow each student to be excused from taking a quiz or test at a given time as long as he/she provides the teacher with documentation as to why he/she is not able to take the test and what he/she will do in place of the test. Completing the Test Substitute Form gives the student something constructive to do while the class is taking the test and it gives the teacher an indication of what the student will do to fill the place where the test mark would be.

17. Give students a prorated test of about twenty questions that requires all students to answer the first ten questions, then gives the option of answering additional questions from the remaining ten. Inform students that they can stop after ten, answer one or more of the optional questions (in any sequence), or complete all twenty. Students are given extra points for the optional questions if they are answered correctly, but if answered incorrectly, extra points are taken away.

18. Design a simple quiz on a topic being studied that asks the student to (a) write a fact about the topic; (b) state an opinion about the topic; (c) give an example related to the topic; (d) draw a conclusion about the topic; (e) make an inference about the topic; (f) issue a judgment on the topic; and (g) compose a summary statement on the topic.

19. Design a single test question on a topic of study that requires the student to record only his or her LEARNINGS: WHAT I AM TAKING AWAY FROM THIS STUDY.

20. Prepare a set of review questions and use them to simulate the tic-tac-toe game show format of Hollywood Squares. Arrange students so that three sit on the floor, three sit on chairs, and three stand behind the chairs. All nine "celebrities" are given cards with a big X printed on one side and a big O printed on the other side. Two volunteers serve as contestants (designated as either an X or an O) and pick members of the celebrity squares to answer the game's questions read by the teacher. Celebrities answer the questions and contestants either AGREE or DISAGREE with their responses. Contestants try to form a tic-tac-toe through this process.

21. Divide students into groups or teams of equal number. Provide each team with a short set of review questions and have them answer the set of questions individually. After the questions have been given and individual responses written down, provide team members with the correct answers. Group members pool their scores and get ready for Round Two of the game. The team with the most points at the end of several rounds wins the Learning Tournament.

22. Prepare a set of 5 x 8 file cards so that one half of the card has a question and the other half of the card has the correct answer or answers. Cut the cards in half and randomly distribute them to members of a class. Ask students to mingle around the room and match up the correct question with its corresponding answer(s).

23. Prepare a set of statements about a topic under study (some of which are facts, some of which are opinions, some of which are true, and some of which are false). Write these on large cards and have students determine the answers through discussion and debate.

24. Provide each student in the class with a file card and have them write out a question (to which they know the answer) on the topic being reviewed for a test. Collect cards and then randomly redistribute them to students. Ask each student to read the question and attempt to answer it as best they can. Require the question's author to certify whether the question has been answered adequately or not.

25. Divide students into small cooperative learning groups and have each group create a one-minute commercial that tells the others all about something important, interesting, or controversial that they have learned about a topic studied in class.

1. FINDING:

Robin Fogarty states: Traditional assessment often focuses on grades, grade point averages, and rankings. Included in traditional assessments are class work, homework, and criterion-referenced and standardized measures. In this situation, teachers teach and test students. Typically, traditional assessments tap primarily the verbal/linguistic and the logical/mathematical intelligences, although the visual/spatial may also be included.

Portfolio assessment tends to focus on the growth and development of student potential. Phases of the portfolio development process include collecting and selecting items, reflecting on the significance of the items as indicators of growth, and inspecting the portfolio for signs of progress. In this situation, students take some control of assessment. Students get the opportunity to "show" teachers what they learned. Often, portfolio development calls into play the intrapersonal and interpersonal intelligences as well as the verbal, logical, visual, and naturalist intelligences used in the traditional measures.

Performance assessment focuses on the direct observance of a student's performance. Procedures for using performance assessment effectively include developing scoring rubrics and using predetermined standards, criteria, and indicators. Performance assessment also allows students to take some control of assessment. Students get to "do" what they learned. With this assessment, the bodily intelligence becomes a vehicle for showing what a student knows and can do. The visual, verbal, logical, musical, interpersonal, and naturalist intelligences are also critical components.

SOURCE: Fogarty, R. (1998). Balanced assessment. Arlington Heights, IL: Skylight Publications, Inc. 7 & 8.

2. FINDING:

National Education Association states: A wide variety of methods are available to teachers for assessing student learning. Regardless of the particular methods employed, effective classroom assessment is guided by three fundamental principles.

Classroom assessment should: (1) promote learning; (2) use multiple sources of information; and (3) provide fair, valid, and reliable information.

The first principle is based upon the premise that the primary purpose of classroom assessment is to inform teaching and improve learning. This premise suggests that classroom assessment be viewed as an ongoing process instead of a single event at the conclusion of instruction. Rather than waiting until the end of a unit of study or course to assess students, effective teachers employ formative assessments at the beginning of instruction to determine students' prior knowledge. They assess regularly throughout the unit or course of study to obtain information to help them adjust their teaching based on the learning needs of students.

A second principle of sound classroom assessment calls for a synthesis of information from several sources. The classroom context offers a distinct advantage over large-scale assessments in that it allows teachers to take frequent samplings of student learning using an array of methods. Applying the principle of multiple sources is especially important when the assessment information is used as a basis for important summative decisions, such as assigning report grades or determining promotion.

A third principle of classroom assessment concerns validity, reliability, and fairness. Validity has to do with whether an assessment measures what it was intended to measure. Reliability refers to the dependability and consistency of assessment results. Fairness in classroom assessment refers to giving all students an equal chance to show what they know and can do. Fairness is compromised when teachers assess something that has not been taught or use assessment methods that are incongruent with instruction.

SOURCE: McTighe, J. & Ferrara, S. (1994). Assessing learning in the classroom. Washington, DC: National Education Association. 7-9.

3. **FINDING:**
Laura P. Stowell and Janet E. McDaniel conclude: Students have been encouraged to take part in their own assessment and are now being asked to take part in sharing the information as well. Reflecting on one's performance can be a powerful learning experience as proved by portfolios. Young adolescents have sufficient metacognitive ability to realize what they do and do not understand. They also are more aware of their own perspectives when confronted with different perspectives; therefore, student-led conferences can offer a powerful learning experience, as well as demonstrate to the student that his or her voice is valued in the assessment process. Successful student-led conferences require a great deal of preparation on the part of students and teacher. Class meetings, journals, conferences with peers, self-evaluations, and portfolios can be used with students to prepare. Schools which have implemented student-led conferences found that students felt more ownership of their work, were less interested in teacher approval and more

interested in the pride derived from their own work, felt more accountable for their behavior and academic work, gave teachers feedback on their work, and even began to devise strategies for improvement during the conference.

SOURCE: Stowell, L. P. & McDaniel, J. E. (1997). The changing face of assessment. Irvin, J. L. (Ed.). What Current Research Says to the Middle Level Practitioner. Columbus, OH: National Middle School Association. 145-146.

4. FINDING:

Elliott summarizes: Assessments that work best for accountability (and other large-scale applications such as program evaluation) lend themselves to standardized administration in a relatively short amount of time; they can be scored quickly and reliably for relatively low cost. The most efficient large-scale assessment methodology is multiple choice. But as we have seen, multiple-choice tests for large-scale assessments, particularly when high stakes are involved, has had a negative effect on instruction. On the other hand, trying to incorporate more instructional-friendly assessments (e.g., performance tasks or portfolios) into large-scale efforts has proven quite difficult because of the costs in time and money and the technical issues involved. The most meaningful information for informing instruction and providing explicit feedback to students is collected daily by teachers working with students. And yet, although a teacher's view is most valued when parents want feedback on their own children's progress, large-scale assessment is valued when examining the performance of states, districts, schools, or teachers. If we are to have any hope of accomplishing our assessment goals, large-scale and classroom assessment must be meaningfully linked.

SOURCE: Asp, E. (2000). Assessment in education: Where have we been? Where are we headed? Brandt, R. S. (Ed.). Education in a New Era. Alexandria, VA: Association for Supervision and Curriculum Development. 147-148.

5. FINDING:

Grant P. Wiggins emphasizes: I would prefer that school systems develop an Assessment Bill of Rights to protect the inherently vulnerable student from the harms that testing easily leads to. It would be supported by explicit audit or oversight policies to ensure that the rights were protected. Here is my rough draft of such a set of rights: All students are entitled to the following:

(1) Worthwhile (engaging, educative, and authentic) intellectual problems that are validated against worthy "real-world" intellectual problems, roles, and situations

(2) Clear, apt, published, and consistently applied teacher criteria in grading work and published models of excellent work that exemplifies standards

(3) Minimal secrecy in testing and grading

(4) Ample opportunities to produce work that they can be proud of (thus, ample opportunity in the curriculum and instruction to monitor, self-assess, and self-correct their work)

(5) Assessment, not just tests; multiple and varied opportunities to display and document their achievement, and options in tests that allow them to play to their strengths.

(6) The freedom, climate, and oversight policies necessary to question grades and test practices without fear of retribution

(7) Forms of testing that allow timely opportunities for students to explain or justify answers marked as wrong but that they believe to be apt or right

(8) Genuine feedback: usable information on their strengths and weaknesses and an accurate assessment of their long-term progress toward a set of exit-level standards framed in terms of essential tasks

(9) Scoring/grading policies that provide incentives and opportunities for improving performance and seeing progress against exit-level and real-world standards.

SOURCE: Wiggins, G. P. (1993). Assessing student performance. San Francisco, CA: Jossey-Bass Publishers. 27-28.

6. FINDING:

Kay Burke says: Assessment is the ongoing process of "gathering and analyzing" evidence of what a student can do. Evaluation is the process of "interpreting" the evidence and "making judgments" and decisions based on the evidence. If the assessment is not sound, the evaluation will not be sound. In most classrooms, teachers assess a student on the basis of observations, oral conversations, and written work. They make instructional decisions based on these assessments. If the assessment is ongoing and frequent, changes can be made immediately to help the student achieve the desired outcome. If the assessment is flawed, the final evaluation will be based upon invalid and unreliable data. The quality of the final evaluation is only as valid as the ongoing assessment data upon which it is based.

SOURCE: Burke, K. (1999). How to assess authentic learning. Arlington, Heights, IL: Skylight Publications. xviii.

7. FINDING:

Wiggins, Grant & Jay McTighe conclude: Understanding . . . involves sophisticated insights and abilities, reflected in varied performances and contexts . . . We also suggest that different kinds of understandings exist, that knowledge and skill do not automatically lead to understanding, that misunderstanding is a bigger problem than we realize, and that assessment of understanding therefore requires evidence that cannot be gained from traditional testing alone. There are six facets to describe the levels of understanding. When students truly understand, they:

(1) Can "explain": provide thorough, supported, and justifiable accounts of phenomena, facts, and data.

(2) Can "interpret": tell meaningful stories; offer apt translations; and events; make it personal or accessible through images, anecdotes, analogies, and models.

(3) Can "apply": effectively use and adapt what we know in diverse contexts.

(4) Have "perspective": see and hear points of view through critical eyes and ears; see the big picture.

(5) Can "emphasize": find value in what others might find odd, alien, or implausible; perceive sensitively on the basis of prior direct experience.

(6) Have "self-knowledge": perceive the personal style, prejudices, projections, and habits of mind that both shape and impede our own understanding; we are aware of what we do not understand and why understanding is so hard.

SOURCE: Wiggins, G. & McTighe, J. (1998). Understanding by design. Alexandria, VA. Association for Supervision and Curriculum Development. 5, 44.

8. FINDING:

Heidi Hayes Jacobs stresses: We need to change the process used in making curriculum decisions because most curriculum committees are ineffective at actually producing work that directly affects student performance. Curriculum committees usually come together to formulate lists of objectives, skills, and concepts that are optimum goals for teachers to implement. Occasionally these lists inspire and focus teachers' actions, but too often they remain nothing more than lifeless inventories of isolated skills. The lists may discuss 1st grade writing skills or 3rd grade reading skills, but they offer little or no focus on precisely when specific skills will be addressed during the course of a school year, let alone a group of school years. Without a commitment to when a skill will be taught, there is no commitment. Furthermore, skills are not taught in a vacuum. They are addressed in application to content, and the learner evidences them in a product or performance. In short, though committees anguish over the skill list, most end up with the feeling that it is not a useful document. As one teacher put it, "There is a sense of let's get through this, because they're making us."

SOURCE: Jacobs, H. H. (1997). Mapping the big picture: Integrating curriculum and assessment, K-12. Alexandria, VA: Association for Supervision and Curriculum Development. 4.

9. FINDING:

Phillip Schlechty writes: Ten critical qualities of student work should be:

(1) PRODUCT FOCUS: Work that engages students almost always focuses on a product or performance of significance to students.

(2) CLEAR AND COMPELLING STANDARDS: Students prefer knowing exactly what is expected of them, and how those expectations relate to something they care about. Standards are only relevant when those to whom they apply care about them.

(3) PROTECTION FROM ADVERSE CONSEQUENCES FOR INITIAL FAILURES: Students are more engaged when they can try tasks without fear of embarrassment, punishment, or implications that they are inadequate.

(4) AFFIRMATION OF THE SIGNIFICANCE OF PERFORMANCE: Students are more highly motivated when their parents, teachers, fellow students, and "significant others" make it known that they think the student's work is important. Portfolio assessments can play a significant role in making student work "more visible."

(5) AFFILIATION: Students are more likely to be engaged by work that permits, encourages, and supports opportunities for them to work interdependently with others.

(6) NOVELTY AND VARIETY: Students are more likely to engage in the work asked of them if they are continually exposed to new and different ways of doing things. New forms of work and new products to produce are as important as new techniques.

(7) CHOICE: When students have some degree of control over what they are doing, they are more likely to feel committed to doing it. Schools, however, must distinguish between giving students choices in what they do and letting them choose what they will learn.

(8) AUTHENTICITY: When students are given tasks that are meaningless, contrived, or inconsequential, they are less likely to take them seriously and to be engaged by them. If the task carries real consequences, it is likely that engagement will increase.

(9) ORGANIZATION OF KNOWLEDGE: Students are more likely to be engaged when information and knowledge are arranged in clear, accessible ways, and in ways that let students use the knowledge and information to address tasks that are important to them. Content should be organized so access to the material is clear and relatively easy, and the students' work has enough attractive qualities to keep them engaged.

(10) CONTENT AND SUBSTANCE: Educators should commit themselves to inventing work that engages all students and helps them attain rich and profound knowledge.

SOURCE: Schlechty, P. (1998, Summer). Ten critical qualities of student work. Journal of Staff Development, National Staff Development Council, Oxford, OH. 42.

10. FINDING:

Scott G. Paris and Linda R. Ayres argue: Achievement testing, even when done with the best of intentions, may undermine self-regulated learning because:

(1) Neither teachers nor students have many choices about the tests they take, when they take them, or how the results are used.

(2) Standardized testing, grading on the curve, and normative comparisons of performance inhibit risk taking and optimism because half of the population will always score below the average.

(3) Most traditional achievement tests do not allow students to control the pace of administration and do not depend on the self-controlled learning strategies that they use on a daily basis to seek and clarify information.

(4) Testing is solitary and competitive, which prohibits help seeking and collaborative learning and contradicts many instructional practices.

(5) Traditional achievement tests inhibit appropriate text comprehension because (a) the passages are often brief, contrived, and decontextualized; (b) the multiple-choice format restricts opportunities to express constructed meaning adequately; (c) the test format fosters strategies of searching for answers in text rather than reading the text for meaning.

(6) The consequences of standardized testing may be devastating for many students because the costs of increased anxiety and self-doubt outweigh any individual diagnostic help provided by the test results.

(7) Traditional tests do not assess students' awareness of their own learning processes and do not provide opportunities for students to use the metacognitive strategies that teachers emphasize on a daily basis.

SOURCE: Paris, S. G. & Ayres, L. R. (1994). Becoming reflective students and teachers with portfolios and authentic assessment. Washington, DC: American Psychological Association. 41.

Assessment Teacher's Wrap-Up, à la Bloom

KNOWLEDGE:
Recall three to five important definitions important to understanding assessment. State their implications for measuring student achievement.

COMPREHENSION:
Summarize the important concepts associated with product, performance, and portfolio assessment.

APPLICATION:
Construct a set of true/false, matching, sentence completion, and essay questions related to authentic assessment.

ANALYSIS:
Compare and contrast the advantages and disadvantage of teacher made tests, standardized tests, and student performances as methods for measuring student growth.

SYNTHESIS:
Design plans for conducting a "Test Pep Rally" for your school that could be used before administering important standardized tests to students.

EVALUATION:
Defend or criticize this statement: "Grades have become more important to parents and students than the learning process."

BIBLIOGRAPHY

•

INDEX

•

ASSOCIATION LISTINGS

Bibliography

SCHOOL STRUCTURES AND CLIMATE

Arnold, J. & Stevenson, C. *Teachers' teaming handbook: A middle level planning guide.* Orlando, FL: Harcourt Brace College Publishers 1998.

Beane, J. *Middle schools under Siege: Points of attack.* Middle School Journal 30(4) 1999, March.

Breeden, T., and Egan, E. *Positive Classroom Management.* Nashville, TN: Incentive Publications, 1997.

Classroom Connection. NMSA Volume 4, Number 1. 2001, August.

Jackson, Anthony W. & Davis, Gayle A. *Turning Points 2000, Educating Adolescents in the 21st Century,* Teachers College Press, Teachers College, Columbia University, New York, NY. Copyright 2000.

Conners, N. *If You Don't Feed the Teachers They Eat the Students: Guide to Success for Administrators and Teachers.* Nashville, TN: Incentive Publications, 2000.

Gossen, D.C. Restitution: *Restructuring school discipline.* Chapel Hill, NC: New View Publications. Xv, 1997.

Hackmann, D., & Valentine, J. *Designing an effective middle level school.* Middle School Journal 29(5) 1998, May.

Jackson, Anthony W. & Davis, Gayle A. *Turning Points 2000, Educating Adolescents in the 21st Century,* Teachers College Press, Teachers College, Columbia University, New York, NY. Copyright 2000.

Lipka, R. & others. *The eight-year study revisited: Lessons from the past for the present.* Columbus, OH: National Middle School Association 1998.

"Structuring Schools for Student Success: A Focus on Ability Grouping." The Massachusetts Department of Education, January, 1990.

This we believe: A position paper of National Middle School Association. Columbus, OH: National Middle School Association, 1995.

Thompson, R., & VanderJagt, D. Fire Up For Learning: Active Learning Projects and Activities to Motivate and Challenge Students. Nashville, TN: Incentive Publications, Inc., 2002.

INTERDISCIPLINARY TEAMING AND BLOCK SCHEDULING

Arnold, J. *Teams and curriculum.* In Dickinson, T. S., & Erb, T. O. (Eds.). *We gain more than we give: Teaming in middle schools.* Columbus, OH: National Middle School Association, 1997.

Carr, C. *Teampower: Lessons from America's top companies on putting teampower to work.* Englewood Cliffs, NJ: Prentice Hall, 1992.

Dalheim, M. (Ed.). *It's about time.* TIME Strategies, National Education Association, NEA Special Committee on Time Resources, 9, 1994.

Epstein, J.L. and MacIver, D. J. *Education in the Middle Grades: Overview of National Practices and Trends.* Columbus, OH: National Middle School Association, 1990.

George, P., Stevenson, C., Thomason, J. and Beane, J. *The Middle School—and Beyond.* Alexandria, VA: Association for Supervision and Curriculum Development, 1992.

George, P. S., & Alexander, W. M. *The exemplary middle school.* Orlando, FL: Harcourt Brace Jovanovich College Publishers, 1993.

Hackman, D.G. *Ten guidelines for implementing block scheduling.* Educational Leadership, 24-27. 1995, November.

Harrington-Mackin, D. *The team building tool kit: Tips, tactics, and rule for effective workplace teams.* New York: American Management Association, 1994.

Irvin, J.L. *Transforming Middle Level Education: Perspectives and Possibilities.* Needham Heights, MA: Allyn and Bacon, 1992.

Katzenbach, J. R., & Smith, D. K. *The wisdom of teams.* New York: Harper Collins, 1993.

Lounsbury, J.H., ed. *Connecting the Curriculum Through Interdisciplinary Instruction.* Columbus, OH: National Middle School Association, 1992.

Merenbloom, E.Y. *The Team Process: A Handbook for Teachers.* Columbus, OH: National Middle School Association, 1991.

Ramano, L. G., & Georgiady, N. P. *Building an effective middle school.* Madison, WI: Brown & Benchmark, 1994.

Rettig, M., & Cannizzaro, J. *Block scheduling: An introduction.* Prentice Hall Social Studies Educators Handbook. Upper Saddle River, NJ, 4, 1996.

Thompson, R., & VanderJagt, D. *Wow What a Team: Essential Components for Successful Teaming.* Nashville, TN: Incentive Publications, Inc., 2001.

ADVISORY AND AFFECTIVE EDUCATION

Cole, C. *Nurturing a Teacher Advisory Program.* Columbus, OH: National Middle School Association, 1992.

Forte, I. *The Me I'm Learning to Be.* Nashville, TN: Incentive Publications, 1991.

Forte, I. and Schurr, S. *Advisory: Middle Grades Advisee / Advisor Program.* Nashville, TN: Incentive Publications, Inc., 1992.

Heidel, J., & Lyman-Mersereau, M. *Character Education, Year 1, Grades 6-12.* Nashville, TN: Incentive Publications, Inc., 1999.

Heidel, J., & Lyman-Mersereau, M. *Character Education, Year 2, Grades 6-12.* Nashville, TN: Incentive Publications, Inc., 1999.

COOPERATIVE LEARNING

Breeden, T. and Mosley, J. *The Cooperative Learning Companion.* Nashville, TN: Incentive Publications, 1992.

Breeden, T. and Mosley, J. *The Middle Grades Teacher's Handbook for Cooperative Learning.* Nashville, TN: Incentive Publications, 1991.

Forte, I. and Schurr, S. *The Cooperative Learning Guide & Planning Pak for Middle Grades.* Nashville, TN: Incentive Publications, 1992.

Forte, I. and Schurr, S. *Curriculum and Project Planner for Integrating Learning Styles, Thinking Skills, and Authentic Assessment.* Nashville, TN: Incentive Publications, 1996.

Forte, I. and Schurr, S. *Integrating Instruction in Language Arts: Strategies, Activities, Projects, Tools, and Techniques.* Nashville, TN: Incentive Publications, 1996.

Forte, I. and Schurr, S. *Integrating Instruction in Math: Strategies, Activities, Projects, Tools, and Techniques.* Nashville, TN: Incentive Publications, 1996.

Forte, I. and Schurr, S. *Integrating Instruction in Science: Strategies, Activities, Projects, Tools, and Techniques.* Nashville, TN: Incentive Publications, 1996.

Forte, I. and Schurr, S. *Integrating Instruction in Social Studies: Strategies, Activities, Projects, Tools, and Techniques.* Nashville, TN: Incentive Publications, 1996.

Hill, S. and Hill, T. *The Collaborative Classroom.* Portsmouth, NH: Heinemann, 1990.

CURRICULUM AND INSTRUCTION OVERVIEW

Beane, J. A. *A middle school curriculum: From rhetoric to reality.* Columbus, OH: National Middle School Association. 24, 1993.

Caldwell, B. J. *Education for the public good: Strategic intentions for the 21st century.* Marsh, D. D. (Ed.). ASCD Yearbook, 1999. Alexandria, VA: Association for Supervision and Curriculum Development. 56-57, 1999.

Clark, D. C. & S. N. *Developmentally responsive curriculum and standards-based reform: Implications for middle level principals.* Bulletin, National Association of Secondary School Principals. 5-7, 2000, April.

English, F. W. *Deciding what to teach and test.* Newbury Park, CA: Corwin Press, Inc. 16, 1992.

Fogarty, R. & Bellanca, J. *Cognition in practice: Best practices for the learning-centered classroom.* Palatine, IL: IRI/Skylight Publishing, Inc. 73, 1995.

Foriska, T. J. *Restructuring around standards: A practitioner's guide to design and implementation.* Thousand Oaks, CA: Corwin Press, Inc. 35, 1998.

Glatthorn, A. A. *Performance standards and authentic learning.* Larchmont, NY: Eye on Education. 28-29, 1999.Foriska, T. J. *Restructuring around standards: A practitioner's guide to design and implementation.* Thousand Oaks, CA: Corwin Press, Inc. 35, 1998.

Parnell, D. *Why do I have to learn this?* Waco, TX: Center for Occupational Research and Development. Inc. 8-9, 1995.

Spear, R.C. *Appropriate grouping practices for middle level students.* Irvin, J.L. (ed.). *Transforming middle level education.* Needham Heights, MA: Allyn and Bacon. 262, 1992.

Tomlinson, C. A. (1999). *The differentiated classroom: Responding to the needs of all learners.* Alexandria, VA: Association for Supervision and Curriculum Development. 2.

TUDENT ASSESSMENT AND EVALUATION

Asp, E. *Assessment in education: Where have we been? Where are we headed?* Brandt, R. S. (Ed.). Education in a New Era. Alexandria, VA: Association for Supervision and Curriculum Development. 147-148, 2000 .

Brandt, R.S. *Performance Assessment: Readings from Educational Leadership.* Alexandria, VA: Association for Supervision and Curriculum Development, 1992.

Burke, K. *How to assess authentic learning.* Arlington, Heights, IL: Skylight Publications. Xviii, 1999.

Fogarty, R. *Balanced assessment.* Arlington Heights, IL: Skylight Publications, Inc. 7 & 8, 1998.

Forte, I. & Schurr, S. *Making Portfolios, Products, and Performances Meaningful and Manageable for Students and Teachers.* Nashville, TN: Incentive Publications, Inc., 1995.

Griswold, P. *Assessing Relevance and Reliability to Improve the Quality of Teacher-Made Tests,* NASSP Bulletin. Reston, VA: National Association of Secondary School Principals, February 1990.

Herman, J.L., Aschbacher, P.R. and Winters, L. *A Practical Guide to Alternative Assessment.* Alexandria, VA: Association for Supervision and Curriculum Development, 1992.

Jacobs, H. H. *Mapping the big picture: Integrating curriculum and assessment, K-12.* Alexandria, VA: Association for Supervision and Curriculum Development. 4, 1997.

McTighe, J. & Ferrara, S. *Assessing learning in the classroom.* Washington, DC: National Education Association. 7-9, 1994.

Paris, S. G. & Ayres, L. R. *Becoming reflective students and teachers with portfolios and authentic assessment.* Washington, DC: American Psychological Association. 41, 1994.

Paulson, F., Paulson, P., and Mayer, C. "What Makes a Portfolio a Portfolio?" Educational Leadership 43, 3:30–33. Association for Supervision and Curriculum Development, 1991.

Schlechty, P. *Ten critical qualities of student work.* Journal of Staff Development, National Staff Development Council, Oxford, OH. 42, 1998, Summer.

Stowell, L. P. & McDaniel, J. E. *The changing face of assessment.* Irvin, J. L. (Ed.). *What Current Research Says to the Middle Level Practitioner.* Columbus, OH: National Middle School Association. 145-146, 1997.

Wiggins, G. "A Response to Cizek," Phi Delta Kappan, 729, May 1991.

Wiggins, G. & McTighe, J. *Understanding by design.* Alexandria, VA. Association for Supervision and Curriculum Development. 5, 44, 1998.

Wiggins, G. P. *Assessing student performance.* San Francisco, CA: Jossey-Bass Publishers. 27-28, 1993.

Index

348

ASSOCIATION LISTINGS

ASSOCIATION NAME / ADDRESS	TELEPHONE / WEBSITE	PUBLICATIONS
National Council of Teachers of English 1111 Kenyon Road Urbana, IL 61801	(NCTE) (217) 328-3870 www.ncte.org	• English Journal • Language Arts
International Reading Association 600 Barksdale Road Newark, DE 19714-8139	(IRA) (302) 731-1600 www.reading.org	• Journal of Reading • The Reading Teacher • Reading Research Quarterly
National Science Teachers Association 1840 Wilson Boulevard Arlington, VA 22201-3000	(NSTA) (703) 243-7100 www.nsta.org	• Science and Children • The Science Teacher
National Council of Teachers of Mathematics 1906 Association Drive Reston, VA 201	(NCTM) (703) 620-9840 www.nctm.org	• Arithmetic Teacher • Mathematics Teacher • Journal of Research in Mathematics
National Art Education Association 1916 Association Drive Reston, VA 22091	(NAEA) (703) 860-8000 www.naea-reston.org	• The Art Education Journal
Music Teachers National Association 441 Vine Street Suite 505 Cincinnati, OH 45202	(MTNA) (513) 421-1420 www.mtna.org	• American Music Teachers
Phi Delta Kappan *(Professional association in education)* Eight and Union P.O. Box 789 Bloomington, IN 47402-0789	(812) 339-1156 www.pdkintl.org	• Phi Delta Kappan • Fastbacks

ASSOCIATION NAME / ADDRESS	TELEPHONE / WEBSITE	PUBLICATIONS
American Educational Research Association 1230 17th Street, NW Washington, DC 20036	(AERA) (202) 223-9485 www.aera.net	• American Education Research Journal • Journal of Educational Statistics
American Federation of Teachers 555 New Jersey Avenue, NW Washington, DC 20001	(AFT) (202) 879-4400 www.aft.org	• The American Teacher • On Campus
National Staff Development Council P.O. Box 240 Oxford, OH 45056	(NSDC) (513) 523-6029 www.nsdc.org	• The Developer • Journal of Staff Development
National Council for the Social Studies 8555 16th Street Suite 500 Silver Springs, MD 20910	(NCSS) (301) 588-1800 www.socialstudies.org	• Social Education

National Education Association
1201 16th Street, NW Suite 310
Washington, DC 20036
    School Systems Capacity Department
    Director, Mr. Buoy Te
    (202) 822-7367
    Student Achievement Department
    Director, Stephanie Fanjul
    (202) 822-7946
    Teacher Quality Department
    Director, Gayla Hudson
	(NEA)
	(202) 822- 7848
	www.nea.org
		• NEA Today

Association for Supervision and Curriculum Development 125 Northwest Street Alexandria, VA 22314	(ASCD) (703) 549-9110 www.ascd.org	• Educational Leadership
National Middle School Association 4151 Executive Parkway, Suite 300 Westerville, OH 43081	(NMSA) (800) 528-6672 www.nmsa.org	• Middle School Journal • Middle Ground • Target